THE STORY OF POLOCROSSE IN ZIMBABWE

CHRIS POCOCK

ISBN-13:
978-1495492945

ISBN-10:
149549294X

DEDICATION

To my good friend Ian Brown [Brown Dog] who did so much for polocrosse and still had more to offer. K.i.a. 1979

CONTENTS

Foreword

by

Barry Burbidge

IT IS A TRUE FACT THAT IN ALL COMMUNITIES and societies, there are many talkers and very few doers. The world of polocrosse can be thankful that Chris Pocock is a doer, and has taken on the daunting task of penning the history of polocrosse. The timing of writing up this valuable history is appropriate, and ensures that there is no further loss of key and important information. Chris has spent countless hours in contacting individuals, organizations and associations around the world, in an attempt to gain factual historical information on the game of polocrosse. Those who have willingly given up their time and contributed are to be thanked. In his own words, Chris has stated that there may be some inaccuracies, as certain information was provided from individuals' memories. We all grow old, and there are times when things are not as clear as they used to be!

The game of polocrosse is truly a family sport, where all members of the family derive pleasure in participating. At club level we have witnessed a grandfather, his son and grandson, all playing in the same team at a tournament. There are few sports available to us that can provide that special opportunity. At the 2003 polocrosse World Cup hosted by Warwick in Australia, it was interesting to read the newspaper sports headlines. Two of those headlines amply prove that this is truly a family sport. One being, *"A family that plays together stays together"*, and the other, *"The battle of the siblings"*. One example was where two brothers captained two different countries at this world cup. There are a number of cases where family members have represented their clubs and nations at the highest level.

In recent times there have been local and global events that have placed pressure on the game. The global financial recession has played its part, but there is no doubt that the game is sufficiently robust to survive. The key factor is that this is a one horse; one man sport, greatly reducing the cost. The future of the game is reliant on the youth playing, and every opportunity must be afforded them. Being involved with polocrosse has provided numerous individuals lasting friendships, at country and global levels.

The core ingredient of polocrosse is the emphasis placed on the horse by the sport. The rules of the game ensure the safety of this noble beast, and should be adhered to at all times. Horses participating in matches from club, all the way through to international level, are recognized at the prize giving ceremony at the end of the event. There are many horses that have left indelible memories from the past, and many in the game at this time. There is no doubt that the key to any individual's success is in the ability of their horse. It is reasonable to allocate any success as 40% of the player's skills and 60% to the horse's ability.

In conclusion, a huge thank you, to you Chris, for bringing this book to print. This has been a sterling effort, and will be appreciated by all who read it. This book will not only be of interest to those people involved in the sport of polocrosse, it will be a good read for anyone.

Barry Burbidge

ACKNOWLEDGMENTS

THERE ARE A NUMBER OF PEOPLE WHO HAVE been a great help to me sending photos and copies of their private collections and to mention them all by name would take up a lot of space. You know who you all are and I thank you sincerely.

I owe it to Sheila Barry for getting me off the mounting block in the first place.

I must thank my old friend and rival on the field, Tim Savory for keeping me focused on this book when frustration was getting the better of me. Typical of Tim, I wasn't getting much help from him until he heard I may have a ticket to depart from this world. Only then did he become very useful and telling me that I had better hurry up and finish this book. I am still here Tim and the book is finished. Thanks mate.

A lady that I used to think absolutely gorgeous when we were at school together is Trish Tomlinson who became Mrs Dave Jackson. Thanks to Facebook, I was able to link up with her after all these years and as she is an author of several books, I was able to charm her into rescuing my work after my attempt at formatting.

This is a story in itself. Transferring my work from an A4 size to the Amazon template was like playing hide and seek. Pictures would disappear and remerge somewhere in the 400 page pack and whole paragraphs would simply walk of the page into the blue yonder of the screen and nothing I did would coax them back. Fortunately my laptop is immune to my choice language and I eventually got it all on the white that depicts the page and bundle it off to Trish. Trish, you are a star and I cannot thank you enough.

My son Nick surprised me by coming up with a new hidden talent. Sitting at the dining room table he came up with some sketches on some of the stories in this book. I seized them and really proud to add them to my book and make it a little family affair. Thanks my boy and now your works have been published.

Ken and Sandy King, old mates and party animals, made available on two occasions their superb Safari Camp on their Kwe Kwe ranch. This was the site of the original Rhodesdale field and so it was appropriate to call in my old 'dugger boy' friends to a weekend of reminiscing over several beers.

Ken and Sandy are one of very few who still remain on their land. Probably the reason why, is that the war vets consider Ken perfectly mad and a little story that must be told will illustrate this.

Farmers, like Ken, live in constant fear of a bunch of thugs turning up on their doorstep and evicting them, often violently. On this occasion, a bunch turned up and thinking the worst and before any demands were made, Ken stripped himself totally naked and countermanded that if they wanted his ranch they should take his clothes as well. The embarrassed gathering managed to splutter out that they simply wanted to buy some meat. One very naked and dumbfounded Ken meekly referred them to his wife.

Ken and Sandy, thank you for the wonderful time and the use of your camp. With a group like this, one is able to discard the accumulated years to the wind and once again live our youth, or so we think.

To my wife Heather, I must apologise for all the time robbed from our time together that I spent hunched over my lap top writing this book. I know it was an irritation and I thank you for being tolerant.

Dugger group from our first session.

Chris Pocock, Jill Wilmot, Ted Wilmot, Eleanor Lowe, Jenny Mannix, Ian Mannix, Heather Pocock, Alan Malloy, Arlene Crook, Julie Cossey, Mike Cossey, Ken King.

Dugger group from the last session.

Rich Mostert, Ken King, Ian Mannix, Jen Mannix, Heather Pocock, Mariana Mostert, Ted Wilmot, Jill Wilmot, Sandy King, Chris Pocock, Allan Malloy, Arlene Crook, John Harris.

And just to prove we did work

THE STORY OF POLOCROSSE IN ZIMBABWE

INTRODUCTION

AS A KEEN LAND ROVER ENTHUSIAST I GAVE some thought to driving my Series 1 across the African continent to England where Land Rovers across the globe were gathering to celebrate 50 years of Land Rover production. That was 1998 and, as it dawned on me, so too was polocrosse in this country. My sport was having its 50th birthday and no one seemed to realise it. Two years later the 'War Vets' started their rampage and polocrosse in this Country came close to extinction.

By 2008, now its 60th birthday, polocrosse had survived albeit in much reduced numbers and I felt the desperate urge that the history of our sport MUST be recorded before it is too late. So I approached my friend and author Mary Leared, the most qualified and experienced person to do this. Alas she was too busy to take this on and suggested I do it. What a daunting thought. I had never done anything like this in my life before and wasn't sure if my command of the English language would be up to it. Certainly my English school teacher had long given up on me. But it HAD to be done and I admit the challenge of it all excited my imagination. So here it is, warts and all, after six years of frustration,

1

feelings of inadequacy, but more than anything, pride at being a part of this great sport.

From its formation in 1951, our polocrosse association executive has run a professional administration through their various sub committees. Minutes were always taken and records kept in safe keeping. I know this; I was a part of it for a period, so I did not think it would be too difficult in my research.

How wrong I was. With the Clubs folding up around the country, records disappeared. So many of the old players that were such a big part of the history migrated to various parts of the globe taking with them personal archives they managed to rescue as they fled their farms. I nearly gave up on the whole thing but how could I after exciting those still in the sport? I could not lose face on my commitment. I came to a compromise; I would not mention the word HISTORY in this book. So to the historians amongst us, use this information at your discretion. I have had to depend a lot on people's memories and they can be faulty, but I have pursued the reality as close as I possibly can. Likewise, there are some gaps that I have failed to fill.

If for nothing else, this book revives cherished memories of our sport that we all enjoyed so much and that it makes for easy reading, then I consider my work done. For the new generation of players, I hope this book gives you an insight into your sport's roots.

Ant Keith was the polocrosse president when the farm invasions occurred. For safety's sake he made the wise decision to mothball the sport until the future could be determined. That was the end of an era of polocrosse administration. What revived after this was different. We had moved from a democratic system to a virtual dictatorship. Under normal circumstances this could have proved fatal to the sport, but instead proved to be its lifeline. From my perspective this was tough, as record-keeping was of nuisance value, but I was intrigued by its success and I call it that despite all the controversy surrounding it.

Wayne Parham was the man of the hour. He was an organiser, a man of means and fortunately, passionate about polocrosse. He ran polocrosse like a business. It had to be—there were so few members and clubs left. Most of the previous generation of top players and officials, with their long-standing status in polocrosse, had left. What remained was a new generation, eager to fill the void but without that established ranking that maintains a natural progression. Discipline and direction, through the personality of a leader, was needed to get the motion forward and Wayne was that man.

The 2011 World Test Series, played in England with eight competing nations was a real test for Zimbabwe. Possibly three clubs could submit players of sufficient ability for selection—or lack of selection, as many complained of favouritism. I went along to watch as the squad was put through their paces, and old friends, Barry Burbidge, John Harris and myself formulated our own selection based on what we saw. The final choice was not ours to make, and we were not completely in agreement with the team that was chosen. Yet despite this, the Zimbabwe team played the finals of the Test Series, just missing the title of World Champions.

So how is it that Zimbabwe with its limited depth of selection could put up a team of mostly inexperienced test players with a coach relatively new to that exposure and achieve such good results? All these players came out of one club, something that has never happened before. Certainly the other clubs had players of at least equal talent.

These youngsters were provided the means; some were lent top horses and some financial support to meet the task ahead. This is not the ideal recipe for a winning side even if it does help. Youngsters of talent need to be disciplined and moulded if they are to perform as a cohesive team. This was achieved through the dictatorial structure of command and reward, and in this case was very successful.

I do not advocate this method. Far from it, but until stability returns to our country and polocrosse is allowed to return to its former numbers, strong leadership is paramount to the survival of our sport.

CHAPTER 1

OUR HERITAGE

IF ONE TAKES SPORT AROUND THE GLOBE, AND considering where the top sportsmen and women originate from, then one will realize that Zimbabwe, per capita, must surely be high up on the leader-board in world class sportspersons. Hockey, swimming, golf and motorsports, to name a few are among the lesser known disciplines that this country has excelled at, and proudly. Polocrosse is another. Yet what made a small third world country like ours feature so prominently in world sport? The answer surely lies in the character and discipline that was developed into a population, through diverse and sometimes traumatic growing pains.

Ever since the flag went up in Salisbury at the end of the Pioneer's trek in September 1890, the evolution road map of the country to the present day Zimbabwe has been ambushed with events that can only develop character of a determined nature.

Cecil John Rhodes, a mining magnate and Prime Minister of the Cape Colony, extricated a concession from the Matebele Chief, Lobengula, to exploit the mineral resources from the country under his control but instead settled it under the guise of a Royal Charter with the name of the British South Africa Company. One hundred and ten years later, this document of dubious intent initiated the greatest disaster the country has seen, with the current politicians using it as justification to steal land and assets under the guise of land reform, but in reality to subjugate the population in order to retain power.

In 1923 the Company's charter came to an end and Winston Churchill, then British Colonial Secretary, offered the population home rule or incorporation with the Union of South Africa. Despite pressure from General Jan Smuts to form a 5th province of South Africa, the country voted for home rule. Then the thirties brought in the great depression and many farms and mines were forced to close, their owners and workers taking up government part-time work, many building strip roads of tar to eke out a living.

The highest percentage in the world, per capita of the country's men volunteered to fight the evils that Nazi Germany under Hitler brought to the world. The Federation of the three countries of Northern and Southern Rhodesia's and Nyasaland was formed in 1953, but was short-lived. It broke apart after only 10 years due to pressure from the newly formed nationalist movements, and the struggle for black independence began.

In order to prevent majority rule in Rhodesia, the government of the day declared unilateral independence from Great Britain in 1965. Sanctions and isolation from the world at large were enforced. The guerrilla bush war took place from the mid-sixties to the first majority elections in 1980 that brought Robert Mugabe to power.

Soon after Independence, the country flourished with the expectation of it becoming a model multiracial state. Despite this, dreadful atrocities where happening behind the scenes in Matabeleland that would secure a one party state. By the '90's the hand of dictatorship was exposing its presence and the results of the Constitutional Referendum at the turn of the century brought about a tantrum from the government that removed some 90 percent of white commercial farmers and their labour through violent means. Over the following eight years the economy was reduced to an inflation rate of three million percent; unemployment of 80% and a GDP of 2%. Food commodities became scarce; fuels were purchased on the black market and electricity and water outages at times lasted for days and sometimes months. The exchange rate to the American dollar in 1980 was eight U.S. dollars to one Zimbabwean, diminishing to one U.S. dollar to two Zimbabwe dollars by 1995, whilst in 2008, thirteen years later, it had devalued to three million Zimbabwe dollars after having removed thirteen zero's, the highest inflation rate ever recorded in the world.

This then was the background in which polocrosse developed and survived!

Horses have played their part over the period and have graduated from satisfying private, military and commercial transport requirements through to sports. They were a large factor in suppressing the Matebele and Shona uprisings of the early 1900's and were again deployed in the more recent guerrilla bush war when the Mounted Infantry Unit, the predecessor to the Grey's Scouts, was formed with polocrosse players as its founding members.

After the Second World War ended, ex-servicemen were offered easy credit and encouraged to settle and open up farms in the colony. Immigrants were also urged to settle in the then Southern Rhodesia, and vast tracts of land were opened up from virgin bush to become highly productive commercial farms, the mainstay of which was Virginia tobacco. These farming communities, having generally started up gymkhana and riding clubs through their local community clubs, became ideal recruiting centres for polocrosse. This is where Minto Strover started the sport out in Fort Victoria in 1948.

Polocrosse grew in stages until the bush war escalated in the '70's. Members of the general white population were conscripted into the armed forces where they were called up for periods of six weeks active duty and six weeks off. Not only did this have an impact on commerce, but also on sport, where a large portion of the 392 registered polocrosse club members [1979], was subject to call up. This had the effect of lowering the standard of the game, through lack of practice time, and thus reducing the strengths of the teams fielded. In order to combat this and to improve the quality of tournaments, and indeed to assist some clubs to participate, the Polocrosse Association introduced sectional tournaments, the first host being Horseshoe Club.

Not only were the military call-ups disruptive but so too were the conditions prevailing in the country at the time. Vehicles travelled in protected convoys for fear of ambush. The ever-present threat of landmines, particularly on the rural gravel roads in the farming communities where most tournaments were held, presented another nightmare. A case in point was when the Shamva lorry belonging to Keith and Tilly Laurent struck a land mine ferrying horses to a Club practice.

The birth of Zimbabwe in 1980 ushered in a period of tranquillity from the '80's through to the '90's and the sport rapidly grew in members and in registered clubs. The sport was still predominantly rural, with only five of the 28 registered clubs being urban. The influence of international polocrosse had a positive effect on the standard of our play and resulted in Zimbabwe achieving World Champion status when it won at the 1997 Quadrangular Test Series held at Pietermaritzburg in South Africa.

A dramatic turnabout in the politics of the country occurred at the turn of the century, when, as mentioned, the Government embarked on its ill-fated and violent land reform exercise. Overnight 18 of the 30 registered clubs ceased to exist as so-called *war veterans* of the bush war forced the occupants off their farms and whole districts ceased to exist. As a result, a large number of rural folk left for new pastures in the hope of picking up their lives again. Talented Zimbabwe players boosted the standards of polocrosse in new countries. Others moved into the towns and cities with what they could rescue, and engaged in a variety of new vocations.

What was once predominantly a rural sport now moved into the towns and cities. Only Hippo, Enterprise and Chipinge clubs could still be classed as rural. Ventersburg, a new club in the Harare area opened up to help accommodate these players and to add a little more variety of venues.

From an all-time high of 43 clubs, polocrosse had shrunk to a mere five clubs, all of which, bar two, were in Harare and the surrounding area. The environment, with all its negative aspects, was ripe for the sport to die a natural death. Yet, contrary to this, the sport has maintained a world class standard of polocrosse and featured admirably in International Test Matches.

Those early Pioneers indeed set the standard. No obstacle was insurmountable and through adversity came resilience, for Zimbabweans have always made a plan.

CHAPTER 2

BACKGROUND

IN 1948, SOUTHERN RHODESIA'S MINTO STROVER, as Chairman of the Fort Victoria Gymkhana Club, suggested they might try polocrosse after reading an article by the late Tony Collins in the English magazine "Riding". He wrote to Porlock Vale in England for a book of rules, some sticks and balls and the sport kicked off, with Fort Victoria being the first Southern Rhodesian polocrosse Club.

I started my polocrosse career in 1965 with Fred and Sheila Barry from Old Umtali and in all my years in polocrosse seldom did I give any thought as to how and where the sport originated. I was not alone in this. Some believed that it started from social games like scooping up a calf in Peru or a sack in Russia or that even lacrosse had something to do with it. In fact it did. Sally Batton Boillotat in her Australian polocrosse book has written that lacrosse influenced the Australians in putting together the framework for the rules, field and equipment for this modern sport. Lacrosse, she says, goes back to the American Indians. Putting together this book I have unearthed fascinating information that clearly lays down the path of the sports evolution.

But in order to trace the origins of polocrosse one needs to go back in history to the beginnings of polo, shrouded as it is in the airy mists of centuries past.

Polo is one of the most ancient of games using a stick and ball and has existed for some 2,000 years with early records coming from Persia. Here the game is mentioned under its Persian name of 'chaugan' in a piece of eastern literature - 'Shahnamah', written by a Persian poet in the 10th / 11th century. From there it appears to have spread westward to Constantinople and eastward through Turkestan to Tibet, China, Mongolia and Japan. The name polo derives from the Tibetan name 'pulu' meaning 'ball' and has evolved over twelve variations of the game.

The game has been recorded as played in Japan as early as AD727 in Mr Basil Hall Chamberlain's classical poetry of the Japanese: "In the first moon of the fourth year of the period of Zhiuki' the nobles and courtiers assembled in the fields of Kasuga and were diverting themselves with a game of polo, when the sky was suddenly over-cast and the rain poured down, amid thunder and lightning, whilst the palace remained unguarded. Thereupon, the Mikado issued an edict confining the offenders to the guardhouse under strict prohibition of leaving its gates."

It is difficult to establish the beginnings of the sport where it is played using a net as against a mallet. The Encyclopaedia Britannica of 1912 describes the fifth variation of polo where it was played in Constantinople using a racquet and a leathern ball the size of an apple in the 12th century, and during the Byzantine period. However it is also recorded that the game found its way into Japan from China in the 6th century where it was popular in feudal times. Known as 'dakiu', meaning 'ball match', a Japanese print of the 17th century shows the upper strata of Japanese society playing the sport. The riders are resplendent in silks and headdress, with beautifully lacquered wooden saddles and ornate leather ware.

Two sections of four players made up a team and the game was played on a field measuring 160 yards by 60 yards that was fenced all around. At each end of the field and outside the fence, was a board raised 5ft from the ground and measuring 12 feet by 7 feet with a central hole of 1ft, 2in in diameter through which the ball was thrown. Behind this hole was a bag to retrieve the ball. The racquet was very similar to a lacrosse racquet and limited to a length of three feet four inches with the inside measurement of the net being three and a half inches. The ball used was made of paper covered with small pebbles or Bamboo fibre, and Ponies were restricted to 14 hands high.

There were twenty two rules to the game but of interest the 'off side' rule did not exist in Japan.

Some years later, in the troublesome times that accompanied the abolition of the feudal system, the game languished and nearly died out. In later years, it was revived with great activity throughout the Empire.

In England, Strutt mentions a game played at the time of Charles the second, with a stick, ball and iron hoop, at what is now Pall Mall, but this was played on foot and possibly the beginnings of modern day lacrosse. There was also a game played in Wales called 'knappan', played in the time of Queen Elizabeth 1st with sticks and a wooden ball by men both mounted and on foot. This game however fell to disuse due to the rough and tumble manner in which it was played, offering too much opportunity for a free-for- all.

The British played polo in their colonies, in particular India, where it flourished in the 16th century and was finally brought to England in 1869 as a military sport for the 10th Hussars. In England, polo was called 'hockey', whilst Ireland called it 'hurling'. Hockey, derived from polo, was known as 'polo on foot' and together with cricket and golf, came into existence from polo.

Polocrosse is also an old game to Russia especially Georgia and was possibly introduced from the east, as there are certain similarities to the game as it was played in Japan. Again two sections of four players made up a team, only they played on a bigger field measuring 300 yards by 160 yards. Their racquets had similar shafts to a polo mallet with a head that was elongated into a shape like a snowshoe.

They staged the traditional national games of the

USSR in Kiev, the capital of the Ukraine, where polocrosse, known as tskhenburti, was played, and is still played today in some of the former USSR states. Bill Cossey records seeing a photograph of an obvious number 1 receiving a pass on his left-hand side from his number 2.

AUSTRALIA

Although it started in England, Australia must take the credit for shaping the game as we know it today, that is fast spreading as a recognised world sport, and indeed giving it the name of polocrosse. Two British Instructors at the National School of Equitation at Kingston Vale near London developed an exercise to supplement the work at the riding school. It was played indoors with two riders a side and with markers on a wall from which the ball bounced back into play. The goals were deep basketball nets hung at each end of the arena that the scorer would drop the ball into. Racquets were made using an old polo stick with the mallet removed and replaced with a squash racquet head and this was re strung with a loose string net in which to scoop up the ball that was slightly larger than a tennis ball.

Then enter Mr. and Mrs. Edward Hirst of Sydney who, in 1938 read about this new sport in an English Horse Magazine and as keen horse breeders and with a keen interest in horse sports, travelled to England to learn more about it. Realizing the possibilities of this exercise as an outdoor horse sport, the couple returned to Australia with sticks, balls and rule books where they sought the assistance of Alf Pitty, a well-known horseman and polo player.

Mrs Marjory Hirst   *Mr Alf Pity*

After many hours of discussion, practising, and much trial and error, and with constant revision of the rules, they finally came up with a new and exciting game using only one horse which could be played by a person of any age. They called the new game 'polocrosse'. Pitty then helped to give the first recorded polocrosse demonstration at Ingleburn Sports Ground near Sydney in 1939. Interest and enthusiasm was so great that it was not long before all the club members were practising this new game, and soon after, Ingleburn became Australia's first polocrosse club. The first book of rules was then established.

At this time, the Second World War had started and with the men going off to the front, polocrosse did not progress as rapidly as it had started. The women kept it going, holding practice matches which were often organised to benefit the war effort. Only after the war did it pick up again, and Australia's second club, Burradoo, was formed in 1945. From there clubs started to spring up rapidly. By 1946, Marjory Hirst felt the need for a governing body to administer the sport and on the 17th of October 1946 the Australian polocrosse Association was formed with Blake Pelly as its inaugural President.

SOUTH AFRICA

Polocrosse was first played in Natal, South Africa in 1947 at the Muriel Higgs School of Riding, and two years later Matamo Club was formed. In 1959, Fort Victoria received a request from Hendrik de Waal, previously from Marandellas, asking if Pretoria University Polocrosse Club could play at their championships on borrowed ponies. Generally, though, very little progress was made until 1966 when Rhodesia sent films of the game being played to Natal, and played a demonstration game in 1968 at the Tugela Basin Agricultural Show at Ladysmith.

By 1972 there were sufficient Clubs and players in South Africa to warrant the formation of a National Association and thus the inaugural meeting of the South African Polocrosse Association was held at Harrismith in the dimly lit cattle pens on the 9th of July 1972. Nick van der Merwe was elected interim president and Gifford Sparks the Interim vice president. Twenty years later, in 1992, the Association had grown to the extent where there were seven affiliated provincial bodies that represented 54 Clubs and over 900 registered players.

PAPUA NEW GUINEA

In 1959, a Col Sefton from Koitaki Plantation outside Port Morsby started polocrosse in Papua New Guinea but as it was a young developing country attracting foreign expatriates on short term contracts, polocrosse struggled to take off. After a brief recess it finally got going in the late '60's with the help of Australians. Now the native Papua New Guineans, most of whom are stockmen from the various cattle stations, make up the majority of players. Papua New Guinea has some of the best polocrosse fields in the world with breath-taking scenery.

ENGLAND

Modern polocrosse was encouraged by the Pony Club in England but was slow to start as a sport in its own right in that country. In 1961, a televised demonstration game was set up at the Rickmansworth Agricultural Show in which three Rhodesians, Mary Leared, Sir Rupert and Maurice Bromley competed against a beginner English side with the idea of promoting the sport. It gradually spread through the various pony clubs and with the likes of Robert Malden and a number of other Zimbabweans and South Africans that had settled in England, coaching began to improve the standard of their game and resulted in the sport developing outside of pony clubs. With the popularity of the sport growing and more clubs being formed it was inevitable that an association be formed and in 1985 the United Kingdom Polocrosse Association was established.

With the sport now controlled under a central authority, an invitation was sent in 1991 for a Junior Zimbabwean side to tour England to play and coach across the Country. Zimbabwe, under the presidency of Jock Kay, sent two experienced national players in Barry Burbidge and Ted Wilmot with the squad. That went a long way in laying the groundwork for future test series in which England has become a growing force.

NEW ZEALAND

Polocrosse started in New Zealand in 1967 when Denys and Ray Gifford emigrated there from South Africa, bringing the game with them and ultimately forming the New Zealand Polocrosse Council in 1975. Some of the early clubs included Kaitieke, Te Maire, National Park, Chura and Waimiha. By 1990 New Zealand had 13 Associations with 62 Clubs and some 900 registered players. In 1976 New Zealand became a member of the International Polocrosse Council and in that same year sent their first touring team to Queensland Australia.

ZAMBIA

Our other polocrosse playing neighbour is Zambia. Unknown to many, Zambia started playing in the '60's but little information can be gleaned. It appears that Lena Winter who had a riding school at the polo stables would play a bit of polocrosse using the shallow nets and lining up in the manner at the time of facing each other. It never took off as she was concentrating on bringing in new polo players. Then there was Tim and Nicola Fuller who appeared to be a part of those early years, but that was generally the sum of it; only in the early '90's did polocrosse establish itself independent from riding exercises or polo recruiting.

Choma was the first to start around 1992/3. A bunch of farmers, the Becketts, Counsells, Danckwerts and others used to get together on weekends, originally on a field at Demo Farm but had no idea about the rules of the game. Paul Dobson, from Mukushi, was the first to explain the game and rules to them and that is when they started to play the game properly. Their first tournament was at Livingstone in 1997.

Leopards Hill then took it up, learnt the rules and took the game more seriously. They held the first tournament in 1995. It all started when Rachel Jellis was out for a dinner party at Tim and Nicola Fuller's house where she saw some old battered sticks with shallow nets lying around and asked what they were. Tim gave them the sticks and the next day a bunch of hung over people got together and tackled the game. Tim and Nicola joined them and explained the rules and polocrosse at Lazy J was born. Rachel then took some sticks to John Clayton (polo) to ask if he could buy her some and he threw the sticks off the polo club balcony and said "This game will not happen in Zambia!" Their first committee meeting was held under an umbrella on their new polocrosse field on Halloween day. They also played in the main arena at the show grounds at times and when tournaments started they played at Chisamba Polocrosse Club. The club has moved to new premises next to Lazy J.

Andrew and Julie Woodley with Rika and Wilson started Chisamba on a mealie field at the Woodley Family Farm. Their first tournament was the Tiger Feeds Sponsors tournament in April 1997. There was so much dust that no one could see the games, and many people who could not ride a horse played in those days.

Trotover started soon after Leopard's Hill. Lorraine Chalcraft started an equestrian centre with cross country, jumping and dressage and when the polocrosse rage hit Zambia she started that too. Trotover lasted for many years but when a group of their members moved to a new club in Lusaka South (as it was in their area) Trotover did not have enough players to continue. Members then joined up with Leopard's Hill Club and Lusaka South Country Club.

Lusaka West was started by the Cartwright family but is no longer going, whilst Lusaka South started later and is still going. Anthony Barker was with Trotover but as both Lusaka Clubs (Leopard's Hill and Trotover) were on the other side of town he decided to open at his local Country Club. Lusaka South organized and hosted the first ZIMZAM International Test.

Livingstone riders started polocrosse in Victoria Falls on the Zimbabwean side and used to cross the border with their horses each weekend. When Doug heard that it had started in Zambia at Leopard's Hill and Chisamba he decided to open a club on his farm in Livingstone. When Colin Lowe joined they took the game more seriously and held their first tournament in 1997. Livingstone were the first to introduce handicapping to polocrosse in Zambia and had polocrosse affiliated under polo in Zambia through the then Chairman Keith Asherwood.

Anthony Barker encouraged and sponsored Zambia Police to play. They still play occasionally.

Copperbelt Polocrosse was started by Mark Leaver who was very enthusiastic. They played two tournaments and then sadly Mark died in a car accident and no one continued it on.

USA

The United States of America started in 1980 when students at Lake Erie College in Ohio introduced the sport from their academic term abroad in Australia. Michael Polya from Australia was the man responsible for setting up the students' teams in Australia in which Kathy Nelson, one of the students, took back racquets and balls to Lake Erie and started the first club. In 1983 the

Polocrosse Association of the United States was formed and with the sport spreading to other states key players broke away to form a rival American Polocrosse Association in 1986 which has grown to over 12 clubs and 300 players.

CANADA

Canada had started in 1983 with the first club being formed by Jonathan Fox III, a Canadian cattle breeder and Bruce Alexander an Australian cattle breeder, but battled to get going and for a period was mothballed.

IRELAND

David and Ivor Young introduced polocrosse to Ireland in 1990 as an additional tourist attraction to their equestrian holiday business in County Wexford. Soon after, the second club was established in the County of Limerick at Rathcannon by Brian McMahon. This has now expanded to seven Clubs and growing.

INTERNATIONAL POLOCROSSE ORGANIZATIONS

In June 1976 the International Polocrosse Council was formed by delegates from Australia, New Zealand, Papua New Guinea, Rhodesia and South Africa to administer the interests of polocrosse as it spread around the Globe. The first President was Max Walters A.M., M.B.E. from Australia. By 1982 there were five countries officially playing polocrosse under the auspices of the International Polocrosse Association. These were Australia, Zimbabwe, South Africa, New Zealand and Papua New Guinea. The first World Test Series was held in Australia in that year, but South Africa was barred from competing due to world sanctions that were imposed on them.

Polocrosse has continued to spread rapidly around the globe and is currently played in England, Australia, Zimbabwe, South Africa, New Zealand, Papua New Guinea, France, Germany, America, Canada, Norway,

Indonesia, Uruguay, Vanuatu, Peru, Zambia, Ireland, Russia and still growing.

A print of the game being played in Mongolia.
[Date unknown]

CHAPTER 3

A BRIEF SYNOPSIS

1948 to 1958

POLOCROSSE STARTED IN SOUTHERN RHODESIA at the Fort Victoria Gymkhana Club in 1948 and for some obscure reason after a year the club split and Zimbabwe Polocrosse Club was formed some distance away. A few years later they re-joined the club and named it Victoria Polocrosse Club. Some interest was shown in the sport by Umvuma residents who introduced it to the Rhodesdale farming area by alternating the club on three farms before establishing a permanent club site. Then in 1952, Bill Cossey, having seen the game played at Victoria, formed Glendale Polocrosse Club in Mashonaland.

By 1958, after ten years, there were nine clubs registered with the association with a combined total of 98 players. These clubs were - Zimbabwe, Rhodesdale, Glendale, Umtali, Old Umtali, Salisbury, Horseshoe, Marandellas, and Hartley. Most of these clubs came into existence from 1957 onwards with Umvuma only just starting with two members. In that year the highest handicap was Charlie Christensen at a 7 and 69 members out of the 98 were in C Division.

The Polocrosse Association of Rhodesia was formed in 1951 with the first Council meeting held in 1953, and the first Rule Book was drafted in 1955.

The first National Championships tournament was held in 1954 at Glendale, whilst the system of handicapping players started in 1955.

1959 to 1968

During the next ten year period, 12 Clubs played the sport; Borrowdale, Glendale, Gwelo, Hippo Valley, Horseshoe, Rhodesdale, Risco, Ruzawi River, Umtali, Virginia, Headlands and Bulawayo, with total registered players amounting to 170. Four of these were 9 handicap players; Ian Moffat, Nick Leared, Ian Brown and Alan Lowe with Wendy Wolfe the highest woman player at an 8 handicap.

1962 was a depressed year with most clubs in the doldrums having lost a number of members, and again in 1965 after Unilateral Independence was declared many left the country. Zimbabwe Polocrosse Club had reverted back to Victoria but then folded, as did Old Umtali and Marandellas. Umvuma, with so few players, joined up with Rhodesdale, and Salisbury re-formed to become Borrowdale. Sinoia was registered but not seen at any tournaments.

The first Inter Provincial tournament was held in 1967, having replaced the previous Inter Zone tournament, and the first Rhodesian touring side travelled to South Africa to play a demonstration test at Mooi River and Ladysmith in 1968.

1969 to 1978

The following ten year period there were a total of 313 registered players dispersed over 16 clubs; Borrowdale, Chipinga, Eiffel Flats, Glendale, Gwelo, Hippo Valley, Horseshoe, Karoi, Matepatepa, Queens, Rhodesdale, Ruzawi River, Shabani, Sinoia and Umvuma. By 1978 handicaps were dramatically reduced to affect all those from a four handicap and upwards. Therefore there were no nine handicap players in 1978, with only three players at the highest handicap of 8; Ken King, Iain Kay and Phil Wixley. This also was the period of increased military call-ups that had an adverse effect on the sport.

Test matches started in this period, as well as touring sides, the first touring side being from New South Wales, Australia in 1972.

The first Newsletter was published in 1969 with Mary Leared as its Editor.

1979 to 1988

In the next decade, the war ended and the country became Zimbabwe after the elections of 1980. We were now directed to cease playing against South Africa, but entered into the greater arena of international polocrosse, previously denied to us. There were 15 registered clubs by 1988; Bulawayo, Cam & Motor, Centenary, Chipinge, Doma, Featherstone, Hippo Valley, Horseshoe, Karoi, Makoni, Masvingo, Mtepatepa, Ruzawi River, Shamva, Virginia

In 1982 Zimbabwe was invited to compete in the first World Test Series held in Australia against Australia, New Zealand and Papua New Guinea.

The concept of forming a Veterans section was initiated.

1989 to 1998

This was the period of greatest activity for Zimbabwe polocrosse and one that put us on the map as a force within international polocrosse. In 1989 New Zealand came out to Zimbabwe for the first time for a test series and thereafter, every year of this decade, Zimbabwe hosted or travelled to test matches that included the United Kingdom, Australia, New Zealand, and South Africa. Of note, these tours included a lot of junior teams. This exposure to test conditions was invaluable for future top quality players. South Africa became open to us in 1992 and this was kicked off with a tour of four Zimbabwean teams. By 1997 Zimbabwe became the World Champions when she won the Quadrangular Test Series held in Pietermaritzburg in Natal South Africa.

1999 to 2008.

In 2000 Zimbabwe held a referendum to decide the outcome of the new constitution for the country. It was rejected and the government lashed out with its vengeful so-called 'Land Reform'. Sadly this resulted in polocrosse losing most of its rural clubs. For safety's sake, the executive at the time stopped all tournaments within the country, but Zimbabwe was able to continue to send teams to South Africa.

At the height of the land invasions in 2003, there was little polocrosse activity in the country, but polocrosse, with its resilient members, survived the ordeal albeit in greatly reduced clubs and numbers. The few remaining clubs continued to play the sport at club practice level mainly in Harare and its proximity as well as Bulawayo, the two major cities of the country. Amazingly Chipinge, Hippo Valley and Enterprise were also able to keep going. Zimbabwe could still produce a formidable side despite the lack of depth to select from and ultimately, to our national pride, become the runner up to the World Champions in 2011within a far greater arena of playing Nations.

Within this period Zambia was establishing itself as another polocrosse nation. The two nations, Zimbabwe and Zambia formulated what became known as the Zim Zam Test Series that alternated between the two. Selection was based on matching strengths that gave exposure and experience to lower grade players. In years to come this experience was to get Zambia to qualify and participate in the United Kingdom World Test Series.

CHAPTER 4

THOSE EARLY YEARS

AS PREVIOUSLY MENTIONED, MINTO STROVER started the game using the rulebook he obtained from England, but it is one thing to have a set of rules and quite another to interpret how to implement them. One can almost hear them arguing over the finer points of it, especially when you hear Barry Burbidge's story that when Hippo Valley started out, they thought the goal posts where positioned on the edge of the 'D'. It was only when they went to their first tournament that they realized where the goal posts should be and were astounded that anyone could score through goal posts that close.

The players in Rhodesia quite obviously adopted the style as they understood it, whilst Australia, the only other country to play at the time, adopted a different style.

Before any game commenced, there had to be a time-keeper, a goal judge at each end and four linesmen monitoring the two 30 yard lines to ensure no player carried the ball over the line. As this required all six members of a team to oversee the game, the four linesmen were eventually dropped and it was left to the umpire's discretion if the ball had been carried or not.

The umpire was given a pony from a selection of mostly unschooled cattle ponies that the host club had available, and the two umpires, dressed in no particular uniform, would ride onto the field to commence the game. Particular attention was given to the depth of the ball in the racquet, and umpires would scrutinize each one to ensure they met the regulation half ball above the racquet head. Not much notice was taken of tack and players were required to wear hard hats, usually the colonial style pith helmets. The time-keeper made sure each chukka lasted for eight minutes.

The game commenced with the opposing sections lining up facing each other, with a one metre gap between the horses' noses, and the ball would be lobbed into the middle of this gap. The game was underway with a mad scramble for the ball. Invariably the ball would land on the ground with this formation of line-out and it would be the bolder horse that would brave the head on confrontation to reach the ball. The tactic, however, was to rush through the opposing line, catching, or knocking the ball forward whilst still in flight.

Once the ball was in the racquet, it was not difficult to dislodge it. Much cradling was essential to keep possession, and even then invariably lost with over cradling or a sharp flick to the back. The racquet shaft made from 'whippy' Malacca cane, usually from an old polo stick and with a short hand grip, would have a heavy squash racquet head attached that made the whole thing cumbersome. It was therefore not a wise player who would hang onto the ball and accept a tackle. It only required one member of the opposition to rob him of his ball and have his backup player retrieve it.

The tactics of the game then centred on the vulnerability of the ball carrier. The long pass was adopted, as the ball could travel the distance quicker than the horse could carry it there, and so the emphasis was to mark the opposite number to eliminate the options of a pass. Once a pass had been made, it was prudent to back it up, as the risk of a mis-catch was relatively high. This then opened up the mid-field with a lot of sprints commuting the ball back and forth as the tactics of pressurizing errors on the ball carrier persisted. Horses were schooled in the art of dropping a shoulder and pushing the opponent further away from the ball carrier to increase the risk of a bad pass, and towards the same end result, to drive them at greater speed.

The Number 1 player invariably liked to carry his own ball into the scoring area with a fast run over the penalty line and a hard, overarm throw at goal. The efficiency of the scoring rate was not so great but the spectator value was sufficient to ensure that the overarm throw has stayed with us to this day. The likes of Alan Lowe and Barry Burbidge were able to score from the back line corner at a full gallop when visual goal post gap was reduced to a mere slit.

The defence, or Number 3 had few options in defending his goal. The first tactic was to interfere with the penalty line cross-over. A vulnerable point for the attacker taking his own ball in was the bounce over the line. Here he would throw a long forward lob and a wise 3 would meet him at the point of retrieving the ball with a hit to the racquet. Having retrieved his ball, the next option was to drive the 1 hard and fast, away from the goal posts to present a difficult shot.

If the 1, however, had to jockey for position to score his goal, then the 3 had a reasonable opportunity to defend his goal. At no point would he part contact with his opposition, always keeping himself between the 1 and the goal post. Here was where the schooled pony came into play by pushing the 1 away from a scoring position and if successful, out of the penalty area. To watch two 'pushers' fighting it out was quite spectacular with the horses leaning close to forty-five degrees into one another. The impression was that the horse would fall over should the other move away. Sue Keene on Nutmeg and Charles Holland on Spare gave many a performance like this.

If the ball came out of the back line for any reason, then it was cleared from the back line. Therefore a missed goal was cleared by the 3 at the point where the ball crossed over the back line. The 1 was not allowed in the penalty area but had to follow the 3, no closer than 'nose to tail', and had to give him freeway for the first ten yards.

The defence now had three options to clear his area. The first was to take his own ball, but this involved two lines to bounce over and with the attack breathing down his neck. The second was a direct pass to his 1, or over his head for him to run onto, and third, a pass to his mid field player (the Number 2) to take up-field. From then on he stuck to his 1 like the proverbial 'shit to a blanket' and made it as difficult as possible for him to get to the ball.

A number of 3's liked to take a run at the back line and throw a long high ball up field in the hope that the One would retrieve it. On some occasions, the ball would travel from the back line and land in the opposite penalty box, but it was not uncommon for the ball to travel three quarters the distance.

Midfield was the domain of the 2. In attack, he was required to feed the 1, or hold the 3 to clear a passage for his 1. In defence, he was required to spoil the opposition ball-carrier or to prevent a pass. There were two styles played by the mid-fielder, the selection of which was dependant on the particular requirements of the game in play.

The first was the 'marking' 2, who was required to keep the opposition away from the ball, and to clear the passage of his 1, and at times, his 3. This requirement came, more for reasons that invariably this player was the weakest, than from any tactical comprehension. The 1 and 3 were 'glory' positions and consequently players favoured these births as the most rewarding. The weaker player, in the 2 birth, would be intimidated and nervous to play the ball, lest he infringe on his fellow players, so he would invariably settle down to an inglorious and simple marking game.

The second style of the 2 was the 'ball player' approach. His primary function was to secure possession of the ball and bring the game to the attack. His first and most important opportunity was to possess the ball from the lineout, where he was in the best position to retrieve it, and with a quick and bold pony, to recover it anywhere midfield, should that fail. In defence, he would attack the ball carrier, or place himself in a position to retrieve a lost ball.

Contrary to a lot of belief, the 2 is a key element to the success of the game. The 1 and 3 are constantly marking or being marked and are susceptible to being out of position. The 2, on the other hand, is free from these inhibitions and generally is a free spirit. He can influence the game from the defence to the attack and is arguably in the best position to oversee the progress of the game from his relatively unencumbered scouting position. After all, the 1's and 3's have their specific and skilled tasks to perform without losing their focus on too much mid-field work.

Australia's first visit to Zimbabwe influenced a number of changes to our game. They arrived in 1972 with exceptionally deep nets in their racquets, so much so that the ball in the net could almost be wrapped around the neck of the shaft. As a result they were unable to throw the ball any distance but gave the advantage of being able to retain the ball from any form of heavy tackle. Since then they have reduced the depth of their nets to much the same as we have it today, allowing for a stronger throw including overhand. However, the deep net set the form for a very different game plan than we had. Instead of the open format with the long pass, the ball carrier was now confident of retaining the ball in a tackle that it closed the game up and allowed for manoeuvring his way up the field, with the occasional pass at close quarters when needed. This then emphasized the need for schooling the pony to deal with scrum conditions.

This style of game produced a lot more contact and consequently a lot more tactical thought than the previous style. As a result the rulebook has been adapted over the years to meet new requirements of the game. As an example, the lineout has changed so the players now face the umpire and stand knee to knee with the opposite number rather than facing him. The method of deploying a penalty has been revised, and with the increased work load of the pony, the game time has been reduced from 64 minutes a game to 48 minutes and provision made for an "Impact Player" [dreadful terminology], to come on with a fresh pony.

From a spectator's point of view, one cannot compare the two styles of game, both are very exciting to watch, but the change has brought about new skills that are constantly improving with each generation. The player must be a better rider and position his horse more precisely whereas in the previous open game a rider could sacrifice contact with his horse and stretch out for the ball.

CHAPTER 5

HANDICAPS

HANDICAPS WERE INTRODUCED IN 1955 AS A means of establishing the scoring potential of a team and to even the prospects for a win by giving the weaker team the benefit of the difference in the score rating. To arrive at the team's potential score rating, the individual players were, and still are rated on their ability to contribute goals for the team, and the team potential being the total of its six members. A player is rated from 0 goal potential to the maximum 10 goals, and is reckoned on by a committee who compare his standard against his opposition. This is done at each tournament by a handicapping committee and adjusted accordingly.

With the handicapping system, tournament organizers were now able to grade teams into divisions and to seed teams to a more even match, thus putting greater spectator value to the game. Players too could now be grouped into divisions, as 0 to 2 became C Division, 3 to 4, B Division and 5 and above was taken as A Division. No player in the early days made a 10 as it was considered too perfect, whilst not many achieved the prestigious 9.

This then was all very well on paper, but the gremlins of the system would raise their heads and disrupt the equilibrium. A player was rated on the horse he played on and at the previous tournament that he played at. Whilst the horse was not that great a factor in the early years, it definitely became one later where the horse represented a large share in the player's potential. So if a player changed mounts for any reason, the quality of that mount would affect his standard of play against his handicap, and to a lesser or greater degree, affect the overall team's potential. The powers that be then decided to handicap the horse and average the handicap between rider and mount. This became such a nightmare for the administrators that it was abandoned after a trial season.

Another gremlin appeared in handicapping the B Division where probably 70 percent of players were in this 3's and 4's bracket. The difference in performance between these two handicaps was so great that it was difficult to establish a uniform standard, and especially when compared to A Division which had six handicaps to spread over. The remedy to this came by moving C Division down to –2 to 0 and opening up the spread of B from 1 to 4. This is as it is today.

In the early years of polocrosse, women were not considered 'tough' enough to play with the men and so were handicapped within their own standard. When eventually they were allowed to mix in with the men, they were given a second handicap for that purpose. But time was to prove that they were 'tough' enough and at times better, that the dual handicaps fell away.

Up to the 1960's, children of 14 and under were not allowed to play polocrosse. If any exception was made it was done with a letter of consent from the parents. All this has since changed and tiny toddlers can now be seen playing on the field, but for a time, when children were ultimately allowed to play, they were handicapped on what was known as a junior handicap. Kids, who were able to play with the adults, then received dual handicaps in order to do so. Again this has been dropped.

As the name implies, the handicap is a burden to a team, particularly if players do not play to their standard. Any club captain worth his position will fight to keep his club handicaps down when representing his members at the handicapping meetings. But to the individual player, a handicap is a yardstick to measure his progress. To be a 9 handicap had a social standing and would put you into the 'hero' bracket. Only recently has anyone achieved a 10-goal handicap and this was conferred on Gavin Cocker in the 2006 season.

At the other end of the scale, players can come down in handicap, but never to the point where they re-enter C Division. Jill Keith, a veteran player and brilliant horsewoman, and the late Doug King also a veteran player, were the only exceptions.

With the game rapidly evolving the way it is and in which high level games can achieve scores of 64 goals in 64 minutes, handicapping as we know it will become irrelevant. The sport is rapidly spreading around the globe with widely differing opinions and methods of applying handicaps, if at all, that I believe it will either be dropped altogether or a more effective system adopted that will be uniform to world polocrosse.

CHAPTER 6

BEHIND THE WHISTLE

'See that down hit!'

IT'S A TOUGH LIFE BEING AN UMPIRE. NOT only does one have to control over-enthusiastic and potentially explosive players, but also sometimes very rowdy crowds that have no problem in venting their opinion of you, or pointing out your shortcomings from their biased outlook.

It is imperative that an umpire should have absolute confidence in himself and the courage of his convictions to control the game fairly, regardless of influence from any quarter. A tough task!

As an umpire, one needs to have a good understanding of the rules, but more importantly one should be able to read the game that one is controlling in order to apply those rules with effect. One should always be aware that players come onto the field full of pent up energy and focused for victory, and it doesn't take much to bring out their frustration and sometimes, simmering anger. It is generally believed by anyone who has umpired that the application of the rules literally, as written in the rulebook, has a tendency to stop the flow of the game and cause it to become scrappy. This in turn brings player frustration to the fore and creates more fouls, generally serious, and so the game can deteriorate.

It seems to work better if minor infringements, where no obvious advantage is gained, are ignored. Of course no harm is done to point out the infringement to the offending player on his return to line up, if one feels he is making a habit of it.

Authority is all-important in controlling a game. The secret is to impose one's authority in the first chukka of each section, so that the players are aware that one means to control the game. Thereafter one should strive to encourage the game to flow in order to minimise fouls.

Apart from portraying decisive self-confidence, one should be on a good horse that will keep up with the game, and also 'get you out of the way'. A good loud whistle is very useful in gaining attention at the instant you need it, as there is nothing so feeble as a nervous sounding squeak attempting to halt a full blooded charge—such an anti-climax.

The old Metropolitan Police used a specific technique when teaching people to drive a car. Learner drivers had to commentate to themselves, describing all that they saw around them whilst they were behind the wheel. This was to encourage greater awareness of their surroundings. This technique can be very useful to umpires and can help an umpire to foresee a foul developing before it happens, and thereby prevent a serious and dangerous accident before it takes place.

In polocrosse, all committee members are appointed, usually on the basis of popularity more than from ability. That, to my mind, is a political process. Unfortunately, the positions of 'chief umpire' and the 'umpire and rulebook' committee members, and to a lesser extent coaches, are also elected on this basis, whereas, in my opinion, umpiring, like coaching, is a profession. I think a separate body of professionals should elect their own chief and committee based on ability. Surely this would go a long way to professionalising umpiring on the field and indeed encourage recruitment of quality umpires in joining a recognised professional body. I would go so far as to venture that some players would quit their mediocre standard of play, where they have peaked out, and put their all into becoming a professional umpire. I know of many cases of B division players who made exceptional umpires, only to fade away through lack of recognition and promotion.

The referee's position is equally important, especially in a potentially controversial game, or one of great contention. His verdict is final. His role should not necessarily be to police his umpires on the field, or to overrule them whilst a game is in play but should rather be that of a mediator and judge, and a good referee is also a 'general' who directs and encourages his umpires between chukkas, just as he would lead his troops into battle. Not only does this have the effect of bolstering the umpire's confidence on the field, knowing that he has an overlord, but in discussions between chukkas he can sound out the correctness of his decisions, and the referee, in turn, can highlight any omissions.

In all my years of umpiring, I have only experienced the confidence that an umpire derives from a good referee in New Zealand where I was privileged to umpire the Test Series under exceptional referee Jack Christian. Jack, for years was New Zealand's chief umpire, and a most professional one at that. He would call us in between chukkas and we would debate how the game was progressing. The confidence it gave us in our job was phenomenal and helped us through some very emotional patches.

In my time I have had to deal with some very awkward situations. I have always stuck on principal, which at times, has landed me on the end of a red-hot poker. During an inter-provincial final at Hippo, a player, from pure habit (a habit that should have been eliminated at its infancy), was overzealous and dangerous with his stick. Having gone through all the customary warnings and 'goal on the board', I arrived at a situation where a warning of removal from the field was necessary. No player had ever been removed from the field before, so my decision was not given lightly. Hoping that this would be the end of it, we re-commenced play, but to my annoyance, the offense happened again

Unfortunately, all through the game, this player was egged on by a particularly rowdy crowd of his team's supporters. I feel sure that without it, he may well have controlled his habit. After I threw him off the field, half of the spectators continued heckling me, whilst the other half cheered and supported me. Immediately at the end of the game, I was summoned to an 'inquisition' by the chief umpire and his committee at the end of the field; I think to pacify the crowd. Their findings were fortunately in my favour.

Here was a case where a good referee was needed. In the pub afterwards, this player was the first to buy me a beer, and I'm pleased to say he went on to represent his country and managed to kick the habit

Talking of crowds, I was one of a pool of umpires at the 1997 Quadrangular Test Series in Pietermaritzburg and the first time I have ever been paid to umpire. Our Zimbabwe supporters were rather over enthusiastic in supporting their team, and the umpire pulled up the game, and awarded a 'goal on the board' against the Zimbabwe supporters for heckling and they were told to keep quiet.

The first I have seen a crowd score, and for the opposition!

There are times when the umpire can enforce control without the drastic use of the "red card". At one tournament, an argument erupted between the 2's in the line-up, and was heading for a punch up. Neither I nor my fellow umpire had seen anything that should have caused this furore. I called for time off, told the offending players to dismount, and sent them walking up their respective sides of the field and told them not to return until they had calmed down It wasn't long before they returned, apologising profusely and shaking hands. There was no further incident in the game, and I never got to the bottom of what really transpired.

As I have said, having a good horse to umpire on is all important. I remember a tournament in Gweru where I was presented with a rather good-looking grey to umpire on. This animal proceeded to snort at my approach with very flared nostrils, ears back and a look of total disgust in his eyes. I asked the owner, who was playing in the game I was about to umpire, if this horse was suitable for me to ride. He assured me it was. So up I got and immediately had a bronco under me. Fortunately, in time it froze, and I grabbed the opportunity to evacuate before my dignity did and suggested to the owner that if he thought the horse was ok, then he should ride it. This he did, and the animal took off for the stables, pig rooting as it went until the owner fell off and broke his leg. I was told later that he had just bought the beast and was assured it was schooled. However I never saw horse or rider ever again.

Umpires need to be suitably dressed, if only to distinguish themselves from the players they are umpiring. At a tournament in Karoi, Mike Cossey, heavily bearded then, was umpiring a game between Horseshoe and Matepatepa. Roger Birdwood, playing in the 2 birth for Matepatepa was instructed to hold out the Horseshoe 3, who happened to be a heavily bearded Richard Games. Roger, who's eyesight was never that great, but none the less, a very effective and aggressive 2, immediately took the umpire out of the game thinking he was Richard, much to Mike's chagrin.

A national colours scheme was introduced in 1985 for qualified umpires able to umpire at test match level and the following umpires have been awarded their colours:-

Iain Kay
Anthony Keith
John Harris
Jim Parker
Chris Pocock
Don Cocker
Barry Burbidge
Ted Wilmot
Henry Harris
Richard Mostert
Allan Malloy
Shannon Burbidge

A progression of some of the rule changes:-

1973 seems to be the time when the line-ups were changed to face the umpire.

1978 the depths of the net were deepened and the ball had to show above the racquet. This seems to coincide with the tour to SA when we changed to the Max Watkins racquets. These conformed to the rules and allowed for a deeper net to be used.

1983 the depth of our polocrosse net came under further discussion at Chipinge Polocrosse Club. It was felt at that time that the reason for us losing the tests was not due purely to the depth of the net but also to the high standard of horsemanship of the Australians and the higher level of competition that their top players were subject to in their home tournaments. Zimbabwean feelings were that the deep nets would make ball skills easier but would increase wild stick swinging in the attempt to dislodge the ball. We would go to a referendum of 4 handicap players and higher to assess the feelings of our players.

1985 the pooling of horses in order to provide even horse power at international tests was used for the first time.

1985 Subsequent to the failure of the old pith helmet in stopping serious head injuries, the banning of these helmets was considered. It was decided at this time that anyone purchasing a new helmet would be obliged to buy a new fibre glass safety helmet.

1987 was when we had the IPC 'Umpire and Rule Book' meeting in Musselbrook, Australia. IPC had requested all the participating countries to forward their thoughts on amending the international rules. Zimbabwe was the only country that forwarded their proposals and after initial hesitation to support our proposals, many of the ideas were accepted.

1990 the old pith helmets were banned. Umpires dress code was tightened up and all umpires had to wear polocrosse kit. It was also in this year that line-ups were taken on alternate sides of the field after a goal was scored.

1991 The length of chukkas and games came under discussion, the final decision was to play 8 minute chukkas but the length of game could be varied between 4, 6 or 8 chukkas. 6 minute chukkas should only be played in extreme circumstances.

The rule of nose to tail penalty throws for the number 3 from either the back line or penalty line came into being. If the number 1 took a back line throw, the number 3 had to stand off at 10 metres. All side line throws had a 10 metre standoff.

1992 The IPC Rule Book allowed for a number 1, in the act of throwing at goal, to cross the centre line of his horse.

Each test team was allowed to select one umpire from a panel of four to umpire their game.

Whips had to have a flap of 12.5 by 50mm.

Penalty throws in the goal scoring areas could be taken in any direction. Polocrosse balls did not have to be white. Umpires throwing in the balls at line-up came under much discussion.

1994 polocrosse racquet coming in contact with a face or helmet was a goal on the board for the opposite team. A list of illegal drugs for the horses was drawn up.

1996 Werribee, Australia again a successful 'Umpire and Rule Book' meeting was held, where it was decided that the percentage bounce of the ball was to be between 55-65%. At the line-up players should be at a standstill until the moment the umpire throws in the ball. In Zimbabwe, vets were asked for reports on fatigued horses on the field. The vets' findings indicated that, in order to avoid injuries to horses, their time on the field should be reduced.

How not to dress as an Umpire.

CHAPTER 7

COACHING

POLOCROSSE IS PROBABLY THE ONLY EQUESTRIAN activity that attracts sportsmen, as well as horsemen. Horsemen, as we know them, generally take up dressage, show jumping or eventing, and those that take up polocrosse generally make quicker progress in the game as they are better able to ride their horse to position. However, sportsmen once they have learnt their horse skills, tend to end up the better player. There are three distinct elements to polocrosse, One is the horsepower and the ability to ride it, second is an eye for the ball and the ability to work it, and third is gamesmanship with the ability to apply tactics.

Because polocrosse attracts sportsmen with limited riding skills, coaching in the early days tended to emphasise on schooling of the pony as against the other two elements. The sport itself was a good tutor for non-riders as it removed the element of fear and allowed natural instinct to take over whilst absorbed in the adrenalin rush of the game. At club level, a lot of work would be put into the first two elements, in itself a large requirement of the game, whilst the third element of gamesmanship and tactics would come later and usually into A Division. Here it requires the cohesion of the section where each player applies his effort to the overall team plan and is the most rewarding and greatest element in winning a game. A lower handicap side can bring down a stronger side with sound tactical play but for the tactics to be effective, the players must have a full understanding of each other, the weakness and strengths, which obviously require practice as a team.

With the influence of the Australian style of game and one that the world over is following, a greater emphasis is required in horsemanship and horse schooling. No longer should the rider defy gravity by stretching out all over the place and unbalance his horse, but remain in the driving seat and ride his horse to position. The use of the Aussie stock saddle with its 'wings' helps one to achieve this.

The Association saw the need for effective coaching and in 1975 brought in two Australian coaches, Ron Jolly and Ross Balcombe who travelled around the clubs coaching polocrosse. Then again Australia sent over Barry Butterly and Mike Gorman in 1984, the year after Zimbabwe's exposure to international polocrosse at the first world test series and a year before the Australian test series held here in Zimbabwe. The result of this coaching was an improved performance against the Aussies.

In 1988 a coaching committee was formed with representation from the four provinces. They then selected potential coaches, trained them and categorized them after passing tests. These coaches were then sent out to the clubs for coaching clinics that produced a marked improvement in the standard of our polocrosse. Then in 1989, Australia sent over three coaches, Max Walters, Terry Blake and Joy Poole to train 30 Zimbabwean coaches to level 1 status, and in 1991 three Zimbabwean coaches attended the Australian National Sports Centre for further training.

CHAPTER 8

PONIES

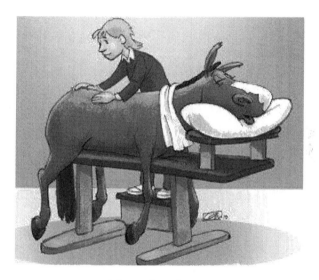

After a hard game

THE EARLY YEARS OF POLOCROSSE WAS NOT SO demanding on the Pony. The sport started off on farm cattle ponies that by nature and breeding were small, stocky and tough. The "bossiekop" as their mixed blood was known, was required, initially, as a mode of transport to ferry the player around the field, whilst most of the skill of the game was in the player and his ball control ability.

Schooling of the Pony was not as critical as it became later; however, as gymkhana's were very much in vogue at the time, they did possess rudimentary basic training. At weekends they would be away playing the sport, only to return to work during the week, rounding up cattle or checking on fences. As the game progressed and the skill of the player improved, so too did the quality of the pony.

Tack used in those formative years was predominantly the old military saddle, with its two padded "ski's" supporting two cast iron hoops, one for the pommel and the other for the cantle, with a leather seat stretched between the two. The bridle was basic with generally a snaffle or Pelham as the bit, and seldom were nose bands or martingales used. Legs were unprotected with bandages or coronet boots.

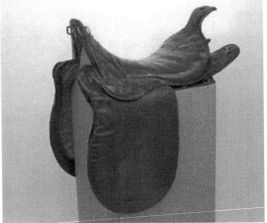

Military saddle

The McClellan saddle, a basic fibre glass tree covered in leather with no padding for the rider and a slit in the middle, was originally designed for women who in those days rode in long skirts. The saddle has its origins in Europe and the Crimea where in 1857 George B. McClellan recommended its use for the military to the U.S. Senate. By 1859, it had replaced the Grimsley saddle and remained in service for nearly one hundred years.

Introduced as a military saddle for the Grey's Scouts and made by Johnsons Saddlery, it soon found its way onto the polocrosse field as it was cheap. Fortunately not for long, as I have always felt that they are too dangerous, and campaigned, unsuccessfully I might add, to have them banned from polocrosse.

McClellan saddle

As the game progressed, speed of the pony became paramount to cope with the long over arm passes. At this time, the speedy and big-hearted Thoroughbred that had completed its career on the racetrack was slowly replacing the bossiekop. These fine looking animals were generally purchased, [at a cheap price in those days], at the annual blood stock sales which coincided with the off season, schooled to hand, and brought in as five year olds.

With the 'professionalism' these horses brought into the game, they became a very much more valued asset and consequently their tack likewise improved. Blankets and sweat rugs began to be used, and saddles were kinder on the pony as well as the rider, with the use of jumping and utility saddles. Bridles became more sophisticated with nosebands and martingales. Bandages and coronet boots were now essential to protect the fine legs of the Thoroughbred. Some enterprising players experimented with the double bridle, so favoured by the polo fraternity, but this was found to be too unmanageable and so it never took hold. Pop Hartley was probably one of the exceptions who used a Pelham with double reins.

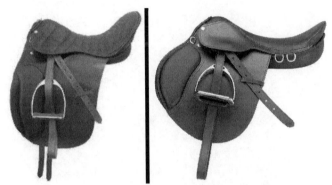

General Purpose Saddle   *Jumping Saddle with the forward   knee roll*

The advent of the first Australian Tour in 1972, introduced the 'saddle with the wings', the Australian Stock Saddle. This saddle came into being some 200 years ago when Australia was a penal colony.

The fugitive criminals often stole horse and saddle during their escape. The hunt saddles brought from England fell far short of providing stability and security for the fleeing outlaws so consequently the saddles were soon modified to include the hunks of leather that eventually evolved into the knee pad or Apoley for which the Aussie saddles are known. Eventually, even rear thigh pads were added.

These saddles started replacing the "easy out" saddles of the jumping and dressage ilk. Here was a saddle most suitable to polocrosse needs with its years of proven acceptability and comfort that generations of Australian stockmen used whilst in the saddle all day, rounding up and 'cutting' livestock.

The Australian Stock Saddle

In the early '70's, The Quarter Horse was introduced into the country in the form of 'Players Compadre', who stood at stud in the then Salisbury. Whilst this stallion produced many progeny, generally crossed with the Thoroughbred, the Quarter Horse made no real impact on the sport although I have seen a few cross breeds playing reasonable polocrosse, but I am not aware of any exceptional ones. Having been privileged to watch some top Australians play the Quarter Horse, I cannot understand why the breed has not featured both here or in South Africa. I can only put it down to sub-standard initial breeding stock that was introduced to South Africa by Gary Player and another, and which filtered through to this country, or that poor promotional techniques possibly failed the Quarter Horse's potential to make any impact on our sport.

The American Quarter Horse

The Australian Stock horse is another amazing animal that has adapted to polocrosse so well. With its unique ability to keep its legs under it, the stock horse dominates Australian polocrosse with its five thousand odd players. In New South Wales, polocrosse is often played under wet conditions and with the stability of the stock horse the game is still played at pace and in mud. I played a stock horse on a field that could have passed as a cattle kraal in the middle of the rainy season, where the ball going to ground would lodge itself in the mud and time off was called to retrieve it. The game was still played at pace and not one horse came down. In fact one felt quite secure in the unusual ability of this horse keeping his legs well controlled and gathered under him.

This is yet another horse that has not appeared on our polocrosse field. Only in recent years has any attempt been made to introduce them. One such person is Dale Scott who has embarked on a breading programme of the stock horse and I wish him every success.

The Australian Stock Horse

Zimbabwe's Independence in 1980, opened up exposure to the international arena of polocrosse, and thus gradually changed the style of our game to conform. The deep-netted racquet coupled with short passes made the sport more contact related and so the requirements of the pony once again changed.

The pony was now required to be schooled to take up a greater share of the talent required for the game. His fitness training required a lot more 'wind jammers' in order for him to come to hand and be highly manoeuvrable. The long sprints now being out-dated for the preference of more tactical play that required a greater degree of ball possession.

Polocrosse has always been known as "The King of the One Horse Sport", but with the game evolving to greater levels of skill required of the pony; this claim can never be maintained. Already game times have been reduced by 16 minutes, played in either 8 Chukka's of 6 minutes or 6 Chukka's of 8 minutes, as against the previous 8 Chukka's of 8 minutes. We are beginning to see substitute ponies coming into the game, particularly in test series, where fatigued ponies are becoming more frequent. In the past owning one pony was all that was required to play polocrosse. Even talented A Division players could get by with this although it was prudent to have a youngster being schooled up in the wings to take over when the old retired. Nowadays, a player is not likely to last in A Division selection if he doesn't have at his disposal, two quality schooled ponies of similar stamp and available on call.

Over the years of polocrosse's history are some outstanding ponies that have played for their country and have been admired and loved by both players and spectators. This book would not be complete without their stories and here are some of them.

BRAZERO

Brazero was owned by Simon Budgen who bought her from a polo player as a reject and unstoppable pony. Charley Christianson then took her over and reached a 9 handicap on her. This horse was honoured by having the horse of the year trophy named after her. She was played by a number of people at national level.

LADY OF LEASURE as told by Barry Burbidge.

Very fast, bold, totally balanced, and in her early years was all but impossible to stop. It required a long run off behind the goal posts, in order to stop her. In the third season of playing, it took Jill Keith's wise council to put matters right. She was played with a tight standing martingale, with a Pelham bit, with the reins attached to the bottom ring and a tight curb chain.

Jill advised me to remove the martingale, and play her in a snaffle. To be sure, my first thought was that she was joking. Having talked me through it, she was convinced that the horse was fighting the martingale and the bit. I took her advice and put Leisure into a snaffle. There was an immediate change for the better, and she became a different horse.

We were on the show jumping circuit, and this was an event at the annual agricultural show. The horse I used to show jump, and all the children learnt to ride on and play polocrosse, Prince, pulled up lame and could not enter the show jumping competition, so I entered Leisure, who had limited experience from cross country. She won the A Grade, and continued to do well for many years. Son Jason won the power jumping competition on Leisure, when she was 20 years of age. This wonderful horse died at the age of 33, and was always a part of the family.

CHIEF ATTRACTION as told by Iain Kay.

We bought Chief as a three year old at the mid-winter sale. She was the second horse on offer, and had no bid. She became ours for the princely sum of $375.00.

As we left the sale, her previous owner, 'Boss' Lilford asked Kerry if we were going to race her. He was horrified to be told that she would be used for polocrosse, and said it was a complete waste of a good horse!

She was very nervous when I first rode her, but I could tell that she was a natural athlete, and she was exceptionally willing. It did not take her long to gain confidence, and for the first five years with us, I was the only one who rode her, perhaps one of the reasons for the incredible rapport I had with her.

Her schooling started straight away. Just 10 to 15 minutes every evening, using an eggbutt snaffle. Although I always had a riding crop in hand, I seldom, if ever, used it. She was a pony that only needed leg aids and your voice.

For the first two seasons, she was only played at club practices, and then I brought her into A-Division tournaments as a five-year-old. Had I brought her in any younger, I don't believe she would have achieved the standard she did, let alone lasted.

Even when she was an experienced polocrosse pony, we still did a short schooling session each evening. Her fitness work used to be just trotting with the odd 'wind jammer', but we found that if we did interval training with her, we could just peak her around National Championships, and she was super fit.

In all her years of top A-Division and international test series, she never once went lame or was vetted out for stress. She played eight seasons in a row as my top pony. Chief was attentive and enthusiastic from the beginning to the end of every game, and genuinely enjoyed her polocrosse. She was awarded 'Pony of the Year' five times during her polocrosse career".

BLUE SKIES [1952 – 1975]

As told by Jon Parkin.

Blue Skies was put to sleep last year. He was born in 1952 in Natal and came to Rhodesia in 1956 when Joan Keene paid twenty-five pounds for him. He began as a cattle pony and was introduced to polocrosse in 1957. Until 1962 he played for Joan in the Marandellas team, enabling her to become a 7 handicap, at that time the highest handicapped woman in Rhodesia.

In 1967 Joan's daughter Sue, with Blue Skies, was selected to ride for the Pony Club team touring South Africa. 1968 introduced Sue to the polocrosse world on Blue. By 1970 he had taught her enough to get on Buzz Bomb and let Joan back onto the field.

During the last years Blue was still playing for Joan for Ruzawi River in the B team. 1975 seemed to be a year of rejuvenation for the old man. I started playing and what better teacher could I have than Blue! Still carrying on with Sue, he played in the ladies team at the Inter-Provincial Championships, and for his last outing we took him to Umtali again for the Eiberg Trophy. Tiring as he was, Blue still put up a magnificent display. And long will he be remembered by those frustrated 3's who had to play against him.

A fine life for a fine horse and it will be many a year before the old stalwarts of polocrosse forget Blue Skies.

STALLION

The Stallion was owned by the Nel family who had bought him and another mangy mare as a job lot for 500 Zimbabwe dollars. Known as Stallion because he once was until he was gelded as an eight year old, was a horse of no particular breed that we call bossiekop. He went on to establish a large number of kids into the sport. The stallion had a huge heart and was at all times willing to give his rider the best opportunities in the game. He is now retired on the Nel's Binder Farm.

BRUNO

The Bruno field at Sebakwe Country Club is named after a 14hh bay gelding of that name, who was a stalwart of Rhodesdale's A team for over 20 years.

Bruno was purchased in 1953 from Ridgeway Riding School by Gordon Tolmay, then captain of Rhodesdale's team for the princely sum of £25. He was then about 6 years old.

Charles Christianson, playing in the No 2 position, rode him in his first national championships, at Glendale in 1954. It was not an auspicious beginning as the team lost and it was not until 1955, when Bruno and Charles were changed to the No 1 position, that he began to weave his spell on the game.

This combination remained the spearhead of the Rhodesdale attack until the 1960 Nationals, again held by Glendale, when Alan Lowe entered the scene and took over riding Bruno.

Selection of the Rhodesdale side of this period centred on ensuring Alan and Charles received maximum support.

Bruno's dominance of the game can be attributed to his phenomenal acceleration and speed over 50 yards and his superb balance which enabled him to manoeuvre in the 30 yard area as no other horse of that time.

Bruno developed a sense of position of the ball, would give Alan just one sight at goal, expect him to score and would then trot back to the centre of his own accord, as soon as the ball had been thrown.

On the few occasions that the throw was wide of the posts, he became visibly upset when forced to return to the area.

Bruno with Alan Lowe

PRINCE

Richard Games on Prince

ROUSTABOUT

Roustabout was one of those horses that appeared on the polocrosse scene in A-Division and rapidly made a name for himself. In his very easy going manner he helped bring Karoi into the top ranking of national polocrosse with both Clive and Glenn Johnson making full use of his talent. In this photo, with Clive at 3 feeding Glenn in the 1 birth and Roustabout in his most effective position, made a formidable combination.

Roustabout with Glenn Johnson

KINGS AFFAIR

Kings Affair was bought from Ted Wilmot by Don and Faye Cocker as a 21st birthday present for son Gavin. Most of Gavin's polocrosse career in Zimbabwe was played on Kings Affair and they only retired him at 19yrs after the 2001 test match.

Kings Affair

RHOMA

Rhoma was a three quarter thoroughbred bred by Lance Nicolle and belonged to Jock Brown of Glendale. Don Cocker purchased him in 1977 as a 5 year old and went on to have a distinguished polocrosse career playing at national level. As a scholar, Gavin played him at provincial and national level and then took sister Fern through her scholars and provincial polocrosse. In all his polocrosse career, Rhoma never went lame or was sick and lived to the age of 25yrs before having to be put down.

Rhoma with Don Cocker

Alan Jack on Fergus.

FERGUS

Fergus was a horse everyone knew and admired. Owned by Alan Jack he would continue to play despite the rider having fallen off.

Ant Keith on Mopani

TROUTSTREAM

In 1961 Nick Leared bought Troutstream from Doubles Draper. He was an ex-polo pony and 14 years old. Nick noticed the tell-tale white marks on the horse's tendons. He had been pin-fired. He needed extra care with his tendons and Nick put cold-water bandages on them after every hard game of polocrosse.

He took Trout into the paddock and began his re-education. polo was quite a different game from polocrosse and only required straight gallops with time to pull up or make wide turns at the end of them. In polocrosse, a horse had to be able to stop immediately and turn a tight circle in order to remain within the lines.

Turning on the forehand was Trout's first lesson. Nick took him out to the paddock with a long stick. It was only to tickle him with, so he could feel it as an extension of the hand.

Nick got off and stood holding the reins very close to Trout's near side. He touched him on his rump with the stick in his left hand. Trout was electrified and jumped all over the place. Quietly Nick walked him forward for a few paces and then stopped and tried again. He once more touched Trout's left rump with the stick. After three or four attempts, Trout eventually got the hang of it. He moved his backside away from the stick. Nick immediately patted him, mounted and set off for a ride. He would go to bed on a good memory. He had learned that trick now. Always, when a horse did what was asked, Nick stopped the lesson.

Turning on the forehand was the first step. Once a horse could do that, turning on the hock came quite easily. He trained Trout every evening until that horse could almost stand on his head when asked to. Nick never had to pull on the reins to make him stop and turn; it took a small pressure behind the saddle, in place of the long stick, and Trout responded.

Nick always played Number 3. He schooled Trout, gradually making him into the top polocrosse pony of the country. Trout would hear the opposite Number 1 galloping up the field and start fidgeting; as soon as Nick touched his sides he would break straight into a gallop, throwing himself against the opponent's horse with all his strength so Nick could rob him of the ball. His handicap went up to a 9.

Trout played for Horseshoe in A level, Mashonaland in the Inter-Provincials and for Rhodesia against Natal.

CHRISTMAS

In 1969 Nick bought 'After Xmas' off the racetrack. He changed the name to Christmas and found it far easier to train a race horse than a polo pony.

To begin with he constructed a school, about 40' square, just outside the garden, with fencing of gum poles. Corners were necessary in order to teach the horse to turn tightly to left or right.

First Nick saddled him, with the stirrups dangling loose. Then he attached long canvas reins to a cavesson bridle, without any bit, and strung them through the stirrups, so that he could drive Christmas from behind. With a long thin stick in one hand and the two ends of the long reins in the other, he drove the horse forward to begin with and walked him round the school. To make him turn to the right, Nick pulled the right rein tighter and touched Christmas's near side with the stick.

Each time the horse responded, the lesson would end. It wasn't long before Nick could make him do anything in the school at a canter; turn in tight corners, stop fast on his hocks, reverse, jump small jumps and even passage.

Christmas played for Rhodesia against South Africa – and for Australia against Rhodesia

ORPA

In 1963 Mary Leared bought Orpa from Hendrik de Waal, who had bred her. Mary sort of trained her; she learnt to change her legs at a canter in a straight line, with a fluid movement that was almost like dancing. She could stop and turn on a tickey and never stepped over a line if she could help it; she learned to weave in and out of other ponies when galloping for the goal. She just loved polocrosse, but was almost unstoppable in a steeplechase. She took Mary to a 6 handicap – at the time the highest ladies' handicap.

Mary played Orpa for Mashonaland in Inter-Provincials and for Rhodesia against Natal; Nick played her against Australia.

A painting by Mary Leared of Tout Stream and Orpa on their Farm.

THE HARRIS HORSE CLAN

To single out any particular horse from the Harris family would be to leave out others equally good. John had Voldin, Dawn, Cocky Queen and French Melody, all of whom played at top level polocrosse. Henry started his distinguished polocrosse career on Mini Tonka before progressing to Kim, J.C., Comedy, Silver and finally Copper Rhythm. Sally started on Mandy then Breathing Fire, Persian, Big Talk and Its My Party [IMP], and Nola rode Cocky Queen and Easy Coup.

Sally used Easy Coup when she played in the World test series, and Dawn was a remarkable horse that John played over many seasons for the National side. Dawn became a household name in the top Ruzawi sides that featured so dominantly at tournaments over the years.

Copper Rhythm was Henry's top horse that probably featured in more national sides than any other horse. The combination of Copper and Henry in the next generation of top players was to set a standard that encouraged others to emulate and to spectators was awe inspiring.

Copper Rhythm

Dawn

Henry on Mini Tonka . Henry on Kim, John on Melody.

ICY TOUCH

Jenny Mannix bought Icy in 1993 as a four year old. Being as clever as she was, Icy always had her own plan, so training her was quite the task. But it all paid off and last season Jenny had no choice but to do the signature 'Icy' stop, duck and turn as she had it all figured out.

Icy has won many best horse prizes in her life and has played countless test matches for Zim men's, ladies and veterans. She also played in almost every open ever played up until 2010 and won a few best horse prizes.

Icy was not only an amazing horse but also an amazing character. She loved playing "Piwi's" but was more than happy to give an occasional "voopsy" to any adult that got on her back.

Icy Touch

CHAPTER 9

AROUND THE CAMPFIRE

POLOCROSSE MEMBERS HAVE ALWAYS BEEN, AND continue to be, a big family unit. Whilst on the field there is keen rivalry; off the field exists a bond that few groupings of humanity can equal. Although predominantly farmers, they come from all walks of life: lawyers, doctors, accountants, business executives, through to poachers and hunters. All socialise and interact on the same level with a common interest and a strong feeling of well-being for their fellow members. Should adversity befall any one of them, it is quickly restored by others. No one is out in the cold in this community.

The start of every season was and still is a time of excitement and anticipation to renew friendships. Loading the van and travelling off to distant tournaments around the country was a great thrill and one would endeavour to make the pub on the Friday night to meet up with all those who would share the weekend with you. The old pick-up truck, often with a trailer, would be loaded to the roof with horse tack, camping equipment, food and booze and not neglecting the medicine box containing healthy supplies of aspirin, Brufen, Garonson, diarrhoea and nausea pills, and wads of cotton wool and plasters. You could recognise them on the open road, polocrosse racquets and helmets taking pride of place in the back window, with bumper stickers proclaiming 'Polocrosse - King of the one Horse Sport'.

Rural venues were particularly personal, as the district would rally even the non-player members of the community to put on a great show. Some would be behind the bar serving, others, usually the wives, preparing food in the kitchen, and in the early days when numbers were not so great, accommodating players in their homes, with hospitality second to none.

Horses often travelled by train, getting off at the nearest siding where they would be collected by transport from the host club; usually a flotilla of farm tractors and trailers as farm lorries were not a common item on farms in those days as it is now. Hiring commercial road transport was usually too expensive, so rail was the next best thing. Railway regulations did not permit people to travel in wagons, but the authorities made a concession to allow grooms to accompany their charges on condition that the doors remained open for them to escape should there be an accident. But usually, the trains were frustratingly unreliable. Very often they would not keep their timetable, or they would abandon the wagons in some obscure siding that would prove difficult to find. A club would appoint a member to track the train's movements and be called on to ferry water to the poor parched animals sitting it out in some sun-scorched siding. Gwelo once sent their horses to the Eiberg tournament in Umtali only to discover the wagon was dropped off on route at Macheki, this despite Bob Gardner being an employee of the railways. The advent of farm lorries eliminated the need to use the railways and is still the predominant means of transport to this day.

But the means to get your horse to tournaments came in other forms apart from lorries. I know of one Rhodesdale player who would walk his horse to the Gweru tournament, some 80 kilometers away, play the tournament and walk it home again. Then again, up to the 1970's, there was a trend where horses were transported in the back of pick-up trucks supported inside a pipe frame, with the horse's head peering over the cab. I have done this with an opened up Series one Land Rover Station Wagon and the horse nuzzling my bald plate as we drove. But what takes the cake is Ronnie Palmer, from

Karoi, who regularly squeezed his two huge animals in the back of a Peugeot 404. Graham Crook on one occasion, had his little mare Twiggy join him on the front seat of his Mazda B1600 when he stopped too suddenly at the traffic intersection. And Prickle Thorn, a Horseshoe player, had his mare fly over the bonnet when he did much the same thing at a traffic intersection. Richard Norval's horse, Planet, objected to the sight of a donkey and pummelled in the cab roof with his front feet and thereafter Rich wore his helmet inside the truck as well as on the field.

Stable accommodation used to be makeshift blocks of stables constructed of eucalyptus poles and rough thatching, with the grooms camping alongside. A tournament committee member would be appointed to oversee the stabling arrangements and by and large, was quite satisfactory. Today, with the clubs centred on cities and towns, the means to provide stables is limited. The trend has developed that individuals accommodate their horses within ropes, or electric tape they bring and string around trees or poles dug in the ground and are removed at the end of the tournament.

Campsites, looking like a Gypsy encampment, used to be set up with a variety of tents and sometimes caravans, all gathered in club groups with a communal campfire blazing away in the chill evening. Players, reminiscing over the finer details of their games, or nursing injured knuckles, sat around on deck chairs amongst the smoke of log fires and the aroma of grilled boerewors and steak, yarning into the early hours of the morning.

The club bar, the social nerve centre, was usually packed to capacity with beer by the gallon flowing across the bar counter and not all of it reaching its intended destination. Players, some still in brightly coloured team shirts with numbers on their backs, and once white jodhpurs, but now saddle stained up to their crotch, engaged in youthful energy. Some showed off their assets in poorly choreographed strip shows, whilst others like Iain Kay, took the legs from under you whilst torpedoing on their sides along the beer soaked floor. Still others, like Ken King would entertain you, stark naked except a rolled up newspaper nipped in the crotch and lit at the rear end, called 'flaming arseholes'. Or Nick O'Connor would proudly drink a beer upside down whilst hanging from a chandelier.

Around the campsite entertainment went on with capers like Sheila Hamilton impersonating Lady Godiva cantering through on her horse, with men desperately trying to latch onto the reins. Once a daring and unfortunate Clive Teubes streaked on a way-too-small monkey-bike, hit a sand patch with his front wheel, somersaulted over the handle bars and knocked himself out in front of startled campers.

"Do you think he needs mouth-to-mouth resuscitation?"

Late revellers from the pub staggered back to camp at varying hours throughout the night. Some, romantically inclined but past effectiveness, crawled into tents they thought belonged to their wives, as was the case when

Colin Jenkins poured himself into Julie Cossey's bed and promptly fell asleep. Julie, unaware but annoyed at the duvet snatching and persistent snoring uncommon for Mike, proceeded to scold the comatose pseudo-husband, until she overheard the camp fire conversation in which Fiona was asking where Colin was. Only when she heard Mike reply did she realise that the man in her bed must be Colin. In a panicked frenzy, she tore out of the tent, protesting profusely, but Mike was hard to convince, Fiona not too fazed, and Colin, too embarrassed to come out of his own tent the next morning.

Then there was Alan Lowe and Brian Bowles, who both had amorous feelings for Eleanor, Alan's wife. Feeling two hands groping her from either side, she cleverly clasped their hands affectionately together, and both men slept happy and contented for the rest of the night.

The mornings would be ablution rush hour. Not many clubs could claim adequate facilities to cater for the numbers. Featherstone, who held the record for hosting the greatest number of teams, built their ablution building over a large long-drop trench. This proved to be the best cure for hangovers, as one visit to the methane chamber would stimulate nausea and induce the alcoholic bile to purgatory. Ruzawi on the other hand invented the urinal reservoir. Here was a beautifully white tiled trough filled with water that could pass as a communal basin to wash your face in, and that is precisely what some did. And I could never figure the thinking behind Gweru's architect who constructed field latrines with 'Desert Lilies', a funnel in the ground, that were so high that it required a 'python' with siphon abilities to feed it.

As with all horse owners, polocrosse players are proud of their mounts and often brag, some with exaggeration, about the exploits of their four-legged friends. After a particular Umguza Club practice, Allan Malloy once boasted about his big dun, Gladiator, being a superb cowboy horse, and that one could leapfrog on from behind. Malcolm Sergeant duly took up the challenge, and the entire pub turned out to witness the event. The unsuspecting Gladiator, snoozing under a tree and waiting to be taken home by his boss, was rudely awakened to a yelling madman charging at his rear end. Glad, having the fright of his life defended himself from this hooligan with a 'double barrel' expertly leaving his hoof prints, either side of Serge's thighs.

Then Tony Pemba, after a drunken session in the pub, decided to express his affections to his horse before calling it a night, and gave the animal a boozy blow up the nostrils. The poor unsuspecting horse took exception to the stale alcoholic fumes and promptly bit him on the face, whereupon Tony, in a fit of rage, lashed out with a hefty kick and broke his foot.

Amongst our members were some very competent and agile horsemen and women. Nick Leared, for instance, was such a competent rider that he demonstrated his skill by riding no less than six horses at full gallop down the polocrosse field by standing upright, like a circus rider, and astride the two centre horses. He had such control that he was able to keep all six in line. Some of the kids were also incredibly agile. Howie Baker was so small that his legs could not reach beyond the saddle flaps, yet when he bent down to reach for the ball, he would disappear from sight and re-emerge with the ball at the end of his racquet that was probably taller than he was.

One thinks of all the talented horsemen and women who not only rode well but also were master trainers. Jill Keith and Sheila Barry, who trained all their family horses over the years, Arlene Crook, Ted Wilmot, Iain Kay, John and Henry Harris, Sean Minter—the horse whisperer', to name a few. Charles Holland put a new dimension into polocrosse by schooling his mounts to be outstanding pushers and to reverse at a fair pace. Then there were those that combined so magically with their mounts that it was 'poetry in motion' to watch. Barry Burbidge on Lady of Leisure, Tony Blake on Pegasus, Alan Lowe on Bruno, Nick Leared on Christmas, and

Mikie Craynor on anything. In fact I rate Mikie the best male rider of all time in that he gets the best out of any horse he rides without the use of crop or spurs.

But there were many that learnt the art of polocrosse before they understood the techniques of riding. I remember an incident when Chris Russell from Umtali, phoned me asking to buy a horse. The only mount I had for sale was rather hot and required a competent rider and I knew he was only a beginner. Not to be dissuaded by trivia like that, and egged on by Neil Gordon, he duly mounted the horse and took off at a full gallop around the paddock. Seeing that there was clearly nothing connecting him to the horse save the reins which he held above his head, I decided to intervene and try and stop the horse by standing in front of it, waving my arms frantically. The horse did a perfect turnabout and discharged its wide-eyed and hydraulic-jointed rider into a torpedo-dive straight through a barbed wire fence. Thinking the worst, we rushed over to retrieve the body that had buried itself in a pile of lawn clippings and discovered his jeans and shirt torn to shreds, but not a mark on his body. Undaunted by it all, he pronounced the horse sold, as it would 'take him into A-Division in no time at all.' Some years later, at a tournament at Ruzawi, I was conscious of a game behind me where the umpire was calling for time off more often than was usual. Having turned around to investigate, I discovered Chris spread eagled on the floor with the same horse disappearing in a hurry to the stables. I don't recall seeing Chris play since then.

I doubt if there are many players who do not suffer 'butterflies' or 'nerves' before a match at a tournament. It is, however, interesting how people deal with them in their own way. Some go completely silent and a little off colour. Others become very talkative and annoy the silent ones. Yet others remain perfectly composed but the odour of their flatulence is a dead giveaway.

It's not a bad thing to suffer from nerves. It gets the adrenaline pumping and ensures you are totally tuned in. Usually moments into the first chukka are sufficient to settle you down and it is straight sailing from then on. But there are those who mistakenly try to suppress natures 'turbo charger'! They will have a couple of beers before the game, and whilst that suppresses the nerves, it generates 'Dutch courage' and becomes a nightmare for the umpire. Others take tranquillisers and you can detect them in the line out, fighting gravity to hold their eyelids up.

Umguza had the answer as to how many tranquillisers one should take. Malcolm Sergeant had a big bay Mare called Sabrina that had an evil temper and would kick anybody in reach. If a player was that relaxed that he could walk up to Sabrina and slap her on the rump, then that player had had too much. Then there was Jean Scotcher, as she was, whose nerves derived from her horse Trampy who would deliver a few unsettling bucks before the game commenced. To sort her own nerves out, she decided to tranquillise Trampy, but unfortunately an overdose was administered. Trampy went on to the field without a buck, much to Jeans delight, but promptly fell into a deep slumber when they reached the line out.

One should not forget our followers and spectators who contribute in their own way to the sport. Tommy Wright originated from South Africa where he ran a hostel for wayward girls. He worked for Mazoe Citrus Estates and befriended Bill Cossey in a relationship that lasted until Bill's death. Not one for the niceties of protocol, he was fired from Mazoe and went to work for Strath Brown where he would often work weekends in order to be free to attend polocrosse tournaments. Small in stature, he had an infectious giggle that rocked his body from the head down and always kept everyone amused. Doug King put up a trophy especially for him as the best supporter and named it the Doug King Floating Trophy.

Rhodesdale had their supporters in Sandy King and Jenny Swift. When their husbands were playing these two brought gesticulation to perfection by rushing up and down the side of the field in complete animation, so much so that someone filmed them and had a showing at the club one evening. Without seeing the game one could tell from their body language precisely what was going on with the game, and of course Jenny shouting "come on precious" being her affectionate name for husband Bob.

At Ruzawi with the home team usually in the final, Iain Kay would have his personal supporters amassing at one end of the field. These would be farm workers come to see their hero at work, enthusiastically shouting "doba doba" referring to his ability to retrieve a ball anywhere, and would add a wonderful atmosphere to the final.

Billy Hughes, from Horseshoe, was a man that I doubt ever sat on a horse, yet he supported his two children, Craig and Julie, to the full. He became thoroughly involved in the sport, lending his transport to South African tours and becoming a knowledgeable national selector. Countless wives fit into this category too, as they follow their husbands around tournaments, feeding them and sorting out all their trivia. Notable amongst them were the Featherstone ladies who would bring along kitchen paraphernalia that could feed an army, and certainly they could do it with delicious Afrikaans cuisine.

*Off to watch the finals "That was some final -
Another drink?"*

Grooms play a large part in the success story of polocrosse, the majority of them dedicated and devoted to the well-being of the horses in their care. Thomas, an old wizened man from Malawi who worked for Sheila Barry for many years, had little time for the human species but was totally devoted to his charges. He took time to train youngsters in the art of clipping and shoeing horses, as he himself was a master farrier. Kezi was one that he trained who ultimately took over from Thomas on his retirement.

Bones was another of these grand old men who worked for John Harris and who served three generations of the Harris family. Bones started working for John in 1962 and went on the first tour to South Africa that went down by train in 1968. Since then he accompanied all the tours and it was generally reckoned that Bones looked after his horses better than all the other grooms. Being the most experienced, Bones was made head of the grooms on a lot of the tours. Sadly, he died in 2011.

Magaba was Ian Brown's groom for many years. Not only was he good with horses but was well schooled as Ian's personal 'Batman', polishing boots, setting up the braai and generally seeing to his well-being with drinks. I inherited him on Ian's death and he gave me great service whilst we continued with 'Brown Dog's' well tried arrangement. Magaba was always a cheerful chap, a bit weak kneed on the booze, but usually dependable and between Ian and I he travelled on many tours. He finally retired to his home in the Zambezi Valley.

Then there was Mandevu, short with a big grey bush for a beard and looking much like the garden gnome, who was known to cure a colic horse that a vet had given up on. He came from the Lowvelt to work for the Nels outside Harare.

The Australians, on tour to Zimbabwe, would frown at our use of grooms arguing that it restricts bonding time with our horses. This may be so but is not necessarily the case as there are many ways one can form a bond with your mount. Grooms do give you an element of freedom, handling the tedious task of mucking out stables and cleaning tack etc. as well as walking the horse between chukkas.

Australia does not use grooms, so walking a horse between chukkas is usually done by themselves or a member of their family. Whilst on tour to that country, our wives would take on this task, but my wife at the time, Sue, who was petrified of horses, bravely decided to do the right thing and offered to lead my horse. No sooner had she taken the reins, than she shrieked "take this horse away, it's following me".

Morgan Freeman, a well-known African American movie star, came out to Zimbabwe on a Safari. He came to watch polocrosse being played at Bulawayo, Ruzawi and Matepatepa. When he was standing watching the game from behind the goal posts in Bulawayo, Ian Mannix dismounted and handed Morgan his horse to walk, thinking he was one of the grooms. Morgan, delighted that he was now a part of the sport, happily walked his horse but Ian had no idea who Morgan was and was highly embarrassed when told.

Talking of tours, I recall one to South Africa where all the horses', feed and kit was jammed into Mike Foresters old Hino that had been modified with an extended back over a double axle and was pulling a trailer. The horses took up most of the space with a portion of the trailer for feed and hay bales. The rest, tack, buckets and grooms were suspended or perched on the top rails. The truck was grossly under-powered for the task resulting in a long and tediously slow journey.

I remember the grooms would take turns in sleeping on top of the feed or perched like chickens on top of the frame, for there was literally nowhere else to go. Every gradient was taken at a snail's pace, grinding away in low gear and the grooms, high up on their perch, would nod away with head tilted in the African sun.

I was Hunty's co-driver, and I developed the tactic of speeding the downhills to gain momentum for the climb on the other side. This proved to be a near fatal mistake. When rounding a crest in third out of the six gears, the road suddenly disappeared down a steep escarpment with hairpin bends. At that particular moment the brakes failed with the air gauges sitting on zero and there was now no option of engaging a low gear but to remain in third.

Feeling a good wind in their face, the grooms woke with excitement that the tedium had been broken, shouting "hunday Baas" [lets go] but little did they know the circumstance I found myself in. Coming around one hairpin bend was a lorry crawling down in low gear and it was either to rear end him or take my chances that nothing was coming up around the corner. Only then did the grooms realise our predicament and in one movement the perches were cleared as they took cover amongst the horses.

After what felt like an eternity, we finally ramped the narrow bridge at the bottom of the pass, and as the speed died on the up gradient, the air gauges picked up pressure. Hunty then released his grip on the passenger seat where he had been absolutely motionless, and launched into a rapid diatribe something about that this happens periodically but the workshops could find nothing wrong and wouldn't believe him. We took five to recover our shattered nerves and recount the ordeal with the likes of Bones and Magaba.

'Must be somewhere up there!'

'Who needs the ball, I'll whack you anyway!'

Gary Jollif highjacked an Aussie Guitar on tour.

Chris Pocock

Zimbabwe supporters at their best.

CHAPTER 10

THE NEWSLETTER

THE IDEA OF A NEWSLETTER STARTED IN 1968 WHEN it was decided that an annual publication was required to keep the membership up to date and informed. The first edition came out in the 1969 season with Mary Leared as its first editor. Mary, an English school teacher, had the added ability of ferreting out worthy material and the skill to edit it into a very enjoyable and readable magazine. In fact, the second edition sold 260 copies doubling the first issue. All of this had to be banged out on an old typewriter, sent into town and rewritten on to a stencil to be printed out on the outdated Roneo Machine. How the modern computer has made all this work so much simpler! In 1976 the association purchased its own Roneo printer and Mary was able to print her own copies. Mary wrote a column under the title of 'With an Ear to the Ground' in which she would draw attention to humorous issues that would occur off the field.

In 1979 Mary wrote the last edition of the Rhodesia Polocrosse Newsletter and handed over to Judy Wilson whose first edition came out in 1980 as the Zimbabwe Polocrosse Newsletter. Then in1983 Ian Taylor became the editor, changing the name again to 'Time off'. He produced a full magazine of interesting articles until 1987 when it was handed over to John and Pauline Fairly. Ian returned with his able wife Lynn to continue editing the magazine in 1990 when John became the Executive

Chairman of the association. The couple continued to produce the magazine until the end of the '90's when polocrosse administration collapsed due to the farm invasions.

Much informative information came out in these newsletters with highlights from the council meetings, updated handicap lists and news from around the clubs. The Chief Umpire was able to use this medium to remind the players of rule changes and to promote better umpiring as when Charles Holland, the 1977 Chief Umpire, put it all down in verse:

It is really simple and easy
Though players say they are queasy
The rules are the same
To umpire a game
With manner sure and breezy

Committees sweat over organisation
Ponies always the greatest vexation
Too slow and inert
Themselves to exert
So the umpire receives condemnation

This year it will all be quite new
With teams self organised too
Their own ponies they'll use
So can only abuse
Themselves if they put up a blue

A team to a match is assigned
So make sure you are not left behind
All study your rules
So you won't look such fools
When the fouls in the game you must find

Teams given a game to control
Line judges and one in each goal
Two others to see

Fouling isn't for free
Only six players justice to dole

Line Judges on stick side will be
Thus it is simple to see
The ball in the net
If it hasn't left yet
The pony's foot of the line must be free

Captains of teams must decide
His players to arrange on each side
Instead of complaints
Umpires now will be saints
And teams in there work will take pride

If you're unhappy about the selection
Or the controlling team's imperfection
Then you have to go
To the ones who know
How to reorganise to your satisfaction

When your play gets to such a contrival
That you find yourselves in for a final
Then you can toss
For who will be boss?
Of the game for your mutual survival

Then there was this advertisement in the 1969 edition that went -

WANTED,
By broken-hearted Mike Cossey, who has lost his
horse and is looking for comfort—black hair, good legs
sound teeth and size 36-24-36.

Also in 1969 Monica Marsden interviewed ten year old Jan Teede and sixteen year old Barbara MacLauchlan on the radio programme 'Young Rhodesia', part of it went;

Monica,
"Are you from Horseshoe too Jan? And what Division do you play in?"
Jan,
"No I live in Salisbury, I play at the Borrowdale Club. I am in C Division because I am not good enough yet for B Division. Anyway I am not old enough—you have got to be 15 to play in B or A Division tournaments, and youngsters have to be 11 before they are allowed to play in a C Division tournament. But all the younger ones have plenty of chance to play at home."
Monica,
"So the top Division is really for grown-ups is it? And do men play as well as women?"
Barbara,
"The men would be MAD to hear you say that! It is quite the other way round really—the women are welcome in C and B Division, but the men are not keen on them playing in A, because it is pretty rough."

By the early 70's so many new members joined polocrosse that a suggestion was made that everyone be made to wear a name tag, gone were the days when everyone knew each other like a big extended family. But with the increased numbers, problems soon arose. More females were now playing polocrosse and threatened the comfort zones of the males. Trophies that women played for were transferred to the men's and the women complained that even their mounts that they had schooled up were taken over by husband, son or boyfriend. This letter appeared from *'A. Female'* and the battle of the sexes began.

'FOR LADIES ONLY
Well girls, this is one of the few sports in the world where we are able to play with the chaps on the same level. So we must keep it that way.

Some time ago the men barred ladies from A Division and this decision was only reversed when Marandellas suddenly realised that they needed Joan Keene in their A team. Or maybe they had another, completely altruistic, motive. However it was, merit is now the only criterion.

When we play at home, we may giggle and squeal and do almost anything we like, provided we bring a cream cake for tea. But to be picked for the TEAM for a TOURNAMENT is quite another kettle of fish. Here is a small set of rules that should be carefully adhered to:

1 a] Look tough and sexless on the field. Men don't like to feel they're knocking a LADY about – it upsets their code of chivalry.

But

b] Become feminine and alluring off the field – they love to be surrounded by TALENT.

2 Imitate the men but not TOO carefully, e.g.

a] They are allowed to make an enormous fuss when they topple off their nags—you are NOT. [Otherwise they may decide the game is TOO DANGEROUS for you].

b] They may use all the most dreadful language you've ever heard, and some more—you may NOT. [Men don't like to hear foul language on the lips of the FAIR SEX].

3 a] Listen to all the free advice the men give you, and look FASCINATED.

But

b] NEVER give a man any advice at all—refer him to someone else if he is in desperate need of help. [Otherwise the men might lose their sense of superiority, and that would be CATASTROPHIC].

4 Make sure you are a perfect wife / girlfriend / mother etc. so that your husband / boyfriend / children can't complain that polocrosse has RUINED you, and sulk in their tents. [Sulky men are UNCOMFORTABLE]. It's quite simple; just pop the children into the car with nappies, bottles, hats, shoes, food, blankets, etc. etc.. Lay out your man's riding kit and remember his spare stick, wrist guard, helmet, whip, etc. Organise the horses completely. Make sure you have a stock of medical supplies such as plasters, scissors, aspirin and bandages. Lastly dress yourself, [preferably with Mary Leared padding] and ON NO ACCOUNT FORGET THE CREAM CAKE.'

And excerpts of Bill Cossey's reply on behalf of the men:

'I am no misogynist, but—and here I hear the cries of the female libs—I do not like females playing first class polocrosse!! Confidentially they are a bloody nuisance. They all assure you they wish to be treated like a man, and to ignore the fact that they are females. How can any man, who is a man, do that?

But get a female running amok in her nippy twisting way, driving her opponent up the wall, and notice where the frustration comes from. It's the number of times he can see the chance to fix her but—if he hits that way, and she drops her stick, the smack will travel up her stick along her arm, and there is a good chance that Mary or Celia or Sue will finish up with a scar across her nose, or her front teeth out.

There is only one way to fight a woman, and the prize is not a cup, and the place is not a polocrosse field. I will tell the men how to fight a female, where to fight a female, and that lovely prize that one gets if one wins. That is if there is a polocrosse player that does not know.

BUT KEEP THEM OUT OF FIRST CLASS POLOCROSSE.'

The psychologists amongst us have come to the fore with their contributions. Here is THE PSYCHOLOGY OF POSITIONS taken from the 1976 Newsletter:

'Have you ever-noticed how flashy number 1's are? 1 is beautiful, they seem to think, and as their heads are

generally filled with their own regard, there is not much space for further thought. They are the glory boys and girls—females too revel in this position, needless to say. Woe to the team that does not make enough of them; these vain beings starve for praise and when they are kept short of it, will often retire into a quite unpleasant sulk.

An entirely different kettle of fish presents itself in the number 3's. These fellows see themselves as the bastion of their team, the last bulwark against the enemy. They are grim earnest battlers, not given to smiling or unnecessary chatter. Serious and stubborn they fully realise the match depends on them, especially if they lose it. Then, withdrawn and silent, they are prepared to shoulder all the blame.

How refreshing it is to meet a number 2. He is a cheerful resilient bloke, who is capable at any minute of changing his play from attack to defence and back again. He will take the ball up the entire field and pass it to the number one to shoot, and happily allow him all the praise. He will defend to the utmost and let the three take all the credit for the saved goal. He is a modest kind of chap who looks for no reward save that of the team's victory. Shunning the limelight, and taking every game as it comes, surely the number two is the backbone of polocrosse.'

Another angle from Bill Cossey. 1972:

'I love the man that walks off the polocrosse field and, to the public, loves his horse so much; that he rests it at every chance he gets. It is pure coincidence that he has just scored a goal in rather a dashing manner and the slow walk across the whole of the crowd gives them the chance of admiring him and his manly figure. I've always reckoned that if the horse is not capable of carrying the type off the field, it is not fit enough to play, and the exercise should be carried to its extreme, and the player walk onto the field, not mounting until he has reached the

centre line.'

And an article written in 1984 on 'REAL MEN':

'The controversial book 'REAL MEN DON'T EAT QUICHE' has given food for thought on the subject of the REAL MAN. Someone suggests that REAL MEN PLAY POLOCROSSE!

To play this game a man must possess all the great manly characteristics which females so admire; guts, determination, honesty, integrity, sportsmanship, pride, sensitivity, reliability - the list goes on. But should I have said guts and constitution? Ah yes, what amazing constitutions those men have; not a decent meal from Thursday through to Sunday, several games of polocrosse, and enough beer and gin to keep the breweries smiling and jingling their pockets, whilst our blokes suggest they have holes in theirs. Having smoked enough coffin nails to put the whole of the Zimbabwe Polocrosse Association away comfortably, and a total of a few hours' sleep, only the very fittest could possibly survive. And yet, come Monday morning these brave and superbly fit specimens are up and at it and ready for another week's hard toil.

As far as their honesty and sportsmanship goes, never a cleaner sport was played; rarely a voice is raised or a vile word of abuse exchanged, never a foul swipe of the racquet when the umpire is not looking, or an elbow in the lineout. Such good sportsmanship indicates a real man.

Like all men, the polocrosse player is also most reliable. Always on time, ready to go home early the evening prior to the big final, and always stone cold sober to play. There is no need to ask if the horses are fed or boots polished. No fear of anyone forgetting their saddle blankets, team shirts, helmets, sticks, balls, or what day it is.

Ask any girl, a real polocrosse man is always so sensitive, kind and loving. Just tell him that his horse is out and injured, and you will see how quickly he will fuss. But of course a woman understands and bears the great affection between man and beast and heaven help any women who tries to get between them. Of course there is also great comradeship ~ this is obvious from the way the men share their lady friends around and buy each other drinks ~ such sacrifices and unselfishness in the name of friendship.

And as these men reminisce over past notorious games; the women sit by and ogle at their wonderful memories and their love of the sport. While the ladies discuss such trivia as the price of the lunch, or how to get their hair presentable in time for the prize giving party at the end of the tournament, the men will continue to discuss more important details like 'the Hippo bar fridge door is still not repaired and they never have any ice' or 'how can I have a decent shower when the Ruzawi members refuse to repair their water system' or 'will Mr Wixley give his sons a few days off to recover from this thrash'.

Oh sigh, such supermen!!! All I can say, if you are a real man, you will eat what the bloody hell you like.'

And now for the REAL MAN'S CREDO:

'Since the beginning of time men have lived by rules. Moses had his Ten Commandments, King Arthur his Knights of the Round Table, and Iain Kay his Umpire Rule Book.

Among real men, however, there has always been one simple rule—never settle with words what you can accomplish with a polocrosse stick, a riding crop, or a seventeen hand horse built like a Clydesdale, and amongst today's Real Men this rule still applies, but with a minor modification—never settle with words what you can accomplish with a polocrosse stick, a riding crop, or a seventeen hand horse built like a Clydesdale—unless the problem in question is of the size of Big John

Davidson; in such a case a man to man apology is the best course to take.

Indeed, given the violent state of modern society, it is always best to defer to argumentative meat heads wielding howitzers, tanks, hand guns, nuclear war heads and pump action shotguns, because it is a simple fact of life, that no matter how tough and strong you are, it all amounts to nothing if you are not around afterwards to show it. This is an example known as the survival of the smartest. Besides, you can always get him later with a pick axe handle, when he is not looking.'

A visiting Australian player, Sally Thompson, left us with this thought in verse in the 1984 Newsletter:

'It must be said that while the laws of the game outline the code of behaviour,
It is the spirit behind them which is important.
A game can be spoiled even if it is played to the letter of law,
For if so minded,
It is not difficult to find ways and means of taking unfair advantage over another.
Therefore, be fine sports, play the game, and help the unwritten spirit of fair play.
It is an aim we should be proud to honour at all times.'

And another verse on the 'Antiquity of Polo .'

'For the daring turn and the skilful stroke,
The ever quickening stride,
The ring of the stirrup, the clash of the stick,
And the rush of the furious ride,
The cheer when the ball through the goal is driven,
By the steady hand and eye,
Have a wild delight in themselves alone'
That can never grow old and die.'

CHAPTER 11

PERSONALITY PROFILES

MODERN POLOCROSSE IS RELATIVELY YOUNG in the eyes of world sport, but Zimbabwe can proudly be associated amongst the pioneers of its development, second only to Australia. Zimbabwe polocrosse has amongst its other achievements, survived sixty years of various degrees of turbulence and it still continues to be ranked amongst the top playing countries of the world. This achievement is due to the talent and determination of all its members and this chapter highlights some of those characters that contributed to the overall success story.

DR. MINTO STROVER

Our Founding Father who started polocrosse in this country in 1948.

Minto Strover was born in 1906 and came from a family strong in British military tradition. His father, however, had broken from tradition and become a doctor and Minto followed in his footsteps. His upbringing and school days in England, which included the period of the first World War, led to his having a wealth of anecdotes and mostly highly amusing. He was a witness to a number of German Zeppelin and Gotha bomber raids over England which he recalled with amazing clarity.

He graduated as a doctor from Bristol University and about this time he met Ethelwyn Everett who became his wife. Ethelwyn had been brought up in Salisbury and whose father had been the first Auditor General of Southern Rhodesia. Later she went to school in England where she met Minto.

The newly married couple came to Rhodesia in 1931 / 32 and Minto became a government medical officer. He served in a number of Districts, but those that he reminisced most about were Bindura and Fort Victoria.

Both Minto and Ethelwyn had a lifelong passion for the bush, wildlife, horses and dogs. Later came the interest and enthusiastic support of their sons in equestrian events which led to the interest in polocrosse. Minto, as the founding father of polocrosse in Zimbabwe maintained a lifelong interest in the game and followed events with a passion. With his skilled surgeon hands, he could handle the most intractable of horses with no fuss or bother.

Minto and Ethelwyn had three sons, two of whom are eminent surgeons and one the general manager of a large sugar estate in Zambia. The sons also grew up with a deep appreciation of the bush and wild life and needless to say, horses.

Minto and Ethelwyn spent many years in Fort Victoria and he finally retired from government service from there. He then took up the position of medical officer at Triangle and served there for a good number of years. It was here that their love for long rides through the lowvelt bush developed.

Minto finally retired in the late 1970's and moved to George in the Southern Cape. From George they moved to Sedgefield where they lived for 10 years. Failing health and the persuasion of their family finally saw them moving to England in 1993. They settled near Angus Strover, one of the surgeon's sons, in Worcester.

Minto had that very rare ability of being able to combine the true qualities of a gentleman, with an attitude of compassion and practicality towards suffering. He was ever a realist with both feet firmly planted on the ground. Always courteous, but he did not suffer fools gladly. He was a product of his time, with firm views on what was right and what was wrong.

One of the stories Minto liked to relate was when he and his son, Paddy, were in the bush filming wild life. The sun was setting and whilst walking along a narrow path returning to camp, they were confronted by an elephant, barring their right of way. It had rained and the ground was muddy. The guide motioned Minto and Paddy to keep still whilst he scooped up a ball of mud, rubbed it under his sweaty armpit and threw it at the Elephant. The Elephant gave it a good sniff and with disgust raised his trunk, trumpeted loudly and fled, leaving the path clear to proceed.

Minto had started writing a book on his life experiences in this country, but it is not known if he had finished it. If he had it would make an interesting read.

Minto died in May 1995 and Ethelwyn in December 1995. For those who had the privilege to know them will never forget them.

TED WILMOT

Ted was born in Bulawayo in 1948. His introduction to polocrosse, in the late 60's, was when he was invited to play at Lakeside, on his roman nosed pony, Pocahontas, who was frustratingly slow on getting onto the ball. For a beginner this was daunting, and Ted's enthusiasm could not kick in, until his mentor, John Hartley, advised him to move it on. He then purchased Billy Boy from Graham Ashford. Billy got Ted out of C-Division to a 4 handicap in his first year and continued to play Billy for many years. The highlight of their partnership was playing for Rhodesia B at Queens in 1976 when Billy was at the ripe old age of twenty-three.

Ted has a keen eye for horses, and after this test, he embarked on buying and selling polocrosse ponies. for which he developed a reputation. Bolshevik, who won the Brazera Horse of The Year trophy twice, First Grouse won it once, and Kings Affair, who he sold to Gavin Cocker, not only won the trophy but also got Gavin to his 10 handicap. Bolshevik put Ted into the Zimbabwe A side against Australia when it was played in Zimbabwe Country in 1985

In 1987 Zimbabwe travelled to Australia for the test series and Ted was the captain of the mixed side. Having seen the Australian Stock Horse for the first time, Ted returned home to breed his own stamp of horse. Bolshevik and Grouse were put to the Stallion Madion, and from this union, Grouse produced Petya the next sire. Petya went on to sire many top horses sort after by both

Zimbabweans and South Africans. Some of these were, Running in the Family, Our Family, Desert Rose, Soup Plate, Petya's Nookie and Luckie.

Ted accompanied the Schools tour to the U.K. as the coach, and in 1992 travelled to New Zealand as player, captain and coach. He was A side reserve at the New Zealand Test Series in 1989, and has been the ladies coach for five years. Ted has played in every tournament of the prestigious Greendale Open, accept for 2008 where he was out of action with a broken hip,

ALLAN MALLOY

Allan started his polocrosse career in 1958? With Glendale Club, progressing through Umguza, Hippo, Borrowdale and back to Hippo before moving to South Africa. He has played for Midlands and Mashonaland as well as Rhodesia B and been reserve for Rhodesia A. His greatest contribution to polocrosse has been through the formation of the veterans of which he was a founder member, and has played a large part in its running both here and in South Africa and subsequently taking over the chairmanship from Malcolm Sergeant in 1998.

Allan has been a keen and able umpire, receiving his colours and been Chief Umpire, both here and in South Africa. He was the Horse Co-ordinator for the Quadrangular World Test Series in 1994, and been a South African Convenor of Selectors. He returned to Zimbabwe and started Riverside Polocrosse Club, but is currently playing for Bulawayo. At 61, he must rank amongst the oldest players still playing.

PAUL SCOTCHER

Paul played a tremendous part in the growth of polocrosse into one of Rhodesia's national Sports. As Public Relations Officer to the Rhodesian Polocrosse Association he achieved his ambition of arranging an international team to visit this country. Paul was known as the silver tongue commentator who could command laughter, tension or anger from a crowd at will. He was appointed a senior umpire in 1969, and was Chairman and Captain of Borrowdale Polocrosse Club for many years. He has also represented Mashonaland and toured to Natal South Africa in 1968. He died on the field in a tournament at Glendale in 1972.

DAVID AND PHYLIS CAMPBELL

David Campbell

David started playing polo for the polo section of the Marandellas Country Club back in 1947. The polo section lasted only a few seasons and some of those remaining players became involved with polocrosse when it eventually started there. David confessed that he was no horseman and a mediocre polo player so decided not to attempt this new sport of polocrosse. However Phyllis took up the sport.

David tagged along in support of his wife and became involved by goal judging and timekeeping. Ultimately he and Phyllis became Chairman and

Secretary of the Marandellas Polocrosse Club. At the National Championships held in Umtali 1965, David was asked to be the President of the National Association to succeed the late Ian Ferguson. This he was prepared to do provided Phyllis agreed to be his secretary.

In 1967, David and Phyllis travelled down to Natal in South Africa to explore the possibility of staging a test match and through their efforts this tour took place the following year. This was the beginning of a number of tours to South Africa and in which David and Phyllis took a keen interest to the point of sponsoring a number of them. In 1976 the couple flew to Australia as delegates to the first International Polocrosse Conference. The couple retired from the national body in 1979 when Jock Kay took over. David became a Patron and Phyllis a Hon Life Vice-President of the Association. They were both presented with R.C.C.B. Silver Medals for meritorious services to polocrosse.

RICHARD MOSTERT

Richard started his polocrosse career as a 12 year old in 1968 where he played at Risco Riding Club and at times would occasionally play at Rhodesdale. He went on to play for many clubs including Queens, Macheki, Virginia, started Tara in Headlands and finally with Hippo where he has been their chairman, captain and coach for the past 20 years. In most of these clubs Richard played a leading part in their administration in the same roles. In the difficult years of the 2000's he kept

Hippo Polocrosse Club going by encouraging new and young players and providing them with mounts.

As a natural leader he has been elected to high office becoming Chairman of Manicaland, Midlands and the latter formed Province of Masvingo, ultimately becoming the President of the Zimbabwe Polocrosse Association in 2004.

Richard Coached the under 13's in 1993 and was invited to travel to the U.S.A for 3 months in 1988 to coach in Arizona and California. He also managed national tours in 1994, 1998 and 2001. As an umpire he has been the Provincial Chief Umpire for Midlands and Masvingo ending up as the National Chief Umpire for six years.

Over the years Richard has played for Midlands, Manicaland and Masvingo Provinces and for Zimbabwe B side in 1979.

TIM SAVORY

Born April 1951 in the Midlands town of Que Que, Tim, as a 3 year old had his own horse which was a bomb proof orphan filly his Dad had bottle fed. He loved going out for rides on the ranch with his mother initially on a lead rein but in no time was off on his own.

As a five year old Tim began playing polocrosse. The stick was just an appendage and any chance of picking up the ball was nil. The adults at Rhodesdale were great, as they were quite happy to include all the youngsters in the weekend practices. This was the main reason that so many young Kings, Massons etc. all played top class polocrosse for Rhodesdale at a very young age.

In the early 1960's, C Division was introduced and was exciting as there was now a tournament that the kids could go to but it wasn't long before Tim, along with others, were having to bluff their ages to play in B division.

In 1966 Guy Savory bought Tim a young mare from the Ashburners down in the Filabusi area. The horse was walked via Shangani to Gweru (100 miles plus) and then loaded onto a train to Que Que. Clearly this was one tough horse and he named her Flame Lily. Her training began immediately, and as Tim was at boarding school she was sent to Charles Holland for a few months, a smart move on the parents' part. She took to polocrosse like a duck to water, straight into A division and by the second season Tim achieved an 8 handicap.

Tim recalls that Flame Lily was without doubt the best horse he ever played; she was so bold, and would collect herself for the ride-off which he had learnt from Barry Masson. She virtually threw herself into the ride-off. What a great feeling that must have been, although at times pretty scary.

With national service, Gwebi, Rugby, and the untimely death of his father, polocrosse took a back seat but Tim did manage to get some tournament time and was able to make selection to play for Midlands in the inter-provincial tournament.

In 1973 Tim was working in Salisbury when John and Anne Farrer very kindly agreed to stable his horse so that he could play for Glendale. With the club short on scoring I's, Tim was moved from his position at 3 to number 1 resulting in Glendale beating Ruzawi in the finals. He spent the rest of his life trying to get back to being a number 3.

In 1973, Tim played for Rhodesia B against South Africa, the first time tests were played between the two countries. By 1975, together with Hugo van Reenan, they started up the Darwendale Club. In this same year he married Di at the end of the season.

In 1976 Tim and Di returned to the family farm at Rhodesdale where he took over as Chairman of Rhodesdale Polocrosse Club and negotiated the transfer of the Easter Tournament from Umvuma to Sebakwe. By 1978 Tim took on the development of the fields, installing irrigation and built the new shower and toilet block at the clubhouse.

Tim was an active National Administrator, serving on the Executive Committee; was Midlands Chairman and served time on the Handicapping and Umpires Committees. At the 1979 AGM he proposed a proportional voting system to improve the representation of player's wishes.

In 1985 Tim played for Zimbabwe B against Australia. Zimbabwe had introduced the *horse pool* system for the first time after the debacle regarding horses in Australia during the 1983 tour. Topmarks, Tim's horse was drawn by the Zimbabweans. Alistair Keith selected her as his mount as he was in the A side and had the priority. As usual this is always a bitter pill to swallow.

Tim made selection for the 1987 Zimbabwe A tour to Australia as the No 2 between Ant Keith and Ian Kay. The Perth part of the tour was extremely well organised by Barry Butterly who went out of his way to ensure good mounts. This was the one and only time that Tim has ever played indoor polocrosse. Fortunately the arena was sawdust, hard to pick up and bounce the ball but soft to land on, which many players found out the hard way.

MICHAEL KRYNAUW

Mike Krynauw, tall and spidery with a reach like a Tarantula, is arguably the best all round player the new millennium era produced. Mike started riding as a four year old but was not allowed to play until he reached five. At that time he went for tennis lessons with the late Don Black (father of Cara and her brothers) and was told that he could go to Wimbledon if he wanted to as he had the talent. When he was seven he went to Featherstone for a polocrosse tournament and when sister Sarah fell off, and without his parent's knowledge, Michael leapt on her horse and finished the game. That was the end of all other sports for him. He went on to play several years for Zimbabwe Under 14, Under 16 and Under19, where he scored 9 goals in a 6 minute chukka against the U.K. He can ride any horse, and without the use of spurs, whips or hard bits.

SOME OTHER NOTABLE PERSONALITIES

Nick Leared   *Kobus Meiring*   *Mike McGrath*

Alan Lowe   *Charles Holland*   *Ian Moffat*

Don Granger   *Jim Parker*   *Ron & Les Taylor*

Wayne Parham   *Roy Bennet*

Nick Oostehuizen *Willie Swan*

Alan Jack *Richard Games* *Chris Bishop*

Ian Brown *Kane Mathews* *Charlie Wilmans*

Up to the mid-sixties, it was frowned upon for women to play with or against the men. Men had their status in a tough all male preserve that women, so they thought, could not sustain and were relegated to the female section with their own handicap. Due to shortages of players to make up teams, however, certain of the 'tougher' ladies were accepted and expected 'to take it like a man'. Some of the male-dominant clubs, like Rhodesdale, were most indignant, as they could not play to their ability against a member of the fairer sex. Those early ladies who 'took the beat' opened up the field to future women who were selected to play amongst the best men, and accepted as equals.

Mary Leared

ARLENE CROOK

Arlene came from show jumping and introduced to polocrosse at Borrowdale, by her newly married Husband, Graeme Crook, in 1972. Despite being an excellent horsewoman, she was a slow starter and only came out of C Division in 1975. The move to Hippo brought her into more serious polocrosse where she reached a 6 handicap in the 3 birth. She played for Midlands in the Men's A side until women were banned and she then continued in the Ladies side. In 1976 she made the National Ladies side that had its first tour to South Africa and continued to make the side each year until in 1981 they moved to South Africa.

After a number of years in isolation, she returned to make the S.A. National side in 1992 and again in 1993 where she was Captain against Australia and in combination with her daughter Nicola, in the 1 birth. She received her provincial colours as well as Springbok and Protea.

Arlene returned to Zimbabwe, and with Allan Malloy, started a new club, Riversdale in Bulawayo. With Allan, she moved to the Bulawayo Club.

JOAN KEENE
Top lady player of her time in the fifties.

SUE KEENE
Sue was the first woman to make the Rhodesia A Team in 1974 as a 6-handicap player.

WENDY WOLFE
The first woman to achieve an 8 goal handicap.

MARGO WORSLEY – WORSWICK

Margo came to settle in Marondera from Cape Town in 1985. Being very passionate about horses and having never played polocrosse before, she managed to persuade Sue Parkin, then living in the Marondera North Farming area, to introduce her to the game.

Around 1987 she started playing polocrosse at Ruzawi River and managed to break her leg at her very first tournament, C Division, held at Hippo Valley.

Margo is one of those exceptional people who, having started the sport late in life went on to be one of the top lady players in the Country. A woman with gifted sports talent, she was able to combine this with her riding skills and rise rapidly into top polocrosse.

By 1992, five years since she started, she was selected for the national side and elected its captain. This was the beginning of a career where she played and captained the national sides every year there was selection until 2007. That particular year was the World Series and regrettably, she had an accident in the early stages of the game against England. She suffered concussion and permanent damage to her optic nerve that brought an end to her playing competitive polocrosse.

OTHER NOTABLE LADIES

Rose Palm

Anna Marie Dodd

Pascal Gambeau

Julie Games

Talent in a person can often perpetuate through their offspring, and children will often benefit from the opportunities that their parents lacked, which forms a chain of perpetual improvement in the sport as a whole. The days of disallowing kids of under fourteen to play polocrosse may well have been misjudged. Today, children are learning the sport as toddlers, and becoming highly skilled well before they reach adulthood. Here are some of our great families.

THE COSSEY FAMILY

Bill Cossey   *Mike Cossey*   *Julie Cossey*

Bill flew Lancaster Bombers in the last world war. After the war he moved to Kenya where he was employed in aerial mapping of Kenya, and then moved on to the then Southern Rhodesia where he worked as a butcher's blockman. In 1949 he took up employment with the Mazoe Citrus Estates as a section manager, and in those days, horses were used as transport around the orchards. In 1950 he watched a game of polocrosse being played at Fort Victoria and came home to start the sport at Glendale Country Club. He became a leading light in the sport, playing for Mashonaland and becoming the Vice President to Campbell of the Association. He introduced his only Son, Michael to polocrosse at an early age, where he played his first tournament at the Bromley Shield, Glendale in 1962.

Mike went on to represent his province and played at national level for Rhodesia B in 1980 and at the first World Test Series held in Australia in 1982. He was a coach and a senior umpire as well as Captain of Ruwa. Mike has been a member of a number of clubs, including Gweru, Hippo, Ruzawi River and Salisbury Sports Club. Married to Julie, daughter of Bob Gardner, they have two sons of which Kane is showing great promise for the sport and has played his first test match against Zambia.

THE KEITH FAMILY

Ant Keith   *Alistair Keith*

Terrance and Graham Keith

Ian and Jill started Marondellas polocrosse Club in 1954 and Ruzawi in 1959. Ian played in the one birth on a big bay mare, Mrs H, whom he bought from Mrs. Grimstone in Macheke. At a 5-goal handicap, he was a master, as with Barry Burbidge and Alan Lowe, at shooting spectacular goals from the back line. He was an excellent umpire and was Chief Umpire for many years and a notable influence on the progression of the rules.

Jill played in the 3 birth on Angler from when he was a three-year-old until he retired at 22. She reached a 4 handicap and together with Doug King were the only players allowed to return to C division at the end of their polocrosse career. Jill excelled at schooling ponies and continued to play polocrosse into her late years in order to bring in ponies for her sons.

Ian and Jill have two sons Anthony and Alistair who have both excelled in polocrosse. Ant first represented the national side in 1968 when he was still a school boy and continued right through to his retirement from Polocrosse. On a number of these occasions he has captained the side. Ant has served on the executive and in all its sub-committees as well as been chief and deputy chief umpire. His son Patrick also plays polocrosse and has been included in the national junior sides.

Alistair, the younger of the two, has been selected in the national sides on a number of occasions. Whilst he can play any position, he isknown for his strength as a number 2. He has two sons Terrence and Graham who have played at national junior level.

THE MANNIX FAMILY

Ian Mannix   *Jenny Mannix*   *Nikkie Hopgood*

Alison Mannix   *Craig Mannix*

Jenny was the first family member to take up the sport. Having come from show jumping, she started playing casually for Rhodesdale before starting the club at Umnyati together with husband Ian. Her first tournament was at Gwelo in 1978 and she rose to provincial level, playing for Midlands Ladies in 1983/4. She was one of the early veterans and since 1995 has played in every test match. Ian started soon after Jenny and also made the provincial side. In 1993 he was selected to coach the Junior National Side and continued to do so for the next eight years. In 1991 he assisted Barry Burbidge to coach the national tour to the U.K., and between 1996 to 2006 he was the Convenor of Junior Selectors, and finally, Convenor of Senior Selectors. Ian's father Cecil Mannix joined the sport at Umnyati in 1981 at the grand age of 61 in order to play with his grandchildren.

Craig, the only son of the three Mannix children, started as a nine-year-old at Umnyati, and played his first nationals for Midlands Under 13 side. At 16 he played for the Midlands Men's B-side, and in 1992 made the Under 21 side that toured to Estcourt in Natal S.A. where he won the saddle for the best overall player and pony. In 1995 he played the Western Australia side on tour to Zimbabwe, and the following year was selected to play the return test in Western Australia. Craig, following in his father's footsteps, also did some coaching in the U.K. as well as Ireland.

Nikki, the oldest child, also started her polocrosse career as a nine-year-old at Umnyati. At the 1986 Virginia tournament the combination of Nikki at 1, and Craig at 3, resulted in each winning the best players in their respective positions. She played Midlands Ladies, and in 1991, for the touring Scholars side to the U.K. The following year she was selected for the reciprocal test against the U.K. played in Zimbabwe. In 2001 she made the ladies side on tour to Pretoria. After returning from university she was selected for the 2005 Ladies Tour to the U.K., and the following year made the Zimbabwe Select side that toured to South Africa.

Alison starting playing at six. She played Under 14's, Under 16's and Under 19's for the National sides and again in the Zim / Zam test series. In 2006 she was selected alongside Nikki for the Select side that toured South Africa, and in 2008 won the best 3 in both tests against S. A. and Zambia. She was also a 'wild card' at the Greendale Open. Craig and Nikki have both married polocrosse players and have four children between them that will probably represent the fourth Mannix generation to play the sport.

THE BURBIDGE FAMILY

Barry and Ros Burbidge

Barry started his working career as a section assistant for Hippo Valley Sugar Estates where in those days company horses were the sole form of transport. He was active in local gymkhanas and show jumping until in 1967 when polocrosse was introduced to Hippo by Simon Budgen. A marksman shot with a rifle, Barry was well suited to the number 1 position in which he became a legend in his time. Inspired by Horseshoe with their Thoroughbred horses he started on Lady of Leisure, a Christmas present from Ros, and continued to play her throughout much of his polocrosse career. As a 9 handicap he played for the national and provincial sides for many years as well as captaining a number of them. He was a member of the side that played against Australia for the first time in 1972 and ended his playing career in the squad that played the first World Test Series in Australia in 1982.

Barry became a coach to the Midlands ladies side as well as for the National ladies and the national Under 16's in which he toured to the U.K. with them. He became a national umpire and served under Jock Kay as Vice President and ultimately taking over as President of the National Association.

Ros, Barry's wife, was a competent left handed player in the 1 birth that was able to shoot goals overhand at any angle. Ros captained the Ladies South side in the annual tournaments that played against the Combined Ladies of the North until there were sufficient ladies playing to field ladies teams at national level. Ros is a sister to Neville Baker who played polocrosse for Hippo and Middle Sabie and is married to Wendy Wolfe.

Jason, their oldest son, played for Midlands in the different age groups. Able to play in all three positions, he moved to England where he became a useful coach and ultimately played and captained their national side. As a sound horseman he spends his spare time schooling problem horses.

Shannon also came up through the ranks playing for Midlands at different age groups. Achieving a 9 handicap, he is able to play in all three positions but, like his father, excels in the 1 birth. He has played for the national team on a number of occasions and whilst captaining the Zimbabwe side at the World Test Series held in Australia, he came up against brother Jason who was the Captain of the English side. Shannon represented his country at two World Cup Series. As an outstanding horseman, he has rescued horses of which one he played at national level. Shannon became the coach to the National Junior side and has served on the National Executive committee.

Griffin, the youngest son, likewise followed in his brothers footsteps by playing as a junior for Midlands at different age groups. He was the Under 21 National Team Captain for two years playing against South Africa in the 3 birth, and in the first Schools International against England he played in the 1 birth before he left for New Zealand and stopped playing polocrosse.

Daughter Taige played for Midlands juniors as well as the Ladies side. She represented Zimbabwe in the National Ladies side against South Africa and like her mother is a competent number 1 capable of scoring overhand goals at any angle.

Mike, younger brother to Barry, also started his working career as a section assistant and played polocrosse for Hippo. A competent player in the 1 birth he played for Midlands provincial side. Married to

Heather Jennings, who played for Borrowdale and represented her provincial side in the ladies, they have two sons who play at club level.

THE JOHNSON FAMILY

Gordon   Trish, Clive and Wendy   Glenn

THE WIXLEY FAMILY

Phil Wixley   Clive Wixley

THE KAY FAMILY

Jock   Iain and son David   Iain and Kerry

THE HARRIS FAMILY

Shirley, Sally, Marjory, Nola, John, Henry   *Henry*

John, Nola, Sally, Henry   *. The Harris Clan.*

THE COCKER FAMILY

Brothers Bob and Don   *Father and son Don and Gavin*

Brian   *Jo*   *Karen and Gavin*

THE SERGEANT FAMILY

Malcolm   *Greg*   *Suzanne*   *Paula*

THE ALEXANDER FAMILY

Angus, Rowena and George Alexander

AND THE CRAZY CHARACTERS

Clive Wixley for all his antics on and off the field.

Jean Scotcher, Jim Parker, Graeme Crook and Fred Barry for wild stick work.

Gordon Johnson for taking the law into his own hands.

Jimmy Meikle and Tommy Wright who find everything worth a giggle.

Nick Leared and John Ferrar who don't need team members.

Jeremy Fisher, Toc Arnold and Conal Bunnet for their captivating commentary.

Bill Cossey, Bob Gardner, incomprehensible after a few drinks.

Ken King, dressing up as a woman and seducing the men.

Richard Hinde for loving all the girls

Mary Leared for breast protectors

Rhodesdale for no teeth

Tilly Laurent for choice language.

Renie Maritz for playing with a peg leg

Fleur Ramsey, Tracey McGrath and Don Boyd for quick tempers.

Barry Binder for wearing his horse.

Wendy Wolfe for her smile.

John Davidson, big John and his Jim Bowie knife.

Hornsby Thurlow and Bill McClelland for polite apologies after they knocked your head off.

Sandy King and Jenny Swift for side line antics.

CHAPTER 12

VETERANS

THE IDEA OF A VETERAN SECTION WAS FIRST discussed in the1980's. The concept was to encourage retiring players to stay with the sport and enjoy their game at an unpressurised level with their own age group. These 'oldies' had a wealth of knowledge and experience in the sport, all of which was valuable to the administration of polocrosse, and would otherwise be lost to the sport.

At first, there were insufficient numbers of the golden oldies to get it going and so the age restriction was brought to 45 for men and 40 for women with a limitation of 4 handicap or less.

With South Africa showing an interest in forming a Veterans section, the possibility of tests between the two countries was an added attraction. However, the problem was that South Africa could not meet the age criteria and so Zimbabwe had to reduce the age in order to compete on a level footing.

It was decided to form a Veteran's Association within the framework of the national body and Malcolm Sergeant became the founding chairman, with Allan Malloy taking over on his return to Zimbabwe. Ian and Lynn Taylor, whilst not playing themselves, for many years devoted their time to manage the veteran's tours.

The Veterans formed a great camaraderie within their group and were left alone by the parent body to run their own affairs. Test matches took on a more social atmosphere with past serious contenders now enjoying the friendships that had developed over the years. The first tour started in 1994.

1994. Bulls Tour to Estcourt and Pietermaritzburg.

1995. Tests held at Hippo and Bulawayo.

1996. Zimbabwe toured to Estcourt and Pietermaritzburg.

1997 South African Master's Tour. This was by invitation from the S.A. Masters Sports Association, and was the inaugural Masters games.

Tim Swanson had a hard fall and taken off to hospital. The ambulance arrived and he was put onto a spinal board, with his head held firmly in a block, so his vision was restricted to what was above him. He had no idea there was another patient in the ambulance. A few minutes into the journey, the attendant started banging on the driver's widow, yelling, "It's coming!" The driver stopped and dashed around to hear the attendant shout "The baby is coming now!" Tim in his befuddled state thought, "A BABY am I having a BABY? I only banged my head!"

Second Test held at Louis Trichardt.

As guests of the Louis Trichardt Polocrosse Club they had dinner at the Cloud's End Hotel. The Mayor and Town Clerk of Louis Trichardt were guests of honour, and entertainment was provided by the 'Wondering Hobo' from Johannesburg, who was so convincing that Ian Taylor, the tour manager, lost his dinner and Ted found his long lost Dad!

1998. South Africa came to Hippo.

1999. Zimbabwe toured to Richards Bay.

2002. Zimbabwe toured to Sondella.

Tragically Anna Becker had an accident on the field resulting in her untimely death.

2003. Tests held at Bulawayo.

2004. Tests held at Hippo.
2005. Travelled to Sondella.
2006. Back to Bulawayo.
2007. Zimbabwe toured to Willem Prinsloo.

*Malcolm Sergeant, John Harris, Ted Wilmot, Toppie
Baker, Roy Mathews, Don Cocker.*

*Irene Kilpet, Minky Slater Brown, Arlene Crook, Jen
Mannix, Margo Worsick, Jill Joubert, Lee Anne Bean.*

Malcolm Sergeant, Wayne Parham, Jack Joubert, Pete Evans, Mark Octobra, Mike Gaisford.

Gary Dodd, Paul Huxham, ?

*Allan Malloy, ?, Arlene Crook, ?, Paul Huxham,
Ted Wilmot , Margo Worsick.*

*Tim Swanson, Charley Wilmans, Mike Cossey,
Jen Mannix, Sue Parkin, Margo Worsick*

CHAPTER 13

NATIONAL TESTS AND TOURS

A NUMBER OF MATCHES TOOK PLACE IN THE '60'S and up to 1972 which cannot be classed as official test matches as they lacked the selection and representation of the Polocrosse Association to represent the country and as such no colours could be awarded. Nevertheless, volunteer teams did play and they are worth recounting. The first official representative side was played in 1972, and in that year the first colours were awarded to

Charles Holland,
Tony Blake,
Barry Burbidge,

.

61 ~ 61

Probably the first test to be played in England was in 1961. Sir Rupert Bromley, who was then President of the Polocrosse Association and his son Maurice were over in England at the same time as Mary Leared. He contacted Mary and asked if she would play in a match against an English team at the Rickmansworth Agricultural Show under television coverage.

At the last minute Sir Rupert changed his mind about playing and opted to umpire instead. Maurice played the one and Mary at three, with two ponies each and two English players filled in as 2's with their own ponies. To quote Mary from her book 'A Horseshoe Clown', "We wiped the floor with the beginners, cantering past their trotting ponies and chucking in goals till we were both exhausted. At the end of the match we were awarded silver pencils as trophies".

68 ~ 68

In 1968 Rhodesia travelled to Natal in South Africa where the horses were entrained at Msasa siding and travelled down by rail. The Rhodesian Milling Co. had promised a load of horse feed that only arrived when the train pulled out of the siding. After frantically pursuing the train, it was finally loaded when it arrived at the further most point at Central Station.

The matches were played at Mooi River and at Ladysmith with the A Team successfully beating their Natal counterparts with 13 goals to 4 and the B side did likewise on a score of 15 goals to 5. The touring players were:~

RHODESIA A
M. Leared,
M. McGrath,
N. Leared,
K. Humphries,
K. Meiring [Capt.]
J. Harris,

RHODESIA B
A. Keith,
B. McGrath,
J. Scotcher,

I. Kay,
P. Scotcher, [Capt.]
R. Robertson

MEN'S A

*J. Harris, K. Meiring, K. Humphries, Nick Leared,
M. McGrath, Mary Leared*

MEN'S B

*Iain Kay, B. McGrath, Ant Keith, Jean Scotcher,
P. Scotcher, R. Robertson*

69 ~ 69

Tests continued to be played in 1969 when Natal came up to play at the National Championships at Hippo Valley Polocrosse Club. Three sections were made up and the selectors made up their team from these sections switching through the weekend as results dictated. The names I have are not complete.

SQUAD
Ant Keith
Iain Kay
Mike Cossey
Barry Burbidge
Simon Budgeon
Tony Blake
Ron Yeatman

71 ~ 71

The following players went on tour to Natal South Africa in 1971

John Harris, [Capt.]
Barry Burbidge, [vice Capt.]
Paul Scotcher,
Sue Keene,
Robin Fennel,
Mark de Robillard,
Jean Scotcher [travel res.].
David Campbell [Manager].

B Burbidge, R. Fennel, J. Harris, Marc de Robillard
P. Scotcher, Sue Parkin.

72 ~ 72

As we had World Sanctions imposed on us after 1965, countries other than South Africa could not send an official side that was representative of their country. However Ingleburn Club sent over an unofficial Australian side to play us in 1972. Neville Gilpin their Captain and Graeme Spackman tried out all the horses and matched them to their players, a practice that is seldom seen and goes to show the ability of these two men in pairing off rider and mount for a crucial test match.

Three tests were played at Hippo, Umtali and Borrowdale, and they played as a team in Karoi at the National Championships. This was the first time we had seen the Australians play and their style of game was very different to ours. They used deep nets in their racquets, a lot deeper than they use today, which made for a very tight short passing game.

FIRST TEST HIPPO VALLEY POLOCROSSE CLUB

Barry Burbidge,
Ronnie Yeatman,
Charles Holland [Capt.],
Ian Moffat,
Ian Brown,
Nick Leared,
John Harris. Reserve.

This was a very close fought game. Barry Burbidge opened the score with the first goal in the first 10 seconds of the first chukka. From there on the game remained level until the last chukka when Australia took the lead to win 22 to 20.

I. Moffat, R. Yeatman, C. Holland, B Burbidge, I. Brown, N. Leared

SECOND TEST UMTALI SADDLE CLUB

Two thousand spectators turned up to watch Rhodesia win. Unfortunately Neville Gilpin of Australia was injured in the fourth chukka and their reserve came on to play which may have been the reason for their loss. The final score was 25 to Rhodesia, and 22 to Australia.

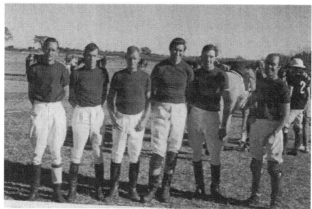

I, Moffat, C. Holland, B. Burbidge, R. Yeatman, I. Brown, N. Leared.

THIRD TEST AT BORROWDALE COUNTRY CLUB

One thousand five hundred spectators turned up to watch this final test; amongst them was the Prime Minister Ian Smith and his wife Janet. Australia won the Barlow Trophy, presented by Janet Smith, with a score of 30 goals to Rhodesia's 24. Nick Leared and Ian Moffit had to withdraw from the team with horse problems, and at one point, an unfit and pregnant Brazera was brought in from maternity leave to play and sadly resulted in aborting her foal later.

At the National Championships, Australia came up against Ruzawi in the finals and was beaten. Australia showed their skill as Horsemen and a lot was learnt by all our members.

A. Blake, C. Holland, I. Brown, A. Malloy, B. Burbidge, J. Harris. R. Yeatman.

73 ~ 73

In 1973, two test series were held with the first played at Inanda Polocrosse Club, Johannesburg with Rhodesia A winning the test 23 to 17 whilst in the curtain raiser Rhodesia B narrowly beat the Junior Springboks 15 goals to 14. The teams consisted of:~

RHODESIA A

Barry Burbidge,
Phil Wixley,
Nick Leared,
Anthony Keith,
Iain Kay,
John Harris.

*J. Harris, P. Wixley, Ant Keith, B. Burbidge, I. Kay,
N. Leared.*

RHODESIA B

Scott Dixon,
Ronnie Yeatman,
Rudi Van den Berg,
Alan Lowe,
Robin Fennel,
Charles Holland.
[Reserves]
John Ferrar,
Tommy Miller.
Mike McGrath, [Manager]

Back home, the test was held at the Salisbury Sports
Club in conjunction with the Inter Provincials. Here the
teams that played were:~

RHODESIA A

Anthony Keith,
Bruce Campbell,
John Harris [Capt.,]

Barry Burbidge,
Iain Kay,
Tony Blake,
Ian Brown [Reserve]

*A. Keith, B. Campbell, J. Harris, B. Burbidge, I. Kay,
A. Blake.*

RHODESIA B

Alan Louw [Capt.]
Phil Wixley,
Nick Leared,
Tim Savory,
Scott Dixon,
John Farrer,
Bob Swift [Reserve].

74 ~ 74

Again in 1974, two test series were held, the first
being at Queensmead Bulawayo, followed by a tour to
South Africa. The first test players were:~

RHODESIA A
Ant Keith,
Iain Kay,
John Harris,
Charles Holland,
Les Yeatman,
Tony Blake.

*L. Yeatman, A. Blake, I. Kay, J. Harris, C. Holland,
Ant Keith.*

SOUTH AFRICA

*P. Taylor, N. Arde, A. Higgs, N. Crooks, E. Seals,
A. van Zyl.*

RHODESIA B

Ian Brown,
Nick Leared,
Ted Wilmot,
Larry Jenkinson,
John Farrer,
Phil Wixley

T. Wilmot, I. Brown, N. Leared, L. Jenkinson, P. Wixley,J. Ferrar

The touring side that travelled to Estcourt were:

RHODESIA A

Barry Burbidge [Capt.],
Ian Brown,
John Harris,
Iain Kay,
Anthony Keith,
Phil Wixley,

RHODESIA B

Charles Holland,
Larry Jenkinson,
Marc de Robillard,
Les Yeatman,

Ronnie Yeatman,
Alan Lowe.
Sue Keene,

*I. Kay, P. Wixley, L Yeatman, A. Keith, I. Brown,
J. Harris.*

75 ~ 75

1975 was the last year that Rhodesia commanded supremacy over South Africa. The First Test held at Milner Park was poorly attended and played on the Oval within the cinder track that barely accommodated the field. Rhodesia-A won the test with a 26-goal lead over 21.

The Second Test at Pietermaritzburg looked like it would be played on a superb field inside the showground. However, it had been over-irrigated some days before the test resulting in a soft and spongy field that tragically resulted in three horses breaking their legs. Despite this, Rhodesia came away winners with the A side beating the Springboks by one goal over their 17 goals. The B side were convincing winners in both tests.

RHODESIA A

Barry Burbidge,
Mark De Robillard,
Tony Blake,
John Harris,
Iain Kay,
Ian Brown,

RHODESIA B

Phil Wixley,
Chris Pocock,
Nick Leared,
Rory McGrath,
Graham Crook,
Al Jenkinson,
John Farrer [Reserve]
Mike McGrath [Manager].

76 ~ 76

In 1976, Rhodesia remained undefeated in the First Test Match against South Africa held at Queensmead Polocrosse Club. Despite a slow start in the first four chukkas, Rhodesia went on to win with 21 goals to 13.

The Second Test at the Salisbury Sports Expo, held on the polo field was a repeat of the first test in that only in the fifth chukka did Rhodesia improve their game. However this was too late to clinch the test and with a superb performance by South Africa's Norman Crookes and Tony Higgs, the Springboks managed a convincing win of 22 goals to 13 to secure their first win over Rhodesia.

In the curtain-raiser matches, Rhodesia B, after trailing by one goal in the fourth chukka, went on to win the First Test 23 goals to 14. In the Second Test, the Junior Springboks beat Rhodesia B 17 goals to 15 having enjoyed a 6 goal lead after the fifth chukka. The teams were

RHODESIA A

Barry Burbidge,
Marc de Robillard,
Iain Kay,
Anthony Keith,
Ian Brown,
John Harris,

RHODESIA B

Charles Holland,
Phil Wixley,
Graham Crook,
John King,
Ken King,
Nick Leared

Reserves

Alan Lowe,
Trevor Rutherford,
Bob Swift.

77 ~ 77

Two tests were held in 1977 in which South Africa now began to dominate the series by winning both tests held in South Africa. This was the year that the bush war in Rhodesia began in earnest and players were called to the front for six weeks in and six weeks out and which began to have an effect on the standard of our game. Played in Pretoria possibly against the S.A. Defence Forces Team. Also of interest is that this was the first year to select a full ladies team.

RHODESIA MENS

A. Keith
B. Cocker
D. Cocker
J. Ferrar
Marc de Robillard,
Prickle Thorn?
?

RHODESIA LADIES

S. Parkin
K. Kay
R. Palm
J. Hughes
A. Crook
?

78 ~ 78

South Africa went on to beat Rhodesia in 1978 at Hippo Valley followed by Ruzawi River. At the first Test, the Springboks annihilated our National side with a 29 – 13 victory. The result improved at the Second Test with Rhodesia coming out victors with 25 goals to 22.

The Schoolboy side achieved two wins, 19 – 16 for the first Test, and a punishing 28 goals to 11 for the second Test.

The B side only just scraped through with a one-goal lead over their 20 goals but by the second Test were utterly beaten with a score of 30 goals to 12.

The Ladies produced a very even game with the first Test results going to them on a 19 goals to 16 win, but with a very exciting draw on the second Test.

RHODESIA A

Anthony Keith [Capt.],
Iain Kay,
Graham Crook,
John King,
Ken King,
Don Cocker.

RHODESIA B

Alan Lowe [Capt.],
Terry Cutter,
Nick Leared,
John Harris,
Alistair Keith,
Vim Schultz.

RHODESIA SCHOOL BOYS

Peter Bowen,
Miles Gaisford,
James Mackay [Capt.],
Clive Johnson,
Mark Zambra,
Barry Thurlow.

RHODESIA LADIES

Rose Palm,
Cynthia Field,
Sue Parkin,
Julie Hughes,
Arlene Crook,
Kerry Kay [Capt.].

RESERVES

Allan Malloy,
John Farrar,
Ian Brown,
Dean Wakefield,
Harvey Leared,
Bunny Auld,
Gail Williams.
Heather Jennings

79 ~ 79

Rhodesia went on tour to South Africa with four teams and played at Inanda and Pietermaritzburg. I have not managed to identify them all.

MENS A and B

R. Mostert
D. Cocker
B. Cocker
T. Cutter
J. Harris
A. Keith.
I. Kay
Ant Keith

LADIES

J. Hughes
S. Elliot
K. Kay
R. Fennell
A. Crook

UNDER 21

P Bowen,
C. Johnson
T. Fennel
D. Wakefield
H. Leared

80 ~ 80

1980 was the last opportunity to play South Africa for many years as the country changed from Rhodesia to Zimbabwe/Rhodesia then to the new Zimbabwe. The new government took exception to the policies of apartheid in South Africa and all sporting contact with that country was stopped. Fortunately the tour had already been organized and the newly formed government allowed the test to proceed. The Polo Association offered their Thorn Park facility but got cold feet when they thought we would chop up their beautifully manicured fields. The compromise was to give us the compacted car park. Again I have not managed to identify all the players.

MENS A and B.

Ant Keith
T. Cutter
I. Kay
J. Harris
J. Parker
G. Crook
A. Keith
Rich Palm
M. Cossey
D. Cocker
B. Cocker
C. Pocock

UNDER 21

H. Leared
P. Bowen
S. McKay
H. Harris
C. Johnson.
T, Fennel.

LADIES

R. Palm
S. Parkin
A. Crook
J. Hughes

Rose Palm in the attack for Zimbabwe Rhodesia at Thorn Park

83 ~ 83

With South Africa now out of the equation, the first opportunity for an international test came in 1983 with an invitation to compete in the first world test series held in Australia. The first opportunity for a polocrosse team to travel and play abroad.

A squad of nine members was to be selected on the basis of sound horsemanship as well as play ability, as the teams would be competing on pooled ponies supplied by Australia. Papua New Guinea was an unknown factor, but we knew that Australia and New Zealand had a very different style of play and that they used deep nets, which was unfamiliar to us, and that our favored over-arm throw was against their rules. Amongst our top players were some exceptional players who were not necessarily good riders but who achieved their status by combining with their own pony and probably could not with any other.

The selectors, of which I was one, had a tough time screening likely candidates. Once we had selected a short list, we devised a system whereby we swapped players around on as many different ponies as we could and put them up against strength to see how they shaped. We eliminated as we went until we arrived at the required nine touring members, which were:

Iain Kay [captain],
Jim Parker [coach],
Ant Keith,
Alistair Keith,
Barry Burbidge,
Mike Cossey,
Clive Johnson,
Ken King,
Chris Pocock.

I have to say that this selection process introduced the most atrocious and ruthless polocrosse I have ever witnessed, as, for the sake of being in the selectors' eye, players were prepared to be suicidal in the hope of making this landmark tour. Horses were ridden aggressively and combinations between players disappeared as individuals vied to outdo everyone else even if it meant fouling. It was sufficiently nauseating, fortunately, to never repeat itself again to the same degree, and with the experience of the test itself, became the pivotal point that changed the whole concept of our game to evolve to what it is today, so ultimately, good came out of bad.

Iain and Jim now took over the squad for serious physical exercise and training. We were allowed to bend the rules and practice using the 'Aussie' deep net, which I might add, Clive Johnson had perfected as he had often sneaked in his deep racquet at tournaments when the umpires weren't looking.

We arrived at Burradoo, New South Wales, where our first hosts were and were introduced to our pool of Australian Stock Horses, and their equivalent to the American Quarter Horse. What magnificent animals they are. New South Wales rains in winter just to add to the cold, and Burradoo's polocrosse field was thick mud similar to a cattle kraal at the height of the rains. We were totally 'gob smacked', that they should even consider playing in this as certainly our horses at home would never stay on their legs in half this condition. But the Stock Horse is an amazing creature, he gathers his legs under him and not once did any of them come down despite the speed at which the game took place. For the first time I witnessed umpires calling 'time off' to recover a ball that would be totally immersed in mud and have to be dug out. The trick was to never let the ball touch the ground.

The First Test was held at Sydney, in weather they said was too cold to snow. The field was under water but fortunately not muddy. Papua New Guinea was an easy match to win, but not so Australia or New Zealand. Our guys found the conditions very hard and their style of game foreign. Clive Johnson was the hero of our side with some spectacular saves in the 3 birth.

Our next venue was the Gold Coast in Queensland, where conditions were closer to home. James King, Ken's brother living in Australia, organized a publicity stunt whereby he advertised in the local papers that they would be throwing a horse out of a helicopter and parachuting it down to earth. This created headline news, and an uproar from animal lovers. The day finally arrived and a dummy horse was thrown out, and the publicity was duly achieved.

Much to our dismay, New Zealand managed to truck their horses up from New South Wales whilst we were issued new ponies of far inferior standard, some of which were C Division kids' ponies. Iain Kay's pony kept falling over and our game never really got going, but we did win the bronze medal of the series.

Ken King, Jim Parker, Clive Johnson, Ant Keith, Alistair Keith, Iain Kay

Clive Johnson, Ken King, Mike Cossey

Zimbabwe supporters

*Iain Kay with our welcoming party, the wild King
brothers.James and Ken.*

85 ~ 85

It was now Australia's turn to tour Zimbabwe and in 1985 it was the first time that we hosted a team from oversees since 1972.

Two teams were selected,

ZIMBABWE A

Ant Keith,
Alistair Keith,
Iain Kay,
Ted Wilmot
Rich Harvey
Jim Parker [Captain]

ZIMBABWE B

Henry Harris,
Chris Pocock,
Richard Games,
Bob Cocker,
Tim Savory,
Don Cocker.

All the Ponies were pooled and drawn out of the hat. I had put in two ponies and hadn't drawn either but was to end up marking my best one with Daryl Smith riding it.

The first test was held at Hippo and the second at Ruzawi. Other than in 1972, this was the first time that our members could watch the Australian style of game that was to ultimately influence ours. As in '83, we were allowed our over arm ruling but the Australians kept to their more efficient under arm, but at the end of the series Mick Gorman, as a crowd pleaser attempted it. The Australians still proved to be the superior side but our teams showed a marked improvement from before. The

First Test Australia beat Zimbabwe A 30 goals to 18 whilst the B side was beaten 49 to 14 goals.

Between tests the Australians were sent off on a conducted tour to Great Zimbabwe, Kariba and Ayrshire where they visited commercial farms. A coaching clinic was organized at the Ayrshire Club were the Australian contingent coached 90 of our members before taking on our under 25.

ZIMBABWE UNDER 25

Rory Muil,
Chris Bishop,
Ron Taylor,
Guy Wixley,
Mike McGregor,
Tim Fennel.

This was a good match with Zimbabwe leading 11 to 7 by half way but falling away to a final loss of 21 to 15.

In the second test Australia were victors at 44 to 21 against the A side and 37 to 17 against our B side to a crowd of 2000 spectators at Ruzawi River Polocrosse Club.

Ted Wilmot, Rich Harvey, Jim Parker, Ant Keith, Al Keith, Iain Kay.

Rich Games

87 ~ 87

1987 was the year to tour Australia. Two teams were selected, a Men's and a Mixed side.

ZIMBABWE MEN

Clive Johnson,
Tim Fennell,
Henry Harris,
Iain Kay,
Tim Savory,
Ant Keith,

ZIMBABWE MIXED

Sally Harris,
Cynthia Field,

Pascal Gambeau,
Ted Wilmot,
Chris Pocock,
Don Cocker.
Malcolm Sergeant, Reserve
John Harris Manager.
[Malcolm Sergeant replaced Chris Pocock].

The tour was a test of thirteen games played at Perth, Western Australia; the Warwick Club in Queensland and Muswell and Burradoo Clubs in New South Wales. The men won 7 out of the 13 games and the mixed won 2. A lot of experience was gained particularly for the ladies.

A saddle shop donated a pink and black saddle for the best rider / pony combination which was won by Pascale Gambeau and fortunately by the fairer sex. Whilst at Perth the players were introduced to indoor polocrosse at the Brigadoon Indoor Equestrian Centre. The arena being too small, the game was played with two aside and the umpire ran up and down outside the glass cage. Later camels were introduced with two riders on each and with sticks extended with broom handles. The game was hilarious as every time someone picked up the ball, the camel would lie down followed by all the rest of the camels.

M. Sergeant, D. Cocker, T. Wilmot, P. Gambeau, C. Field, S. Harris.

*T. Fennel, C. Johnson, A. Keith, H. Harris, T. Savory,
I. Kay.*

88 ~ 88

In 1988 a World Test side was formed with three
players from each country, Zimbabwe, New Zealand and
Papua New Guinea to take on the might of Australia in
the Bicentennial Celebration Test Matches.

ZIMBABWE

Clive Johnson,
Glenn Johnson,
Roy Bennett

NEW ZEALAND

Gary Malcolm,
Ashley Christian,
Errol Gloyne

PAPUA NEW GUINEA

Kepas Kamare,
James Launder
Grant Jephcott

The First Test was played in Melbourne and comprised the Zimbabwe section with the second section of Papua New Guinea players. Zimbabwe managed to beat their opposing Australia section 11 goals to 10 whilst Papua New Guinea lost to theirs at 6 goals to 18.

The Second Test was held at Burradoo with Zimbabwe up with New Zealand. A new Australian side convincingly beat the world team but New Zealand fared better than Zimbabwe having just lost to their opposition.

The Third Test was held at Chinchilla in Queensland with a new selection side drawn from all three countries. This proved to be a nail-biting game with the World Side at one point taking the lead by 13 goals only to be caught up by Australia and an end result of 4 goals in the lead for the World side.

National Ladies Select. Kim Mannix, Sue Parkin,
Sally Harris, Bev McIntosh, Ros Fennel,
Suzanne Sergeant

National Scholars S. Burbidge, R. Fennell, G. Mannix, D. Whaley,   S. Arnold, J. Rutherford

President Select Scholars P. deKlerk, V. King, S. Tait, P. Whaley, C. Mannix, T. Parker

NATIONAL UNDER 13

Susie Baker,
Griffin Burbidge,
Jonathan Cocker,
Kelsey Halkier,
Nikki Mannix,
Paula Sergeant.

PRESIDENT SELECT UNDER 13

Shane Bloxham,
Hamish Michael,
Sean Davies,
Lance Davidson,
Loekie de Klerk,
Mark Colley.

89 ~ 89

New Zealand came out on tour for the first time in Zimbabwe. They played at the Ruzawi tournament to select and settle in with their mounts by mixing in with the teams.

The First Test was held at Ruwa where unfortunately both the Mens side and Mixed could not jell as a team. Both were beaten by the New Zealand side with the Men going down with a 20 to 32 defeat.

The Second Test was held at Hippo the following weekend in which the Mixed lost again but with the Men going into the ninth chukka in a very exciting draw of 35 goals a piece.

The final and decisive Test was held in Bulawayo. Again the Mixed were beaten but the men went on to a convincing win of 37 goals to 25. Sadly Iain Kay lost that amazing horse Chief Attraction.

ZIMBABWE MENS

Glenn Johnson,
 Tim Fennell,
Clive Johnson,
Kane Mathews,
Ant Keith [Capt.],
Iain Kay.
Henry Harris,
Alistair Keith

MIXED SIDE

Sally Harris
Bev McIntosh,
Susanne Sergeant,
Pascale Guimbeau
Ron Taylor,
Roy Bennett,
Gavin Cocker,
Toppie Baker.

H. Harris, Ant Keith, I. Kay, G. Johnston, A. Keith, C. Johnston

90 ~ 90

A Mixed team from Zimbabwe was sent over to play against Australia. I have no details.

Gavin Cocker, Margo Worsick, Kane Mathews, Sally Harris, Henry Harris, Angus Alexander, Paula Sergeant, Suzie Sergeant.

91 ~ 91

Modern day polocrosse has its roots in the United Kingdom with a variation of the sport being used as a riding school exercise. How ironic then that the U.K. should invite Zimbabwe to send a team over to teach Pony Club members to play the sport that would kick start England into the family of polocrosse nations.

Barry Burbidge and Ted Wilmot, as experienced players and coaches took a young schools side to tour England and coach both adults and school children across the country. At some venues there were over a hundred children participating. Ian Mannix and Ed Gundry as travelling parents also assisted.

The squad played several matches against adult sides and finally a test match against the U.K. schools side with the Zimbabweans winning all their games.

The Zimbabwean team were billeted at the Pearl family farm in Stanford Rivers, near Ongar in Essex. A beautiful location with all the trappings, space and facilities to host the guests. Being a prominent hunting and pony club family with Emily, their eldest daughter having got the 'polocrosse bug', a field was always available to play on at the farm.

The Zimbabweans travelled the length and breadth of England and into Wales. Wherever they went the enthusiasm for polocrosse developed and went from strength to strength

UNITED KINGDOM

Vikki Borland, Captain,
Sarah Simkin,
Tim Gearing,
Bonita Moody,
Andrew Schaeffer,

Julie Perkins,
Simon Shearing

ZIMBABWE

Jo Arnold,
Paula Sergeant,
Sally Mannix,
Nicky Mannix,
Brian Cocker,
Lionel Gundry,
Brian Cocker,
Sean Davy

Barry Burbidge, Ted Wilmot, Jo Arnold, Paula Sergeant, Sally Mannix, Brian Cocker, Griffin Burbidge, Lionel Gundry, Sean Davey, Nicky Mannix, Ed Gundry, Jock Kay.

*from right to left – Vix Borland, Sue McGregor,
Bonita Moody, Andrew Schaffer, Julie Perkins, Tim
Gearing, Simon Shearing, Sarah Simkin.*

*Ted Wilmot giving a speech with Ed Gundry
and Jock Kay, Rob Maldon and Charles Mason.*

Sarah Simkin, Tim Gearing, Julie Perkins, Andrew Schaffer, Bonita Moody, Sue McGregor, Vix Borland and Ed Gundry.

92 ~92

Lehanna Van Zyl, Susanne Sergeant, Bev McIntosh, Pascal Gambeau, Gavin Cocker, Ted Wilmot, Henry Harris, Phillip Whaley. Mascot Joshua, Manager Chris Pocock.

In 1992 an invitation was received from the New Zealand Polocrosse Association to send a mixed side and men's side to New Zealand to compete in a three test series against that country. The side was comprised of up and coming young talent some of whom had not played in a test match before but would gain invaluable experience from the tour. Ted Wilmot, with his experience was selected captain and coach as well as player to give the side depth of experience, Pascal Gambeau and Henry Harris being the only other two to had competed in International Tests.

ZIMBABWE LADIES

Lehanna Van Zyl,
Susanne Sergeant,
Bev McIntosh,
Pascal Gambeau.

ZIMBABWE MEN

Gavin Cocker,
Ted Wilmot, Captain, Coach
Henry Harris,
Kane Mathews,
Guy Wixley,
Pietman de Klerk,
Squacky Whaley.

Chris Pocock Tour Manager and Zimbabwe Umpire.

Zimbabwe lost all the tests but achieved a better result at the final test with Squacky Whaley coming into his own.

The New Zealand hosts treated the delegation to a fun-filled tour of scenic places including the breathtaking mountains of the King Country. We were also invited to a Maori celebration in their modern compound that comprised schools and training centres. The two delegations of New Zealanders and Zimbabweans arrived at the entrance gate where we were challenged by painted warriors wielding spears. On being instructed not to look aggressive but to look away, we were accepted as friends and led into a large courtyard. The Maoris with their chief seated on the ground on one side with us seated on chairs on the opposite side. The Chief then came to the centre with a gift for me as manager of the Zimbabwe delegation and laid it down on the floor. He then proceeded to make a speech in his language with an interpreter. Then it was my turn to reciprocate so keeping it in the traditional style I asked Ted to be my interpreter and I duly spoke in Shona. I did not realise that Ted, a fluent Ndebele speaker, had no idea about Shona and therefore could not understand a word I was saying. Not fazed by this Ted went off on his own version of what he thought I was saying with our delegations back on our side of the courtyard trying hard to keep a solemn face as protocol demanded.

From there we were introduced to the warriors, all standing in a long line. Traditional Maori greeting is by rubbing noses and as I was in the front proceeded to rub what seemed like hundreds of noses. Behind me the rest followed offering their hands in greeting thus getting out of the intimate nose rub. A splendid lunch was had in the hall followed by further speeches, this time in English.

After 12 years of isolation, South Africa was now given permission to join the international polocrosse community and this was the first opportunity we had of playing our long standing rivals since 1980. A large contingent of players and horses were sent to Pietermaritzburg for the first Test then on to Johannesburg for the final test.

The South Africans, in my opinion, were rather over-enthusiastic at this reunion test series wanting to have three consecutive weekend tests spread as far as Pietermaritzburg, down to Port Elizabeth and finally at Inanda in Johannesburg. I felt that this would have too heavy a toll on the horses having to travel such large distances and then play top level polocrosse over the three weekends. After much negotiation and with the support of our National Executive Chairman, Hendrick O' Neil, the South Africans settled on the two venues. I was not particularly popular over this decision even by our own players but I had had experience of fatigued horses breaking their legs.

The touring squads congregated at the Featherstone tournament where Robbie Hitchcock completed his finishing touches to the horse documentations before loading onto lorries very generously lent by Ant Keith, Mike Jamie and Roy Bennett. Everyone at the tournament turned out to see the horses off and to wish the squads good luck. Piet de Klerk did a sterling job Estcourting the horses and generally seeing to their welfare.

The First Test results were:-

MEN'S A, ?
Men's B   Zim 29, S.A. 22
Ladies   Zim 23, S.A. 20
Colts   Zim 18, S.A. 16

Second Test
Men's A   Zim 29, S.A 30
Men's B   Zim 32, S.A. 17
Ladies   Zim 20, S.A. 24
Colts   Zim 23, S.A. 18

Third Test
Men's A   Zim 30, S.A. 26
Men's B   Zim 24, S.A. 16
Ladies   Zim 26, S.A. 9
Colts   Zim 17, S.A. 18

Chris Pocock [Manager]
John Harris [Coach]
Robbie Hitchcock [Vet]

Piet de Klerk [Transport Manager]

ZIMBABWE MENS A

Kane Mathews
Gavin Cocker
Henry Harris
Glenn Johnson
Alistair Keith
Clive Johnson
Roy Bennett

ZIMBABWE MEN'S B

Clive Wright
Guy Wixley
Wessels Eksteen
Tim Fennell
Ted Wilmot
Ant Keith

ZIMBABWE LADIES

Nola Harris
Sally Harris
Bev McIntosh
Johanna Arnold
Jane Woods
Lihana van Zyl
Margo Worswick.

Margot Worswick, Nola Harris, Bev mackintosh, Sally Harris, Jane Woods, Johanna Arnold, Lehanna van Zyl

ZIMBABWE COLTS

Lionel Gundry
Rick Goby
Craig Mannix
Brian Cocker
Pieter de Klerk
Jason Davidson
Phillip Whayley

Brian Cocker, Craig Mannix, Jason Davidson, Philip Whaley, Rick Gobey, Pieman de Klerk, Lionel Gundry.

93 ~ 93

1993 Australia sent over a Men's and Ladies side to tour to Zimbabwe. The tests were played at Ruwa and Matepatepa. This was also the year that kicked off the Africa Challenge Trophy as an annual Test series.

ZIMBABWE MEN

Ron Taylor
Clive Johnson
Roy Bennet
Glenn Johnson
Henry Harris
Ian Taylor
Gavin Cocker

Ron Taylor, Clive Johnson, Roy Bennet, Glen Johnson, Henry Harris, Ian Taylor, Gavin Cocker.

ZIMBABWE LADIES

Margo Worswick [Captain]
Sally Harris
Lehanna van Zyl
Paula Sergeant
Kim Mannix
Jo Arnold
Susanne Sergeant

*Back Row Zimbabwe, Margot Worswick, Captain,
Sally Harris, Lehanna van Zyl, Paula Sergeant, Kim
Mannix, Jo Arnold, Susanne Sergeant.
Front Row Australia, Vikki Copeland, Wendy
Barlow, Lesley Jeffries, Bev Hughes, Captain, Annette
Henry, Avis Wotton, Vicki Morris.*

*Nola Harris, Sally Harris, Lehanna van Zyl, Paula
Sergeant, Jo Arnold, Suzanne Sergeant.*

94 ~ 94

This year the touring party comprised a Men's and Ladies sides that played at either Pietermaritzburg or Kyalami Country Base.

ZIMBABWE MEN

Gavin Cocker
Kane Mathews
Henry Harris
Glen Johnson
Alistair Keith
Clive Johnson

Gavin Cocker, Kane Mathews, Henry Harris, Glen Johnson, Alistair Keith, Clive Johnson.

ZIMBABWE LADIES

Margo Worswick
Nola Harris
Bev McIntosh
Sally Harris
Jane Woods
Jo Arnold
Lehanna Van Zyl

Margot Worswick, Nola Harris , Bev McIntosh, Sally Harris, Jane Woods , Jo Arnold, with Lehanna Van Zyl holding the mascot.

*Our dear Friend Anne Timms pictured at this tour
and sporting a tee shirt given to her in 1978. A South
African, Anne always looked after our touring sides for
many years.*

95 ~ 95

Zimbabwe Men's and ladies toured to Western
Australia. The Squad consisted of
C. Wilmans [Manager]
G. Alexander [Manager]

ZIMBABWE MENS

Z. Alexander,
D. Whaley,
G. Cocker,
S. Brown,

A. Alexander,
C. Mannix
C. Wixley,

ZIMBABWE LADIES

N. Wilmans
M. Worswick,
S. Harris,
P. Sergeant
L. Taylor,
K. Mannix,
J. Cocker,
A.M. Dodd

Z. Alexander, C. Wilmans, D. Whaley, G. Cocker, S. Brown, N. Wilmans, M. Worswick, G. Alexander, S. Harris, P. Sergeant, L. Taylor. A. Alexander, C. Mannix, C. Wixley, R. Taylor, K. Mannix, J. Cocker, A.M. Dodd.

Later that year Tests were held in Chipinge against South Africa, but no details available.

96 ~ 96

In 1996 an Under 19 Tour was sent to South Africa.

Ian Mannix [Coach]
Glen Morgan [Captain]
Sean Minter
Andy Baker
Ian Palmer
Evie Stanley
Matthew Hossack
Benji Hossack

Ian Mannix, Sean Minter, Mathew Hossack, Benji Hossack , Andy Baker , Ian Palmer, Evie Stanley Glen Morgan.

97 ~ 97

1997 was definitely a year to remember as it was the Quadrangular Test Series between Zimbabwe, South Africa, New Zealand and Australia held at Pietermaritzburg in South Africa. In effect this was the second world championships since the first in 1982. Here Zimbabwe came out world champions, beating New Zealand into second place [on goal count], Australia into third and South Africa into fourth.

We had a superb young side in:
Gavin Cocker,
Henry Harris,
Kane Mathews,
Angus Alexander,
Paula Campbell,
Margo Worswick,
Suzanne Sergeant,
Sally Harris,
Charlie and Nan Wilmans, Tour Manager's
George and Cynthia Alexander, Transport Manager's
Ted Wilmot and Ant Keith. Coaches.

Back row. Robbie Hitchcock, George Alexander, Charlie Wilmans, Gavin Cocker, Henry Harris, Ted Wilmot, Ant Keith.
Front row. Kane Mathews, Sally Harris, Paula Sergeant, Margot Worswick, Sue Sergeant, Angus Alexander.

Line up against South Africa

Gavin Cocker recovering an offside ball

In the same year the Juniors toured South Africa for the Africa Challenge trophy. The under 14's lost one and won two tests, whilst the under 19's lost the first test 14 to 22 but won the second with a score of 25 to 16. The touring squad was

Toppie Baker, Manager
Henry Harris, Coach

UNDER 14'S
Garth Perreira,
Ryan Biggs,
Graham Keith,
Ian Taylor,
Jason Biggs,
Mathew Baron,
Mathew Hossack.

UNDER 19'S

David Kay,
Hilton Bellis,
Andy Baker,
Mathew Hossack,
Ian Stanley,
Sean Minter.

Also that year, the ladies toured Western Australia
with
Robin Fennel, Manager,
Barry Burbidge, Coach
Manu Harris,
Joanne Graves,
Jenny Alexander,
Bev Lombard,
Rowena Fairly,
Zelda Smorenburg,
Sandy Millar.
Jenny Alexander
Karen Rae

98 ~ 98

Africa Challenge Trophy, Zimbabwe versus South
Africa played at the Bloemfontein Equestrian Centre,
South Africa.

ZIMBABWE UNDER 14

Toppie Baker [Manager]
James Biggs [Coach]
Luke Hanmer
Terrance Keith
Krystal Shaw
Gareth Barry

Ryan Mee
Jason Biggs
Patrick Keith

ZIMBABWE UNDER 16

Doug Fingland [Manager]
Ant Keith [Coach]
Odette Mostert
Jackie Fingland
Janet Johnston
Cheryl Hanmer
Mathew Barron
Ryan Biggs
Graham Keith
Ian Taylor

ZIMBABWE LADIES UNDER 19

Barbara Panter [Manager]
Richard Mostert [Coach]
Stephanie Fingland
Linda Wright
Hayley Evans
Jennifer Hughes
Tracey Pereira
Hayley Panter

ZIMBABWE MEN UNDER 19

Peter Barron [Manager]
Alistair Keith [Coach]
Andy Baker
Mathew Hossack
Bossie Joubert
Andre Coetzee
Ian Stanley
Murray Evans
David Barron

99 ~ 99

The Africa Challenge Trophy 99 was played at Hippo Valley

Rob Panter [Overall Manager]
Barbara Panter [Overall Manager]

ZIMBABWE MEN UNDER 19

Peter Barron [Manager]
Alistair Keith [Coach]
Andy Baker
Jonathan Barry
David Barron
Bossie Joubert
Ryan Biggs
Mathew Barron
Ian Taylor
Mathew Kay
ZIMBABWE LADIES UNDER 19

Norman Gardiner [Manager]
Isobel Gardiner [Manager]
Sandy Miller [Coach]
Ashley Panter
Cheryl Hanmer
Odette Mostert
Steph Fingland
Hayley Panter
Jennifer Hughes
Hayley Evans

ZIMBABWE UNDER 16

Doug Fingland [Manager]
Jon Jon Rutherford [Coach]

Troy Parker [Coach]
Garth Pereira
Gareth Barry
Graham Keith
Tyrone Joubert
Warren Games
Jackie Fingland
Ashlyn Rowley
Tracey Douglas

ZIMBABWE UNDER 14

James Biggs [Manager]
Toppy Baker [Coach]
Jason Biggs
Krystal Shaw
Allison Mannix
Terrance Keith
Katie Baker
Bradley Clark
Audra Dixon
Heath Games

2000 ~ 2000

The new millennium brought in a catastrophic period for the country that had a serious impact on the future of most polocrosse clubs in rural Zimbabwe. The year 2000 was to be the last season where polocrosse was played out across the country before violent evictions occurred and so it was fitting that Ruzawi River should be the host venue to play out test matches against touring sides from South Africa.

Again for the first time the Zimbabwe teams wore the rainbow colours on their white T-shirts.

*Paula Sergeant, Caroline Bohnet, Lehana Van Zyl,
Rowena Fairlie, Sally Harris, Bev McIntosh, Margot
Worswick, Karen Rae, Kim Mannix, Taige Burbidge,
Leslie Taylor, Evie Stanley, Jo Cocker, Ted Wilmot,
[Front Row]Manou Harris, Nola Harris, Zelda
Rohm.*

*Men's A And B. George Alexander, Angus Alexander,
Greg Sergeant, Robbie Hitchcock, Lionel Gundry, ?
Parker, Henry Harris, Willie Swan, Shannon Burbidge,
Piet De Klerk, Ant Keith, Kane Mathews, Ian Mannix,
John Harris.
Front Row, Gavin Cocker, Jon Jon Rutherford, Ron
Taylor, Phillip Whaley.*

THE SQUAD LINE UP AT RUZAWI RIVER CLUB.

Men's A Standing to The National Anthem. Shannon Burbidge, Jon Jon Rutherford, Ant Keith, Gavin Cocker, Angus Alexander, Henry Harris.

Margo Worswick In Action.

Sweet music after the first chukka.

2001 ~ 2001

In 2001 Zimbabwe sent a large contingent to Pretoria South Africa for a series of test matches. Both men's sides, A and B lost to South Africa 3 – 0 whilst the ladies A side scored a victory of 3 – 0. Gavin Cocker received the trophy for the best 3 of the test.

ZIMBABWE MENS A

Allan Malloy (Manager)
Ted Wilmot (Coach)
Squacky Whaley
Gavin Cocker
Anthony Keith
Brian Cocker
Henry Harris (Captain)
Shannon Burbidge

ZIMBABWE MENS B

Johnnie Du Rand (Manager)
Jon Jon Rutherford
Dale Scott
Pietman De Klerk
Wally Crawford
Ron Taylor
Willie Swan
Connell Bunnett

ZIMBABWE LADIES A

Sue Mactavish (Manager)
Anthony Keith (Coach)
Sally Carey
Karen Cocker
Margot Worswick
Paula Sergeant
Arlene Crook
Lesley Taylor

ZIMBABWE LADIES B

Jenny Mannix (Manager)
Richard Games (Coach)
Taige Stirrup
Nicki Mannix

Jo Graves
Manu Harris
Ann Marie Dodd
Ashley Panter
Sally Anne Van Eeden

ZIMBABWE MEN UNDER 19

Doug Fingland (Manager)
Gary Dodd (Coach)
Ross Shand
Ian Taylor
Graham Keith
T J Joubert
Graeme Hughes
Ryan Biggs
Gareth Barry

ZIMBABWE LADIES UNDER 19

Tony And Caroline Krynauw (Managers)
Hayley Panter
Amy Norval
Odette Mostert
Jackie Fingland
Tracy Douglas
Katy Baker. [Was the Reserve for the Under 16 And Brought Up]

ZIMBABWE UNDER 16

Norman And Isobel Gardiner (Managers)
Richard Mosterd (Coach)
Jason Biggs
Krystal Shaw
Pierre Joubert
Ross Fingland
Bradley Clark
Alison Mannix

Audra Dixon
Katy Baker

ZIMBABWE UNDER 14

Glenn Dixon (Manager)
Ian Mannix (Coach)
Brad Mallet
Lorraine Ferreira
Chrissie Coetzee
Michael Krynauw
Frances Dodd
Stacey Logan
Graeme Pallister

Gavin Cocker

T.J. Joubert, Gareth Barry, Ryan Biggs, Graeme Hughes,
Ian Taylor, Graham Keith,

Tracey Douglas, Odette Mostert, Brad Clarke, Jackie Fingland

2002 ~ 2002

This was the year that the South African Juniors and Veterans were to travel to Zimbabwe but with all the political upheaval going on in the country, Ant Keith, as the current President accepted the South African invitation to hold the test series at Sondella in Warmbaths.

This was the first occasion that a host country provided 'pool horses' for a neighbour and was an invaluable experience for the juniors to play at test level on strange horses.

ZIMBABWE UNDER 19 BOYS

Bradley Clark
Luke Hanmer
Graham Keith
Terrance Keith
Ryan Biggs
Jason Biggs
Ross Shand
Patrick Keith
Shannon Burbidge [Manager]
Greg Sergeant [Coach]
Hamish Michaels [Coach]

S. Burbidge, H. Michael, G. Sergeant, B. Clark, G. Keith, T. Keith, R. Shand, P. Keith, L. Hamner, R. Biggs, J. Biggs

ZIMBABWE UNDER 19 GIRLS

Krystal Shaw
Audra Dixon
Stacey Brown
Natasha Langley
Amy Norvall
Alison Mannix
Ashlyn Rowley
Shirley Norval [Manager]
Suzanne Sergeant [Coach]

ZIMBABWE JUNIORS UNDER 16 MIXED

Michael Krynauw
Pierre Joubert
Ashley Shand
Christian Coetzee
Ralf Joubert
Katie Baker
Frances Dodd
Susan Cocker
Jamie Haasbroek
Natalie Taylor
Glen Dixon [Manager]
Sandy Dixon [Manager]
Ken Flavell [Coach]

ZIMBABWE JUNIORS UNDER 14 MIXED

Stacey Logan
Ashleigh Haasbroek
Derek Cloete
Brad Mallet
Vanessa Birkentoft
Lorraine Ferreira
Ursula Shaw
Mike Mallet [Manager]
Sharon Mallet [Manager]

2003 ~ 2003

The World Cup Was Played In Australia. The touring squad Was as follows.

Gavin Cocker, Captain.
Henry Harris,
Howie Baker,
Shannon Burbidge,
Paula Sergeant,
Suzanne Sergeant,
Eve Stanley,
Margo Worswick,
Toppie Baker Coach,
Allan Malloy, Manager
Allan Jack, President

2004 ~ 2004

Zimbabwe Versus South Africa Played At Hippo Polocrosse Club.

Overall Manager Hedrick O'Neil.

ZIMBABWE MEN

Andy Baker
Shannon Burbidge
Henry Harris
Howie Baker
Kevin Fisher
David Tanner
Graham Keith

Brian Wright

ZIMBABWE LADIES

Susanne Sergeant
Eve Stanley
Margo Worswick
Paula Sergeant
Nikkie Mannix
Susie Whaley
Manu Harris
Nickie Du Toit

ZIMBABWE MEN UNDER 19

Bradley Clarke
Mikey Krynauw
Chrissy Coetzee
Bruce Kay

ZIMBABWE LADIES UNDER 19

Katie Baker
Francis Dodds
Jamie Haasbroek
Audra Dixon

ZIMBABWE UNDER 16

Mathew Donovan
Bradley Mallet
Mark Taylor
Danie Swan
Ashleigh Haasbroek
Kirsten Dodd
Stacey Logan
Ursula Shaw

ZIMBABWE UNDER 14

Damien Harris
Richard Taylor
Stevie Gardini
Zanna Worswick
Leigh Worswick
Shayne Ellman-Brown
Audrey Logan

2005 ~ 2005

In 2005 the under 19 girls travelled to Sondella, South Africa for a test against South Africa. With Nola Coetzee as Manager and Margo Worswick as Coach, the squad comprised:

Jamie Haasbroek,
Stacey Logan,
Urshula Shaw,
Ca-Marie Swan,
Katy Baker,
Audrey Logan,
Leigh Worswick.

Sondella S.A. Tour. Nola Coetzee, Manager, Stacey Logan, Jamie Haasbroek, Audrey Logan, Urshula Shaw, Leigh Worswick, Ca~Marie Swan, Katy Baker, Margot Worswick, Coach.

In April of the same year a junior quadrangular test series was held in Australia. Those that travelled were:

Audrey Logan
Rosanne Worswick
Leigh Worswick
Kirsten Dodds
Brad Mallett
Danie Swan
Ian Winwood
Matt Donovan
Shannon Burbidge Coach.
Rory Logan Manager.
Willie Swan. In charge of the horses.

By august, Zimbabwe sent over two mixed sides to compete in a series of tests in the UK. Zimbabwe president, Richard Mostert, accompanied the tour in which the first test was played at Worcestershire and the second at Henley-in-Arden.

THE TOP MIXED TEAM WAS:-

Shannon Burbidge(Capt.)
Squacky Whaley
Andy Baker
Howie Baker
Ash Panter
Arlene Crook
Nikki Mannix
Margot Worswick
Kevin And Jules Fisher, Managers
Gary Dodd Umpire
Toppy Baker, Coach
 Barry Burbidge, Coach

UNDER 21 MIXED

Mikey Krynauw,
Brad Clark,
Ross Shand
Danie Swan
Kirsten Dodds,
Francis Dodds,
Jamie Haasbroek
Audra Dixon
Willie Swan, Coach

2006 ~ 2006

This tour travelled down to Noodsberg in South Africa around April. Regrettably no information has come to light on this tour.

2007 ~ 2007

The World Test Series was held in Australia. Tim Fennell assisted by Mick Gorman were the coaches whilst the managers were Jules and Kevin Fisher. Tracey Beekes as reserve came on to replace Margo Worswick in the first test who had an accident and was taken off for concussion.

ZIMBABWE

Andy Baker
Howie Baker
Shannon Burbidge
Brad Clark
Margot Worswick
Ash Panter
Kirsten Dodd
Francis Dodd
Tracey Beekes, Reserve

CHAPTER 14

CLUBS

IT WAS IN 1967 THAT THE FIRST INTER PROVINCIAL Tournament was held. Prior to that it was the Inter Zone tournament that was not confined to provincial boundaries. All clubs in the country fell into one of the four provinces of Manicaland, Mashonaland, Matabeleland and Midlands.

Mashonaland captured the largest number of clubs and to even out the competition, some of the clubs on the fringe, like Virginia, were given over to Manicaland, or Featherstone to Midlands. Matabeleland was a small playing province and had to resort to importing borrowed players that had not made their provincial selection.

Provincial colours were awarded if you had represented your province for six games with Mashonaland setting their standard higher than the others.

Each province had its own executive committee with the chairman being the provincial representative on the National Executive and with sub committees that performed the seasonal tasks of handicaps, selection and coaching etc. A Chief and Deputy Umpire were elected. Likewise each province would hold its own championships and on that weekend hold their Annual General Meeting in which new office bearers would be elected.

After the 1994 season, the Government re-zoned all the provinces to eight provinces of which polocrosse was played only in seven. This then caused a problem in that some provinces only had one club and so re-zoning of clubs had to be done by the National Executive.

Inter Provincials became less of a prestigious event as it was and by 2000 had faded from the calendar.

MANICALAND PROVINCE

PATRON
> J. Kay [1984]

Honorary Life Vice President
> F.J. Barry [1984]

Chairman.
> Jock Kay [1971/1979]
> R. Fennell [1980/1982]
> R. Mostert [1983/1984]
> Ant Keith [1985/1988]
> A. Baisley 1989 to 1990]

Secretary.
> Gail Wiggins [1971/ 75]
> D. Boyd [1976/77]
> S. Harris [1978/]
> K. Kay [1979 to 19 84]
> I. Baisley [1989 to 1990]

Manicaland Men's A. Henry Harris, Arthur Baisley, John Harris, Ant Keith, Tim Fennel, Iain Kay

CHIPINGA ~ CHIPINGE
[1961 to present day]
Colours—Green and White quarter

Chipinge Club House Aitken, M.

Aitkin, K.
Allison, G.
Anderson, G.
Baker, N.
Baker, W.
Barron, M
Barron.
Barron. P
Barry, R.
Bennett R.
Bennett, C.
Blignaut, K.
Blignaut, P.
Burbidge, G
Burnett, G.
Carshalton (sister).
Carshalton, D.
Clowes, R.
Colles, A.
Cooper, J.
Cugnet, J.
Cugnet, V.
Cutter, T.

Davies, D.
Dent, J.
Du Plooy, G
Fennel T.
Fennel, R.
Fennel, Rod.
Fennel, Roz.
Fennel, Tim.
Forrester F.
Forrester N.
Forrester, A.
Forrester, M.
Forrester, R.
Forrester, S.
Gambeau E.
Gambeau P.
Gambeau R
Gambeau, L
Gilson, B.
Gilson, G.
Gilson, R.
Groenewald, A
Hanmer, A.
Harding, A.
Herselman, R.
Human, P.
Hurwick, C.
Hurwick, J.
Hurwick, L.
Jahme, K
Jahme, M.
Joubert Bossie.
Joubert M.
Joubert P.
Joubert R.
Joubert TJ.
Joubert W.
Joubert, D.
Joubert, F.

Joubert, J.
Joubert, Juan.
Joubert, Monique.
Joubert, Y.
Keith, A.
Knien, H.
Kotze, A.
Kotze, F.
Kotze, J.
Kotze, S.
Kruger, D.
Kruger, J.
Lamb, T.
Lewis, B.
Lewis, I.
Masson, B.
Meyer, E.
Moffat, I.
Morgan, G.
Morgan, L.
Morrison, M.
Nissen, J.
Olivey, A
Olivey, O.
Palm, R.
Pascoe, G.
Paterson, P.
Peel, A.
Peel, S.
Powell, J
Prince L.
Prince, L.
Prince,G.
Russel, A.
Rutherford Jamie.
Rutherford K.
Rutherford, C.
Rutherford, J.
Rutherford, T.

Scott, Brendon,
Scott, C.
Scott, D.
Scott, Dale
Scott, J.
Scott, R.
Scott, S.
Scott, W.
Shirring, R.
St John, Barry.
Stirrup, R.
Stonier, B.
Stonier, M.
Taffs, C.
Taylor, R.
Titley, H.
Tweedie, J.
Ulrich R.
van der Bet, P.
van der Meeberg.
Van Heerden
Van Zyl, A.
Veldsman, I.
Vermaak, E.
Walsh, C.
Wilding Davies.
Wilson, D.
Wright, P.
Yeatman, H.
Yeatman, J.
Yeatman, B.

Chipinge was originally settled by the Moodie Trek in 1903 and was to be named Melsetter after the village in Scotland, spelled Melster where Thomas Moodie's ancestors came from. Thomas Moodie died soon after arrival and a year later, the Martin Trek decided to move the centre of Melsetter to the present day Chimanimani. Chipinga then became the name after the resident Chief.

On Zimbabwe's independence it changed again to Chipinge.

The fortunes of the district changed significantly when two brothers, Hugh and Robin Fennel migrated from India, Hugh in 1958 followed by Robin a year later, and settled to pioneer the growing of coffee that, together with tea, became the prosperity of the community. Hugh, on his arrival having travelled down Africa from Ethiopia, had purchased the farm Crocodile Creek for four hundred pounds whilst in the Chipinga pub. Robin settled on Fiddlers Green.

Chipinga, Melsetter and Silver streams were very active with gymkhanas and race meetings, but it was Robin who ultimately raised the standards and tempo with the introduction of quality Thoroughbred horses, and later, in 1961 he started the Chipinga Polocrosse Club at the Chipinga Club grounds in the Village.

A tragedy occurred in the first year of inception with the death of Gary Pascoe whilst at a club practice. This put an end to the newly formed club as members felt the sport was too dangerous. Two years later it was revived by Robin, Trevor Rutherford, Tony Olivie and John Tweedie, and in 1974 the club changed its name from Chipinga Gymkhana and Race Club to Chipinga Polocrosse Club.

Despite Chipinga starting polocrosse in 1961, there is no record of the Club attending any official tournaments or any of its members registered on the handicap list until 1970 when they attended the National Championships held at Ruzawi that year. The next year, 1971, Chipinga held a sponsored invitation tournament of 24 top players from around the country. The last game was an exciting match between Hippo and against a selection of the rest to show the district what good polocrosse looks like.

As the club only had one field, the polocrosse section was relocated to Robin's farm, Fiddlers Green in 1980, where more fields could be established to accommodate tournaments. A hundred stables and a magnificent clubhouse was built in 1981 with stone and thatch that unfortunately burnt down in 1988. It was then rebuilt to its original status and continues to this day.

A number of members bred racehorses, and as a result the club fielded magnificent animals over the period of its existence. During the Australian tour of 1972, Robin Fennel and Trevor Rutherford, having watched the first test and been dismayed at the poor quality of horses given to the Australian team, offered to mount the Australian's with Chipinge horses and this produced a better result for the Aussies.

The club produced many top-ranking players, of whom a large number played at national and provincial levels. Terry Cutter was a prominent coffee farmer in the Chipinge District and bred magnificent racehorses that later were brought into polocrosse. He was one of the top club players and played for the Manicaland Provincial side as well as making the national team. His favoured position was in the 3 birth. He died in a tragic motor accident.

Ros Fennel, Robin's wife, was an excellent horsewomen and a competent and aggressive polocrosse player in the defence position. She played in the Ladies Provincial team for Manicaland and for the National Ladies side. She died tragically when her horse ran into the back of a car at a tournament at Ruzawi. Robin's oldest son Tim also played for his province as well as for the National side as did Rose Barry and Richard Palm.

Despite the land invasions that destroyed most country districts, Chipinge has managed to continue with the few members left and is still producing players of substance.

Prize giving at Ruzawi. Mrs Marjory Harris handing over the Harris Trophy to Rose Palm, Terry Cutter and Rich Palm.

Robin Fennel   Ros Fennel   Terry Cutter

Tim Fennel   Mark Winwood   Dave Scott

Joubert Bros, Francois, Jan, Davie.

*Francois Joubert with Tim Fennel being marked by
Henry Harris*

Roy Bennet in pursuit of Robbie Hitchcock.

*Mike Cossey of Ruwa being marked by Terry Cutter
with Mike Jamie in the background*

Roy Bennet marking up Sally Harris.

HEADLANDS
[1968 to 1971]
Colours—Scarlet Red

Eksteen, B
Fischer, G
Labusche, L
Martin, J
Odendaal, O
Oosthuizen, B
Philips, P
Robertson, R
Smuts, F
Truwent, R
Van der Merwe, L
Walls, T
Wright, C
Wright, P

Headlands Polocrosse Club was situated along the Inyati Mine road, just beyond the cattle sales pens and close to the main Harare / Mutare road. It was a registered club in name, in that apart from its members, no facilities existed. The field consisted of a marked out piece of bush that had an anthill in the middle and the grass kept short by grazing.

Seldom were there any more than eight members at a practice and sometimes a spectator would umpire on foot. Going to tournaments they would just scrape together a team with no one in reserve and when they turned up at Hippo for their first match, Jaapie Martin was kicked by a horse and invalided out. This then meant that Peter Baker had to double in his place between chukkas.

Being a small club also meant difficulties with horse transport. The two brothers Clive and Peter Wright rode their mounts from their farm at Eagles Nest to the 1970 Ruzawi National Championships and back home at the end of the tournament.

Later Clive Wright went on to play for Ruzawi and distinguished himself by playing for his provincial side as well as the national side. Gilbert Fischer was more into show jumping than polocrosse and was the captain of the show jumping national team. He is mentioned under Old Umtali Polocrosse Club for his antics in teaching riders the art of falling off a horse.

MACHEKI
[1979 to 1982]
Colours—Orange with Brown Quarters

Cocker, N
Cocker, R
Cocker, W
Eckstein, B
Freshman, A
Freshman, R
Games, R
Hobbs, R
Hulme, R
Mostert, D
Mostert, P

Mostert, R
Oosthuizen D
Oosthuizen, L
Oosthuizen, N
Oosthuizen, J
Rich, D

Nick Oosthuizen seems to be the man who reactivated the main Macheki Club that was forced to shut down during the heat of the war. This was at the end of the war and the period leading up to elections that brought in the new Zimbabwe. With the help of Richard Games he ring-fenced the club grounds and ploughed and prepared the polocrosse fields.

*Dave Mostert, Cork Hulme, Rich Mostert, Rich Games,
Daff Oosthuizen, Nick Oosthuizen*

MAKONI
[1983 to 1989]
Colours—Navy Blue and Red Checks

Brits, B
Brits, C.
Crooks, N
Czerwinski, R
du Toit, K
du Toit, F
du Toit, G

Eckstein, M
Eckstein, W
Green, D
Henderson, Rusty
Langley, A
Langley, M
Lock, H
Mac Alistair, G
McAllister, G
McAllister, P
Nell, P
Oosthuizen, W
Rogers, J
Savona, R
Taylor, Dido
Taylor, J

George McAllister was one of the founder members that established polocrosse at the Maroni Club on a piece of waste land across the way from the main clubhouse. A pavilion was built with three fields in which mini tournaments were held. The first major tournament was held in 1986.

Pete Nell was the coach and in 1987 the Club won the Manicaland Provincial Championships in which five of the club players made selection for the Manicaland side.

OLD UMTALI
[1952 to 1964]
Colours—Green and Black

Barry, B.
Barry, F.
Barry, J.
Barry, N.
Barry, R.
Barry, Rose.

Barry, S.
Barry, W
Bowen, I.
Brown, P.
Burrell, E.
Chatters, J.
De Smite, Miss.
Dixon, S.
Hanmer, A
Hanmer, Mgrs.
Holland, C.
Kenny, J.
McIntyre, E.
Olorenshaw, Miss.
Sewell, C
Sewell, Mrs.
Taylor, B.
Thompson, A.
Vaughan Roberts.
Wilson, R.
Wolfe, Wendy.

Old Umtali Polocrosse Club was situated on Umtassa Farm belonging to Fred and Sheila Barry. There was only one field and a basic brick pavilion. Players came in from around the neighbouring farming communities, like Odzi where Charles Holland and Ivor Bowen worked as farm managers. Later Ivor took on a job in Beatrice and continued to play for the club, driving all the way with his horse every weekend and was usually the first to arrive at the practice.

Fred Barry was one of those defence players who were able to throw the ball from the back line and into his scoring area. However, the women hated marking him as he was inclined to be rough with the racquet. Wife Sheila played at No 1 on a lively, short-strided chestnut named Rhodeen that detested any form of contact and would more than often bite the opposing rider. Sheila was a brilliant horsewoman and horse trainer and was responsible for schooling all the family horses. Later she opened up a riding school and many three phase events took place there.

The likes of Gilbert Fischer and Leslie Lombard would hold courses there and at one time Gilbert would teach his pupils the art of falling off as well as stopping a runaway horse. This was done by sliding up the underside of the horses neck with arms wrapped around the horse's neck and legs gripping precariously somewhere near the withers. The theory being that a horse cannot continue to bolt with that sort of weight around his neck. Evidently, in rehearsing this procedure galloping down the polocrosse field, the pupils could not keep their legs up and would invariably entangle themselves in the horse's front legs resulting in the horse coming a cropper and thereby successfully halting it.

Fred Barry became the Vice President of the National Association in 1964 and donated the Umtassa Floating Trophy in 1959 for the winners of the Tarantellas Women's Tournament. This trophy was then taken over by the association in 1967 for the winners of the interprovincial tournament and renamed The Barry Floating Trophy, much to the annoyance of the ladies.

Lady Borrett was a keen follower of the Club and donated a beautiful rose bowl which may later have been used for international matches. 1957 the Club won the A Division Founders cup.

Remo Barry on Prince, ?, Bill Barry on Loppy Ears,
Fred Barry on Kerry Dancer.

RUZAWI **RIVER**
[1963 to 2000]
Colours—White shirt with black diagonal cross bands

Alexander, A
Alexander, Z.
Baisely, A.
Baker, A.
Baker, H.
Baker, S.
Baker, T.
Barron M.
Barron, D.
Bellis, M.
Bellis, H.
Bryson, R.
Bunnet, C.
Bunnet, K.
Burdett, C.
Burl, A.
Campbell, B.
Campbell, J.
Clayton, T.
Coetzee, A.
Coetzee, A. Snr.

Collett, B.
Collett, W.
Cossey, J
Cossey, M.
Cross, J.
Davies, S.
de Cellain, P.
de Waal, H.
Donaldson, I.
Duff, G.
Duff, J.
Edgar, M.
Fairlie, J.
Fitzroy, J.
Gaylard, D.
Gorman, K.
Gorman, M.
Grant, A.
Grant, G.
Harris, C.
Harris, D.
Harris, H.
Harris, J.
Harris, M.
Harris, N.
Harris, S.
Hitchcock, R
Hitchcock, Rachael.
Hitchcock, S
Hunter, Oonagh.
Jobson, R
Johnson, A.
Johnson, C
Johnson, S.
Johnson, Sally.
Kay, B
Kay, C.
Kay, I.
Kay, K.

Kay, M.
Kay, D.
Keene, J.
Keith A
Keith, Alistair.
Keith, I.
Keith, J.
Keith, P.
Lampard, K.
Lampard, M.
Lampard, S.
Lampard, T.
Lennard, Gail.
Lewis, S.
Malden, M.
Maldon, J
Maldon, R.
Martin, M.
McKay, J.
McKay, S.
Meikle, J.
Micheals, H.
Micheals, L.
Milbank, F.
Milbank, J.
Nel, P.
Parker, T
Parkin Sean.
Parkin, J
Parkin, S.
Parkin, T.
Parsons, A.
Perreira, G.
Perreira, M.
Perreira, T
Pistorius, R.
Rice, R.
Rutherford, J.
Semple, G.

Simpson, T.
Smith, B.
Smith, Molly.
Stacey, R.
Stanley, E.
Stanley, I.
Stanley, M.
Stockhill, R.
Strang, C.
Strang, J.
Swanson, K.
Swanson, T.
Thompson, D.
Thorneycroft, D.
Tozer, E
Travers J.
Viljoen, H.
Watson, P.
Wiehe, M.
Woodhouse, D.
Woodhouse, M.
Worsley-Worsick M.
Worsley-Worsick, P.
Wright, L.
Wright, N.
Wright, C.
Yeatman, R

Ruzawi started in 1963 when the Keith, Harris, Donaldson and Bryson families decided it would be far less travelling if they started a club at Ruzawi River rather than carry on playing in Marandellas. Rated as one of the best venues for polocrosse, the club put in four well-grassed fields under irrigation and later, when numbers coming to the tournaments grew, three more fields were created adjacent to the club grounds.

The club house, built in the old Colonial Rhodesian style construction, was built as the farming community grew, for the social centre of early land settlers from the

Second World War and catered for the sporting needs of cricket, rugby, golf, tennis, squash and bowls. A tight knit community, the district would turn out to help in any sports function to assist wherever they were needed and this was so evident in polocrosse where the membership was never that great in the sport to cater for the volumes that would turn up for the tournaments. An example of this was the 1970 National Championships where 700 people were fed and entertained.

In the early years, visiting teams and their families would be accommodated around the district and invariably in homesteads that were not directly involved with the sport, but as numbers increased this became impracticable and clubs would camp around the club vicinity. An additional campsite across the road from the club house was used when required, and this became the centre of many memorable camp fire parties where players would congregate, beer in hand, around a central log fire and indulge in wild and energetic pranks.

Ruzawi was not particularly known for its good weather. The Whitsun weekend was a regular Ruzawi venue and invariably freezing. The players and umpires, roused by the early morning loud speaker to the start of their games, would have to trundle across the four fields covered in frost to extricate their frozen mounts from the stable block. One particular weekend, spectators lined the side of the field warmly wrapped in duvets and blankets and I remember sitting in with Graeme Crook in the cab of his pick-up truck, exhaling fumes of vapour that misted up the windscreen. In front of us and oblivious to our presence in the cab, was Ronnie Palmer holding his hippo sized bay, when a passerby informed him his overreach boots were upside down. He duly bent down to rectify the problem but his mount would have none of it and lashed out. After calling in his son to hold up the front leg, he managed to raise the offending rear but the horse, standing now on two legs, was able to lash out with both legs that tossed two Palmers back and forth as they desperately hung on. After a few attempts he looked around to see if anyone had noticed and decided to pretend it never happened.

The National Championships were often hosted by Ruzawi. It used to be a three day event and was the time that the executive would call the Annual General Meeting for which we would all gather in the club house at lunch time. When the membership got too big we then sat around on the ground of the B field. The last evening would be a ball and prize giving in which everyone was required to dress up and those with their colours proudly wore them. This was the time the selectors announced the national sides to compete in the forthcoming test series.

Ruzawi had some extremely talented players who were the foundation of the success of the club. Of these John Harris, Ant Keith and Iain Kay were the forerunners. It was generally believed amongst the greater fraternity that for any talented player who wished to get to the top, Ruzawi was the best coaching centre. Even club coaches would study the Ruzawi tactics to take home for their players. John was the king of tactics and spectators would watch in awe as on many occasions he would turn his losing team around to a last chukka win. Up until the club ceased to exist, there was never a national men's side in which Ruzawi was not represented. Ant Keith, as a school boy was a member of the first national team to tour to Natal, South Africa and remained in the national side right through to his retirement from top polocrosse. Not far behind this record was Iain Kay. Since 1982 our national sides have progressed up the leader board to become world champions in 1997 and Ruzawi has played a large part in this success. Names like Angus Alexander, Alistair Keith, and Henry Harris, to name a few have all been moulded at Ruzawi and gone on to represent the country on a number of occasions. Even the ladies have dominated the national ladies sides with Sally Harris, Sue Parkin and Margo Worswick rated high on the world rating for women players. Sue Keene as she was then was the only lady player to be selected in the top men's national side, an achievement no other has accomplished.

Ruzawi has also played a key part in national and provincial level administration. The position of Chief and Deputy Chief Umpire has for many years been in the hands of Ian Keith, John Harris, Ant Keith and Iain Kay. John has been instrumental in developing the rules of the game as it progresses to meet the needs of a developing sport. Keeping the wheels of the National Association turning and guiding it through changes brought about from exposure to international polocrosse has been a string of presidents starting with David Campbell, Jock Kay and Ant Keith. David Campbell and his wife Phyllis received the R.C.C.B. Silver Medal for services to polocrosse. David will always be remembered not only for all that he achieved for polocrosse, but also the final president's speech he delivered, his emotional distress evident.

It was in the Wedza district, adjacent to Ruzawi where it all started. Politicized 'war veterans' from the Rhodesian war, incited villagers from the nearby Sowe Communal Lands to occupy farms and drive the land owners and their labour force off the land, often violently. The government turned a blind eye and Ruzawi, just as all the other commercial agricultural districts, ceased to function and an era of polocrosse went down with it. It was fitting then, that the last test match with South Africa was held at Ruzawi before the association mothballed all inter-club polocrosse activity. Fitting in that Ruzawi had been the host to so many test matches over the years, and, although unknown at the time, this was to be its final epitaph.

The Zimbabwe Teams line up for the last test to be played at Ruzawi in 2000

Ruzawi Juniors versus Virginia Juniors.

Ruzawi's Under 14 contingent

*Left to right. Linda Wright, Shirley Lampard, Kirk Swanson,
Ian Stanley, Evie Stanley, Gordon Duff, James Duff,
David Kay, Andy Baker, Jenny Hughes, Douglas Hughes,
Nicola Wright.*

UMTALI POLOCROSSE AND SADDLE CLUB
Before 1959 to 1985?]
Colours—White Shirt with Green Crossband

Typical Umtali street.

Agnew, B
Alves, J
Anderson, J
Arch Deacon, E
Barron, M
Barron, P
Barron, R
Barron, S
Barry, F
Barry, J
Barry, N
Barry, R
Barry, S
Boyd, D
Boyd, M
Boyd, S
Burrell, Mrs
Burrell, R
Camp Morrison, I
Claason, E
Claridge, P
Clasterns, E
Corbett, V
Craig, B
Dodd G
Eales, J
Eales. J
Eksteen W
Eksteen, R
Ford, P
Ford, G
Forrester F
Forrester R
Fourie, F
Fourie, J
Gardner, C
Gordon J
Gordon, D
Gordon, N

Hanmer, D
Hanmer, J
Hanmer, Q
Hannan, P
Henderson, R
Holloway, M
Hope, C
Humphrey, V
Humphries, K
Jackson, D
Jackson, P
Kellett, P
Lawrence, J
Lennon, P
Lennon, P
Levy, G
Levy, S
Lubecka, E
Macgregor, M
McGregor, G
McLaren, J
McLaren, L
Millborrow, M
Miller, A
Miller, H
Miller, Henry
Miller, T
Milne, B
Milne, Miss R
Milne, R
Milne, S
Minter, N
Mirabelli,
Moffit, I
Moore, R
Morrison, A
Orr, G
Orr, J
Orr, S

Palm, R
Palmer, S
Penfold, M
Penfold, S
Plenderleith, L
Pocock, C
Pringle, C
Rault, S
Rose, P
Russell, C
Rutherford, J
Taylor, P
Taylor, P
Thyne, L
Tomlinson, P.
Van Niekerk, F
Van Rooyen, S
Van Staaden, S
Wale, A
Widdup, A
Wiggins, D
Wiggins, J
Wiggins, S
Willis, L
Winwood, F
Winwood, J
Winwood, M
Wolfe, W
Wolfee, Mrs
Zambra, Mrs G
Vorster, Mrs.

As one descended the Christmas Pass into Mutare or Umtali as it was then, one could see the Umtali Polocrosse and Saddle Club nestled in the valley below and under a large granite kopje known as Hospital Hill. Three fields were put in with a club house and permanent brick stable.

Being a border town with Portuguese Mozambique

had its attractions for team members coming to tournaments. Through the sanctions years after 1965, Mozambique assisted fuel-strapped Rhodesia with abundant and cheap fuel from a fuel station provided specifically for Rhodesians and situated at the border. Here was an opportunity to fill your tank and save the few valuable fuel coupons given on ration. Naturally, people then moved on to Masekese Railway Station Restaurant a few kilometres further on for a plate of prawns washed down with a Manica beer or two. On one occasion, Mike McGrath, standing in the queue had an altercation with a local trying to push in and so proceeded to invite the local to punch him in the face, thinking that he would back down. This was not to be and Mike received a hefty punch in the eye resulting in an embarrassed Mike playing the next day with a black eye.

Up in the hills surrounding Mutare is the Vumba and further on, down in the valley is Burma Valley where the Wiggins, Clyde Wiggins and Wolfee families lived, farming burley tobacco and bananas. Every weekend they would send their horses in by tractor and trailer for practices. Colonel Wolfee was the President of the Pony Club and his daughter, Wendy, the top woman player when she made an eight handicap in 1967.

Don Boyd was a fiery character riding his little white blazed chestnut, Pablo, and possibly should have been the first player to be sent off the field as he would at times lose control of his temper. Sharon, his daughter was a lovely competent player and represented Manicaland at the Inter Provincial Tournaments. Pixie Ford was another of these top lady players riding her very pretty grey mare Solitaire, whilst Gail McGregor; Alison Widdup, Anne Morrison and Rose Barry were also very handy lady players. Rose moved on to Chipinge were she became a national and provincial player for the ladies teams.

Ken Humphries was the main mover behind the club and also a top player where he represented Rhodesia on tour to South Africa in 1968. Steve Rault started his polocrosse career in Umtali and after moving to South

Africa, ended up as that country's National President. Neil Gordon was another handy player and in 1970 Dusty Miller won the John McLaren Memorial Trophy for the most improved player. Tragically, John had died as a schoolboy when playing around a disused mine shaft in the Penhalonga area. The club was fortunate to have the expertise of young Anthony Keith, even then a top national player from Ruzawi, who would come for weekend practises whilst he was boarding at Umtali Boys High School.

The Eiberg Tournament was the club's traditional tournament where the winners played for the Kirkos Trophy whilst the handicap tournament played for the Manica Shield sponsored by the club itself. Around 1975 the club relocated for a brief period to Old Mutare on Neil Barry's farm. The club stopped around 1985 when the Mutare Municipality took it over for a housing development.

An early picture of Old Umtali playing at an Umtali tournament with Fred and Remo Barry

*Iain Kay with Alex Miller in pursuit at an Umtali
Tournament.
Note the lonely penalty line judge.*

*Umtali polocrosse Club with the ladies and gents
loo's enclosed with thatching grass in the background.*

Umtali v Ruzawi. Mark Winward, Steve Rault, Alex Miller.

Ken Humphrey, John Milne, Sharon Boyd, Vaughan Humphrey, Don Boyd, TommyMiller

VIRGINIA
[1964 to 1974, restarted 1979 to 2000]
Colours—[1] Paprika Green. [2] Maroon

Arnold, J
Arnold, L
Arnold, N
Arnold, S
Arnold, Toc.
Arnold, H

Baisely, D
Baisley, Arthur
Baisley, A
Baisley, D.
Baisley, I
Baisley, K.
Barker
Becker, A.
Bell, S.
Bradley, A
Brennan, A.
Cocker, B
Cocker, N
Cocker, P
Cocker, W
Davidovics, M
Engelbrecht, M
Fairly, Jack
Fortesque, J
Gemmel, S
Gemmil, S.
Goff, P
Green, A
Green, D.
Griffin, G.
Hatty, A.
Hobbs, W
Hodgson, S
Hodnett, D.
Hodnett, G.
Huellet, M.
Hulme, F
Hulme, G
Hulme, P
Hulme, Pat
Hulme, R
Hulme, Robin
Hulme, W
Keith, A

Keith, G.
Keith, I
Keith, J
Keith, T.
Kriederman, C
Kriederman, D.
Kriederman, K.
Kriederman, W.
Lewis, M
Masson, B
Masson, D
Matthews, K.
Mostert, D
Mostert, P
Mostert, R
Naude, J
Nel, P
Palmer, D
Palmer, I
Palmer, M.
Parkin, Sean.
Parsons, A
Penny, D
Rose, M
Rose, H
Rose, Maggie
Rose, P.
Rose, V.
Ryan, C
Ryan, T
Schlachter, Ben
Shand, D.
Shand, R.
Smales, G.
Smales, K.
Smales, P.
Stratton, M
Stubbs, G
Trethowen, P.

van der Walt, J.
van der Walt, T.
Walraven, R
Watson, A
Webster, G
Whaley, D
Whaley, L
Whaley, P

Virginia is a vast agricultural district of rolling plains north of the Harare / Mutare highway that was settled after the second world war. Prosperous in growing tobacco, maize and cattle, the community build a superb club at the cross roads that leads to Mtoko. All the sporting amenities were on offer including, golf, tennis and squash and later polocrosse took up its home there.

But to begin with polocrosse started on a dusty field on Bracken Hill Farm in 1964 by Thaidie Ryan. The first C Division tournament was held on this field in 1967 and later in 1971, Mrs. Dorothy Rutherford established the first National Under 13 tournament for which she donated the trophy. With playing members moving away, the club petered out in 1974. Notable players from that period were the Hulme brothers, Pete Nel and Arthur Baisely.

The Club restarted in 1979 where the fields were on the adjacent farm and just a stone's throw from the main club. Later, new fields were developed at the club complete with grand stand to accommodate the scorers.

A new breed of players established Virginia as a force to be reckoned with, some of whom made the national sides. The Whaley family came up with Doug and Phillip known to all as Squacky, Whilst John, the father and a keen sportsman, became the president of the association. Joanna Arnold made the national ladies whilst Alistair Keith's two boys, Terrence and Graham received their grounding at Virginia that ultimately brought them into the national sides.

Toc Arnold, a character of note, had every one enthralled with his commentating and livened up the atmosphere at all the national tournaments.

Virginia playing Ruzawi River.

MASHONALAND PROVINCE

CHAIRMAN
G. de Vries. [1972 to 1975]
W.J. Hughes [1976 to 1978]
Richard Tate [1979 to 1981]
Chris Pocock [1982 to 1984]
P. Lombard [1985 to 1986]
M. Davies [1987 to1990]
R. Bennet [1991 to 1992]

Vice Chairman.
Bill Cossey [1972 to 1975]
Chris Pocock [1979 to 1981]
Richard Homan, [1982 to 1984]
Chris Pocock [1991 to 1992]

Secretary.
Mary Leared, [1972 to 1973 – 1975 to 1978]
Di Ridout [1974].
Sue Pocock [1982 to 1984]
Mrs Pete Lombard[1985to1986]

Mashonaland's Ron Taylor being fed the ball by Gavin Cocker with Manicaland's Henry Harris in defence at the Interprovincial.

AYRESHIRE
[1981to 1996]
Colours—Sky Blue Black Trimmings

Anderson N
Ashton, P
Brown I
Brown K
Brown, N
Brown, S.
Brown, P.
Brown, R.
Brundle M
Brundle, I
Brundle, L
Bunnett, A
Bunnett, I
Bunnett, C

Christian, L
Crees, R
Cripps C
Cripps, S.
Davies Shaun
Dechalin, P
Davies, M
Davies, S
Dodd A
Dodd, G
Duncan C
Duncan Mrs.
Duncan, V.
Dutoit, S
Ford, L.
Fortescue, D.
Garner, V
Green, T
Harris, G
Hind, C.
Kay A
Keith, I
Keith, J
Jones, E.
Latham, B
Latham, C.
Lowe, A
Lowe, C
Ludeke, B
Malan, C
Martin, E
McClelland, B
McClelland, G
McClelland, R
Muir, R
Nel, P
Randall, S
Rous Scrappy
Sands-Thomas, M

Scott, D
Slater-Brown, M
Scott, S
Shelley W,
Shelley, M
Swan H
Swan J
Swan W
Swanepoel, N
Teukes, B
Teukes, F
Vaughan~Davies, A
Vaughan-Davies, S
Venables, C
Willis, C
Willis, K.
Wixley, C
Wixley, G
Wixley, K
Wixley, P.

In 1980, Shane Scott came to watch the test match against South Africa that was held in the car park at Thorn Park Polo Club. She was very excited about the game and had several interested new players keen to start up a club at Ayrshire. The next season, she invited Richard Tate and Chris Pocock to come to the Ayrshire Country Club, where they had marked out a field on a section of the golf course, to coach their beginners and help them get the club on its way.

Apart from Dave and Shane Scott, Mike and Sheena Davies ran the club as chairman and secretary for many years, and later had the benefit of the experienced national player, Phil Wixley and his family. Some notable players came out of this club, such as Bill McClelland, Simon Brown and the two Bunnett boys, Ian and Conal.

Ayrshire was the home to the annual Family Tournament, but the idea of a family tournament originated at Ruzawi at the Whitson tournament in 1981.

Sinoia was playing Virginia in the final of the B Division, and the Mosterts made up one section for Virginia, while the Wixleys played together in the Sinoia section. It turned out that the two families would play against each other, so a bet of a crate of beers was made on the result between their sections. Later in the pub that night, Phil and Richard decided to get a family tournament off the ground. They approached Mike Forrester and a couple of others, who were very keen on the idea, and as Ayrshire had just started and wanted a tournament, it was suggested to Shayne Scott to hold it as a regular feature. The tournament started in 1982 and continued as an annual event although the venue has moved to various clubs since Ayrshire closed down.

Tobacco Auctions sponsored a trophy for the winners of the Family Tournament. The Wixley family were the first winners of this trophy.

By 1983, the Club won the A Division Strover trophy at Hippo, and in 1985 were hosts to the Australian test match against Zimbabwe Ladies and Juniors.

Davies Family

Johnson Family

Sharp Family   Howie Baker, most improved player.

BANKET
[1993 to 1996]
Colours—White with Red Stripes

Bennet W
Buchanan, M.
Christian L
Dodd, A
Dodd, G
Duncan C
Fleming C

Fleming R
Green, T
Hind, C
Hind, M
Huxham, P
Jordaan, B
Mannix, K
Marais, D
Palmer. K
Robinson, S.
Rowe, S
Slater Brown, M
Strause, A
Tuke, F
Wilcox, A

In 1992, six players came together to practice on Gary and Anna Marie Dodd's farm, but would truck their horses to Matepatepa to play for that club. After a season, these six players, the Dodds, Adrian Wilcox, Paul Huxham, Tim Green and Aubrey Straus, decided to register Banket Club and Banket Country Club became the new home. To start with, a field was pegged out on the 9th fairway, and later a second field was added.

When Ayrshire closed in 1996, Banket took over the annual Family Tournament, and in that final year as a club, they won the B Division Championships.

With the Dodds selling their farm and Aubrey and Kim, finding partners to marry and moving on, the club was not able to sustain the loss of these members, and so closed down after the 1996 season. Adrian left to farm in his own right whilst Deon and Paul moved across to Matepatepa.

BEATRICE
[1976 to 1985
Colours—Black / white quarters

Benade, F
Benade, J
Brown, S
Davison, J
Hampson, T
Harley, A
Harley, P
Haxley, T
Madgwick, S
Maritz, L
Oxten, W
Pretorious, A
Sharp, G
Sharp, H
Sharp, L
Sharp, P
Smit, K
Smit, J
Smit, Jaapie
Surtees, M
Surtees, P
Winwood, J
Winwood, M

Beatrice, a small village on the main road to Masvingo, comprising Surtees Farm Shop, a Fuel Station, Police Post, and a Gold Mine, started polocrosse in 1976 on the old polo field at Beatrice Sports Club.

Polo had been played there in the 60's and had packed up in 1968, so the field had returned to bush when the original six, Mark Surtees, Percy, Henry and George Sharp, Arthur Harley, Jan and Jaapie Smit, arrived to get the club under way.

Apart from their cattle ponies, they had nothing to get started with, until Corky Hulme from Virginia came to their assistance with pith helmets, sticks with squash racquet heads and any other 'hand me downs' they needed. Later Simon Brown and Penny Surtees joined them.

Beatrice for many years had been a strong Gymkhana club and held its annual amateur race meetings with six divisions and sponsorship in support. Beatrice packed up as a polocrosse Club in the mid 80's and their members then joined up with the newly formed Featherstone polocrosse Club

BINDURA
[1981 to 1983]
Colours—Red / Blue Diagonal Cross

Birdwood, R
Bishop, C
Bunnett, T
Lamb, N
Laurent, K
Laurent, M
Laurent, R
Newton, O
Niccolle, L
Nicol, Yola
Peak, Dick
Robertson, R
Scott, L
Shelly, C
Shelly, T
Smith, Ted
Strover, Dr Minto
Thurlow, Hornsby
Waterhouse, Alistair
Wheeler, R

Bindura probably started playing polocrosse in 1952 where it was played at the Bindura Polo Club. I can find no record of it being registered as a club or indeed handicaps of players registered to the club. I must therefore assume that it was a satellite section to Glendale for the convenience of those players living in Bindura. Around this period, Dr Minto Strover was transferred as a medical doctor to Bindura Hospital and was instrumental in assisting the polocrosse section get underway. Hornsby Thurlow, who farmed nearby, appears to have been the driving force that generated interest in establishing the section but the section petered out in the '60's.

Interest to revive the club came in 1981 when it became registered as a club in its own right and colours were awarded but was described in that year as an 'uninteresting little club'. However, the next year, 1982, it attracted a number of new players of which the Laurents were the main stalwarts, but again closed soon after when the Laurents moved to Shamva Polocrosse Club.

BORROWDALE
[1962 to 1976]
Colours—1]Red shirt. 2] White. 3] Purple

Anson, F
Beer, A.
Beer, J
Bennett, R
Biddows, B
Blomiers, D.
Bromley, G
Burnett ~Smith, E
Burnett ~Smith, G
Burnett~ Smith, J
Burnett-Smith, Dr
Cameron, J
Charteris, J

Chateris, B
Chetwyn, B
Coghill, J
Corbett, V
Crook, A
Crook, G
Cubitt, V
Curle, D.
Curle, J.
Dankwirts, B
Davidson, A
Davidson, J
Davidson, Jason
Davidson, L.
Davies, T
De Vries, D
Demblon, N.
DeVries, G
Dickson, S
Fairly, C
Fenton, H
Fenton, W
Fish, S.
Fisher, J
Fisher, John
Fisher, T
Fisher, Teresa
Floory, J
Freeman, C
Freeman, P
Garazini, A
Gardener, Ret
Gardiner, N
Geldaart, N.
Grainger, D
Hamilton, N
Hamilton-Ritchie D
Hamilton-Ritchie J
Hill, R

Holderness, D
Hudson, I
Irvine, G.
Jennings, H
Johnson, C
Johnson, G
Johnson, Glenn
Johnson, Miss J
Johnson, W
Jolliffe, G
King, Don
Kyle, B
Lamb, D.
Lambert, D
Lamont, D
Laurence, Don
Long, D
Long. Diddy
MacDonald, D
Malcolm, D
Manchip, S.
Marais, T.
Maritz, L
Maritz, R
Masson, D
McManus, R
Meeken, G
Meeken, H
Miers, E
Miers, Mrs
Moffit, B
Noakes, A
Paweni, F
Paynter, R
Philips, E
Pocock, C
Proudfoot, A
Proudfoot. B
Rabi, B

Ramsey, A
Ramsey, C
Ramsey, F
Rick, S
Ridout, D
Roberts, A
Roberts, N
Roberts, R.
Robertson, Rob
Ross, J
Ross, S
Rushforth, L.
Scotcher, P
Scotcher, I
Scotcher, W
Sewell, C
Shoesmith, R.
Soso, A
Sparks, B
Spilling, J
Steyn, T.
Swift, J
Swift, R
Teede, A
Teede, J
Teede, L
Teede, S
Teubes, C
Thomson, A
Thornton, S
Thornton, W
Tilley, C
Van der Merwe, F
Vaughan, P.
Walker, A
Wallace, Λ
Warren, N
Wilde, N
Wilkins, D

Wilkins, G
Wilkins, L
Wilkins, P
Wilkins, T
Williamson, T
Wilson, R
Wright C
Wright P
Wright, T
Wyde, G
Zambra S
Zambra, M
Zana, Shwinde.

The piece of land next to the clubhouse was not wide enough to accommodate a field and so arrangements were made to encroach on the neighbour's property. The site was not particularly ideal being on a slope but for the first season they played like this where the goal posts at the lower end could not be seen from the top end. The Proudfoots had friends in the earth moving equipment business and persuaded them to do a demonstration by levelling off the field. This was done for the price of drinks and lunch. Only one field could barely fit in with little run off on the northern side before it disappeared down the slope to the valley below. The stables were built down this slope which gave every encouragement for the horses to disappear back to the stables when running out the back of the field.

Paul Scotcher was a leading light in the '60's and early '70's until his tragic death on the polocrosse field at a Glendale tournament. He was also a good commentator and often called upon to commentate at the various tournaments. The war cry of "Up the Dale" originated from him and continued throughout the life of the club. He was also very active within the polocrosse Association, as was Graeme De Vries who became the first Mashonaland provincial chairman. Jeremy Fisher was the association P.R.O. for many years. And Leo

Teede, tragically killed with his wife in the second Viscount shot down in the war, was for many years Secretary to the Executive. Don Grainger took over the role of commentator after Paul Scotcher.

Borrowdale was the third venue for the 1972 Australia Test Match with commentary on the Rhodesia Broadcasting radio service by Bill Malden and with 1500 spectators that turned out to watch the Final Test. Another highlight was when the then Prime Minister, Ian Smith arrived to watch the 1970 Inter Provincial Tournament. Sitting on the side of the field in a deck chair, with minimal security, he was happy to be thronged by admirers seeking his autograph. Two Peruvian polo players arrived at the same tournament to see the game and returned with two rulebooks, sticks and ball as a present from the Polocrosse Association. They hoped to start polocrosse in Peru.

Gordon Johnson leased his farm in Karoi and moved into town in the '70's with his family and horses, and together with Roy Bennett and Dave Masson, doing their national service at the Borrowdale Police Station, brought in new blood to the club. Gordon was club captain for a number of years and eased the lot of the club by providing his lorry for transport, which was sadly lacking and typical of a city club. Up until then, the club had hired Javelin commercial transport at a high fee. Gordon had a keen eye for horses and always had a string of exceptional ponies bought off the racetrack and sometimes in pitiful condition that others would not bid for.

In the latter years some of the members broke away from Borrowdale, and tried to start a new club elsewhere in the city. John Davidson took his wife Angie, son Jason, Zana Shwinde and Jo Beer to the show grounds where John used to operate a Rodeo Show. This did not last long and no record of it being registered with the association can be found.

Borrowdale restarted around 1991 under John Davidson with around 24 members but closed soon after in 1993.

BROMLEY
[1994 to 1995]
Colours—Green with Black Collar

Agiotus, A
Clare, M
Cranswick, A
Duff S
DuToit, R
Forrester K
Gaisford, M
Hertzburg, G.
Jenkins, C
Jenkins, F
Norvall, N.
Norvall, P.

Bromley started as a breakaway from Ruwa and was based at the Bromley Country Club just off the main Harare / Mutare main road. It ran for a couple of seasons but ended when Andy Cranswick was able to secure grounds at the Greendale Country Club. This was more suitable for Andy and Ricky Dutoit who lived in town, and the club was able to field enough players to get going.

CENTENARY
[1986 to 1990]
Colours—Blue and White Stripes

Barnard, H.
Flavel, K.
Forrester A. M
Graham, L.
Havener, C.

Havener, M.
Hewitt B
Hulme, P.
Humphries, D.
Jack A
Lindsay G
MacTavish, I
MacTavish, N.
Ridley, C
Rose, F
Rose, M
Rose, P
Rose. V
Strydom, R.
Taffs, C.
Wallcot, S.
Waller, A.
Wilson Harris, R

Centenary got going when Mick Rose packed up playing polo at the Mvurwi Club. Not having enough horses for polo was a good inducement to convert to polocrosse. The first year they played in a dust bowl in one of Mick's paddocks but later joined up as a section with Centenary Country Club.

Their first year was very successful for a new club in that they won the B Division Plate and the C Division at both Ayrshire and Matepatepa.

Centenary held the Mashonaland Provincial Championships and at this tournament Alex Tait playing for Ruwa, came off his horse in one of those overreach situations that cannot defy gravity. He ended up concussed, sitting in a chair on the veranda of the pavilion with several concerned people gathering around. In marched Fred Rose, a down to earth practical woman, and proceeded to slap Alex across the face and demanding to know who she is in an effort to determine his state of concussion. The problem was that Alex was by now fine but did not have a clue who Fred was, pleading "I really do not know who you are and I am really fine! Please stop slapping me."

CHIWIRA ~ MVURWI
[1980 to 1984]
Colours—Beige

Bentley, S
Burnett-Smith, C
Burnett-Smith, G
Cardwell, K
Chetwyn, E
Darby, I
Duncan, C
Duncan, D
Francis, A
Marfy, M
McDonald, M
Stonier, B
Stonier, M
Strydom, R
Von der Hyde, A

Geoff and Celia Burnett Smith, having just married, moved from Borrowdale Polocrosse Club to manage Celia's parent's farm in the Umvukwes District.

The nearest Club to them was Horseshoe some 50km away, which they joined. They would send their horses over by tractor and trailer, but after a season they were able to attract a sufficient number of new players from neighbouring farms to start up their own club.

A field was prepared on their farm "Chiwira" and reciprocal practices took place between Horseshoe and themselves. At one point, they tried to encourage Mvurwi Club to start, and for probably a year managed to have practises there, but the club is an old polo club and any new male recruit was soon whisked off to play polo .

The club continued for a couple of seasons until

Geoff and Celia immigrated to Australia and the club then folded.

ENTERPRISE
[1993 still playing]
Colours—Orange and Black Squares

Birkentoff, V.
Blake, C.
Blake, P
Blighnought, A
Blumiers L
Blumiers, D
Borlase T
Cameron, M.
Chadwick, G.
Chadwick, Glynis
Clarke, B
Collings, A.
Collings, B.
Crawford, G.
Crawford, M.
Crawford, R.
Crawford, W
Crookes, E.
Curle, J
Davison, L.
Dixon, A
Dixon, C.
Dixon, G
Dixon, S
Dodd F
Dodd K
Dodd, A
Dodd, G.
Dudley, P.
Evans, E
Evans, H

Evans, J.
Evans, M
Evans, P.
Fingland, S
Fingland, A
Fingland, D
Fingland, J
Fingland, R
Forsyth, G.
Forsyth, P.
Freeburn, B.
Gardini, R
Gardini S
Gobey, R
Harrison, K
Harrison, N
Hollingshead, A.
Howard, N
Howson, A.
Hughes, D
Hughes, G
Hughes, Jenny.
Ingram, S.
Johnstone, G.
Johnstone, L.
Kilpit, I.
Kirkman, S.
Krifoff,
Kruger D.
Kruger S
Kruger, L
Krynauw, S
Krynauw, A
Krynauw, C.
Krynauw, M
Langley, T
Lassy, I.
Lombard, P
Ludick, H

Lyle, D.
Moore, M
Norton, G.
Norton, L.
Norton, M.
Norval, A
Norval, K
Norval, S.
O'Connor, C.
Octobra, M
Octobra, Mark
Palmer, K
Pascoe, R
Pretorious, A
Rensburg, M
Rowley, A.
Shand, A
Shand, D
Shand, R
Small, S
Small, Sue
Smit, K.
Sparks, T.
Tait, J
Tanner, D
Tanner, M
Thompson K
Walters D
Walters K
Ward, N
Wilkinson, Sord
Zaal, R

Pete Evans, while managing the dairy farm on Munenga, a section of Howson Trust Estate, started the Enterprise Polocrosse Club on the farm with a field laid out in one of the paddocks. The initial players were his son Murray, Philippa Blake, Dean Blumiers, Sord Wilkinson, Tony and Mike Krynouw.

Over the four years that the Club existed there, reciprocal practices would take place between Ruwa and themselves, alternating between the venues. Enterprise swelled with numbers and soon found that the dairy section field was not enough, so they moved to the main Enterprise Club in 1997, taking over the rugby club which had folded. Pete Howson gave up some land, to extend the rugby field and also put in two more fields, plus a club house and stables for over 100 horses. Paul Scudamore from the UK designed the clubhouse, Peter Lombard supplied all the main weight-bearing gum poles and the club members then paid for the construction of the actual building/bar/showers and toilets, plus thatching of the completed structure.

The first tournament was at Virginia. Pete asked Tony Krynauw to put some soil onto the back of the eight ton UD lorry, but Tony being a little clueless, took some guys and filled up the truck with about a foot of soil throughout. No-one noticed when they loaded the horses. Tony had originally come from the host area so off they went on the main road to Mtoko, knowing that they could cut across through back roads to get to Virginia club. A roadblock of cops stopped them and found that no rear lights were working on the UD, so Tony had to travel in front and Pete in his pick-up, to follow the lorry. They took Tony's "shortcut" and after an hour or so, were only a few kilometres from the club when they came across a new dam which had been built and filled with water across the shortcut road! Back to the tar and then the long way round, arriving at the club at 11pm that Friday night. The lorry drove to the stables and was being directed to the offloading ramp, when the driver went through a patch of water. The soil Tony had put in the truck must have weighed many extra tons, and the entire lorry sank to its axles in the mud where it stayed until mid-morning Saturday. Pete had to 'jump/slide' the horses off the truck.

Horses now safe, they all asked Pete where they were staying. Chalets? Houses? Camping he told them. They had only brought a change of clothing and a toothbrush, so that night they slept on the grass on the golf course with no blankets or anything. One of the ladies woke up the next morning with a spider bite on the eyelid, which made it look like a swollen dog ball!! But they did win the prize of the Best Dressed Team, dog ball eye notwithstanding.

Over the period Enterprise hosted many tournaments and produced some top players who made the national and provincial sides as with Steph, Jax and Ross Fingland, Ross Shand, Brad Clark, Audra Dixon, Mike Krynauw, Murray and Hayley Evans, Ashley Rowley, Ami Norvel, the Hugh's brothers, Stevie Gardini and Sean Ingram. Brad and Mike played in the world cup team.

Mitchell Rensburg and Philippa Blake took their vows in 2004 when they got married on the polocrosse field, and joined in on the Sunday practice with Greendale that had come over for the day.

GLENDALE
[1951 to 1984]
Colours—Blue Birdwood, R

Bromley, M
Bromley, Sir Rupert
Brown, I
Brown, Jock
Brown, L
Brown, N
Brown, S
Budge, J
Budge, Mrs. A
Candy D [Jnr],
Candy, D
Cossey, M
Cossey, W
Crawford, B
Crawford, N

Crawford, S
Dale, P
Economy, P
Economy, S
Fairey, C
Ferrar, J
Fitzroy, J
Flett, D
Francis, A
Francis, V
Gaylard, D
Gibson, G
Harris, R
Huxham, T
Keightley, W
Kemp, A
Langstone, N
Laurent, K
Laurent, M
Laurent, R
Lyon, D
Lyon, G
Malden, J
Malden, M
Maritz, R
McKersie, H
Mears, P
Muil, J
Muile, John
Peek, R
Perritt, J
Phillips, E
Pocock C
Robertson, R
Savory, T
Self, M
Sewell, C
Stone, P
Topping, J

Topping, R
Topping, T
Van Reenan, H
Wallis, A
Waterhouse, A
Wilcock, A
Wilcox

Glendale is a small village in the Mazoe valley serving a community of cotton and grain farms with aromatic citrus trees growing either side of the road on Mazoe Citrus Estates. Bill Cossey was working as a section manager for the citrus estates when he travelled down to Fort Victoria to watch a polocrosse match and returned to Glendale to start a polocrosse club. He applied for registration and Glendale became the third club to play the sport in 1951.

In 1953, a Polocrosse Association was formed between the three existing clubs, Fort Victoria, Umvuma [Rhodesdale] and Glendale and the proposal was formulated to hold National Championships the following year. With stiff competition from Fort Victoria, Glendale became the first club to host the National Championships in 1954.

By 1960, Glendale began holding its own tournaments that coincided with the Queen's Birthday. Later, in 1967, there were sufficient clubs around the country to start the Inter Provincial Championships and again Glendale was the first to host it.

Glendale produced the second president of the association with Sir Rupert Bromley Bart taking office in 1956 and for the next seven years was very active in promoting polocrosse around the country. He put up the Bromley Shield for the winners of the A Division held annually at Glendale that became known as the Bromley Tournament.

Bow legged Yorkshireman Bill Cossey also put a lot of mileage into getting polocrosse going, not only in establishing Glendale, but also throughout the country and was the Vice President of the association from 1966 and continued for the next sixteen years.

Being a longstanding club, there were more than a few characters that came out of it. I think that the last time I ever saw Tilly Laurent actually play was in the early '70s, and that was a good thing, as she was far more useful as a coach from the side lines. Her forceful character and very descriptive vocabulary helped many teams and indeed clubs, as they moved to various locations. Then there was the gentle giant in Jock Brown who played at provincial level, and was later tragically shot by a disgruntled groom. John Farrer was another talented player, also playing at provincial as well as national level. Having said that, he was a dreadful team player, believing he could do it all himself. Young Mike Cossey was probably the only youngster of the early days and did justice when selected to play in the A side. Later he moved to Gwelo where he mastered the art of throwing the goal and losing his mount at the same time. Then along came Roger Birdwood whose eyesight was not that great. The moment his glasses fell off, he would follow them, resulting in his team members tying them securely to his head. Alistair Waterhouse, who spoke and behaved like the old English squire was not that great a player, but would ride up to his opponent with the comment, "move over in the bed Sir!"

Glendale ceased to exist as a club when the grounds were taken over for a housing complex and the field was turned into a football pitch.

Bill Cossey

Neville Brown, Steve Brown on Buttercup the mother to Ian Brown's Happy and Major, and Bill Cossey.

Mike Jame for Chipinga, Tim Savory,
Keith Laurent and Paris Economy

GOROMONZI
[1969 to 1973]
Colours—Yellow

Evans, D
Hughes, Liz
Malden, J
Malden, R
Malden, W
Perrott, J
Rogers, Jane
Rogers, Jo
Rogers, Philip
Self, M

Goromonzi, a club some 40km east of Harare started a polocrosse section towards the end of the 1969 polocrosse season. A handful of interested players led by John Perrot started preparing a field and stable facilities but a heavy storm came along and blew the stable roofs off.

13 players started the 1970 season with a lot of

enthusiasm and were able to hold the C Division National Championships in 1972 but with a number of players moving away from the district, the club survived another year before closing down.

A number of years later, around 2004, Players from Ruwa, disgruntled by the main club's policies, moved across to Goromonzi to continue there. They used the original field and practised for part of the season before giving up on it.

GREENDALE
[1996 to 2007]
Colours—Navy Blue / Red and Green sleeves

Agiotus, A
Atkinson A
Atkinson C
Barnard H
Beekes T.
Beekes, R.
Blignaut, A
Burbidge S
Burbidge Tammy
Campbell C
Corbit, J
Cranswick C
Cranswick, A

Dodd A
Dodd F
Dodd G
Dodd K
Dutoit M
DuToit, R
Evans H
Evans J
Evans M
Fennel R
Fennel T
Fingland, S.
Fisher J
Fisher K
FitzPatrick, L.
Flavell D
Flavell, K
Gaisford R
Gaisford, M
Goodwin K
Gorringer, P
Gobet, R.
Harris C
Harris D
Harris H
Harris M
Huxham P
Kilpit, I.
Keith, P.
Kempen, D
Kotzee, A
Langley T
Logan L
Logan R
Logan R
Logan S
Lyle D
McIntyre D
McIntyre L

Norval N
O' Reedan, K
O' Reedan, M
Ray G
Ray K
Rensburg, M
Rensburg P
Rhodes D
Scott D
Shaw C
Shaw U
Smit Jaapie
Smit K
Smith R
Sophie
Strous, A
Swan C
Swan D
Swan J
Swan W
Tanner, D
Tanner, M
Utton, L
Van der Merwe A
Wilson, Harris

Andy Cranswick approached the Greendale Country Club to form a section of polocrosse. He was given the 'Chip and Put' golf course, which was a hockey field before then and the newly formed members created two polocrosse fields. Mike Gaisford and Ricky DuToit were leading lights in those early days, both serving time as club chairmen.

Two years later, the club approached the polocrosse Executive for permission to run the Greendale Open Tournament. At the time there was some controversy as to whether this tournament would turn polocrosse into a professional sport and introduce an element of 'skullduggery' that tends to raise its ugly head when large sums of money are behind it. However, the idea was to fund-raise through sponsorship for the association to finance international tours.

Provided players were registered with the P.A.Z. team managers could recruit players from any club as long as they had attained a 4 handicap or better. This meant that all the top players in the country were moulded into high powered teams that raised the tempo of the tournament to that of test matches, and was an excellent venue to test the mettle of our international players.

The 'Open' has become a prestige tournament that all top players strive to play at.

On the preceding Thursday night of the tournament, a fashionable ball is held where the top players, known as 'wild cards', are auctioned off to the highest bidding team. Some of these players have been 'sold' for incredible amounts of money. A percentage of the money raised is paid to the winning team.

For the weekend, the club is turned out to resemble a fair, with show stands of commercial products on display, and marquees for the teams and spectators surrounding the fields. It is a lavish affair and one that even non-polocrosse supporters often attend for a weekend of exceptional entertainment. Lately, and due to diminishing numbers of top players, recruiting has extended across borders to top players from South Africa, Australia and some from England, with very favourable comments coming from these international players.

Despite all the difficulties of the 2000 period, Greendale managed to keep going and under various committees held some excellent tournaments.

*?.Tim Fennel. Rod Fennel, Roy Bennet, Bev
McIntosh, Peter Bowen, Henry Harris. Flag bearers,
?Robin Fennel.*

*Andre Kotzee. Ross Shand. Rich Games. IanTaylor,
Lucas Holtshousen, Angus Alexander, Rowena Fairly.*

*Sally Harris, Robbie Hitchcock, Mark Lombard, Ted
Wilmot.Ron Taylor, Lesley Taylor, Greg Sergeant.*

*Jo Cocker. Brian Cocker. Craig Mannix. Gavin
Lindsey, Ant Keith. Alan Jack. Alistair Keith.*

*Piet de Klerk. Doug Whaley. Conal Bunnet, Simon
Brown. Andy Cranswick, Nola Harris.*

M. Kotzee. Margo Worsick, Kane Mathews. Shannon Burbidge.
Murray Evans.

HARARE SOUTH
Colours—Apricot with Black Band on Sleeve and Collar

Mallet B
Mallet L
Mallet M
Mallet N
Smit J
Smit K

HORSESHOE
[1959 to 2001]
Colours—White with Red Bands. 2] Red / White Trimming
Anderson, A
Anderson, R
Anderson, S
Barnard S

Barnard Zippy
Bowen, I
Bowen, P
Burnett ~ Smith, C
Burnett ~ Smith, G
Chetwyn, D
Chetwyn, E
Chetwyn, R
Cross, J
Cross, R
De la Harpe, D
De la Harpe, P
Dixon, S
Fisher, J
Gallaher, B
Games
Games H
Games R
Graves J
Graves L
Gunn A
Harris Jane
Hughes, C
Hughes, J
Humphries, L
Humphries, S
Ingles B
Jack A
Kennedy, J
Kennedy, M
Kennedy, V
Kerrigan, J
Leared, A
Leared, H
Leared, M
Leared, N
Marr, R
McGrath, B
McGrath, M

McGrath, R
McGrath, T
McLaughlan, B
McTavish, I
Meiring, G
Meiring, P
Neville, S
O'Connor, C
O'Connor, N
Pearce, C
Pearce, N
Pocock R
Pocock T
Pocock, C
Savory, P
Schlachter, B
Slater Brown G
Slater Brown S
Slater Brown, A
Stopforth, P
Thompson, N
Thorn, J
Tibbett, B
Wilson Harris R
Wilson, D
Worley-Birch, A
Wirley-Birch, R
Wixley, C
Wixley, G
Wixley, P

Up in the North, overlooking the Zambezi Valley is Horseshoe. A farming district named from the shape of the mountains where the Great Dyke circles in a horseshoe to meet the Mvuradona range. The club started in 1959 on Mike and Barbara McGrath's tobacco and Charolais stud farm. The original 6 players to start out were Nick and Mary Leared, Mike and Barbara McGrath, Jeremy Fisher and Brian Tibbett. They were all beginners

Chris Pocock

then except Nick who coached them to play. Some extras would pitch up but didn't last, like Ian Thompson, who would climb on one side of his pony, and fall off the other, Dave Lilford didn't like the game and Tom Bloomfield had a horse that kicked.

Jeremy Fisher once told me the story that when he employed Brian Tibbett to manage for him, he recruited him on condition that he would play polocrosse as they were short one member to make up the six. Unfortunately for Brian, he had never ridden a horse before, so he learnt to play the game on a bicycle on the front lawn. Brian had a very keen eye for the ball and I remember him at a Goromonzi tournament one year where he was playing the 1, with Jeremy and Mike behind. Brian's riding ability did not match his game skills, and so was usually fed the ball by his team mid field. At this point he would forget his nervous and unsettled seat and take off like a cavalry charge to shoot a goal, which he invariably did. Having achieved this, he then had to stop his runaway horse that he had little control over and the easy out was to bail. Time off would be called to recover his long disappearing mount.

For many years Horseshoe was one of the top A Division clubs, battling it out with Rhodesdale and Hippo, and produced a number of prominent members at national level. Mary was a very affective lady player in the 1 birth on her handy pony Orpa. Always having to play with the men, she would come up against tough and rough male opposition and suffer the body blows that rugged men like to dish out. Mary's answer to this was to secure her breasts in layers of padding and bandages that gave her a rather voluptuous appearance. In 1963 she played against England at the Rickmansworth Agricultural Show. Husband Nick was a very eccentric character but a brilliant horseman who achieved his national colours and his 9 goal handicap in the 3 birth. He had a most outstanding horse in Christmas that went on to win the prestigious horse of the year award. Nick learnt the game when working for Hugh Baker, a farmer in the

270

Marandellas district, and was instrumental in bringing Hugh into the sport that benefited polocrosse with three generations of top playing Bakers. Nick was a master defender in the 3 birth. Most often than not he would recover the ball, but once out of his defending area he would become a nightmare to his other two fellow players by tossing the ball at no specific target and expecting them to retrieve it.

Also from the Marandellas area was Robyn Wyrley-Birch who also achieved a 9 goal handicap. Ivor Bowen, another 9 handicap player was probably the most experienced player in the club having played in the early '50s with Charles Holland for Old Umtali.

Kobus Meiring, another national player, captained the Rhodesian A side that toured Natal, South Africa in 1968, followed by Ian Brown, another 9 handicapper that captained the national side. He played two great horses in Happy and Major and was Deputy Chief Umpire in 1978 until his untimely death in a contact the following year. Ian was a very versatile player and was worth his 9 handicap in any position. Always the life and soul of the party, but never drank any alcohol; he was a master at pressurizing his opponent to frustration and annoyingly maintaining a satisfied grin.

The club was relocated in 1974 to the recently built Horseshoe Country Club. This was designed and built with a Spanish theme by Mike who is a dab hand at building and designing. Two fields were built originally, with a third added later. The club ran the annual Horseshoe tournament but as the adverse effects of 'call-ups' during the war were affecting the club's ability to field full teams, Horseshoe introduced sectional tournaments.

Horseshoe, at its new home continued to produce top players at national and provincial level in Richard and Julie Games, Rory McGrath, Chris Pocock, Peter Bowen, Harvey Leared, Prickle Thorn and Nev Pearce. Richard Games made Chief Umpire and Chris Pocock received colours as a national umpire. Alan Jack became the

Association President and Mike McGrath and Chris Pocock were tour managers, Billy Hughes and Chris Pocock national selectors, and Billy Hughes and Chris Pocock respectively became the second and fourth Mashonaland and provincial chairmen.

Mike McGrath, Ivor Bowen, Prickle Thorn, Ian Brown, Nick Leared, Nev Pearce

Alan Agiotis, Richard Games, Alan Jack, Nev Pearce, Brendon Ingels, Julie Games.

I

The renowned Fergus on the defence

Glen Johnson, Chris Pocock, Rich Games, Gordon Johnson, Geoff Burnett Smith at a Horseshoe Tournament.

Nick Leared marking Alan Lowe   *Harvey Leared*

Mary Leared and Mike McGrath

Ian Brown, Brian Tibbet, Cobus Meiring, Mike McGrath,
Mary Leared, Nick Leared

The fields and polocrosse pavillion after the land invasions taken in 2012

KAROI
[1969 to 1999]
Colours—Red and White Quarters

Bashford, D
Bennett, R
Bezuidenhout, R
Bishop, A
Bishop, G
Bishop, J
Bishop, S
Bishop, C
Bowen, I
Brown P
Brown S
Burger, D
Cochrane P
Corbett, A
Corbett, E
Corbett, M
Corbett, V
Crook, G
Cross
Crawford, J
Cuthbert R
Dabbs, J
Dalkin, M
de Waal, H
Dobbs, J
Eckstein W
Flavell, D
Fuller, T
Gaisford, G
Gaisford, J
Gaisford, Miles
Gundry L
Haasbroek, N
Hamilton, J

Hamilton, N
Hamilton, S
Harris, R
Hoskyns, A
Hulme P
Huxham P
Hewlitt, M.
Hewlitt, C.
Jahme, Graham
Jahme, M
Johnston C
Johnston Glenn
Johnston W
Johnston, A
Johnston, G
Kadonski, Y
Kay A
Labuschane, L
Lee, R
Lindsay, C.
Lindsay, G.
Mackay J
Mackay, S
Mannix, K
McKenzie, J
Oosthuizen, N
Oosthuizen, D
Palmer, A
Palmer, D
Palmer, G
Palmer, R
Palmer, T
Pocock, C
Postlethwate, L
Reid Clarke, M
Robb, A
Robb, J
Rodwell, S
Roper G

Salmon, T
Schlachter, B
Schlacter, Ben
Schlacter, M
Stotter, D
Strydom, K
Strydom, R
Swan J
Swan W
Thomas, H
Thornton, M
Townsend, R
Van Reenan, A
Van Reenan, H
Walters, G
Williamson, T
Winwood, J
Wixley, C
Wixley,

Gordon Johnson with strong backing from Len Lunsted, started polocrosse in Karoi in 1969 when he took over the polo fields at the Karoi Country Club. Gordon, an ex-polo player, was able to fit three fields into the space available and encouraged some of the polo players to join in. At the time he had a magnificent horse in Jet and was able to coach a strong side to be eligible to play at the 1970 Ruzawi National Championships. By 1971 they hosted their first tournament and in 1972 a very successful National Championships which included the touring Australian side from New South Wales. Karoi was able to provide five strong teams at the tournament with the A Team of Gordon Johnson, Ivor Bowen, Ben Schlacter, Andy Robb, Chris Pocock and Graham Crook reaching the semifinals. In 1986 the club hosted the prestigious Inter provincials.

Gordon moved to Salisbury with his young family in 1973 and Joined Borrowdale Country Club which left Karoi somewhat diminished in strength. However the new generation of Johnson boys, Clive and Glen, the Wixley brothers, Clive and Guy, with Chris Bishop and Roy Bennett put Karoi back as a leading side. Karoi produced some very talented and top players that made the national side, Roy Bennett, Chris Bishop, Guy Wixley, Clive, Glen and Trish Johnson and Scott Mackay. Clive Johnson at one time was rated the best number 3 in the world. Clive, Glenn and Roy played for the world side against Australia.

The Johnsons brought some exceptional horses into the game. Roustabout, ageing and gracious was one of them and gave both Clive and Glenn a spectacular game.

Gordon Johnson

Chris Bishop, Roy Bennet, Clive Wixley, Clive Johnson, Glen Johnson.

MARANDELLAS
[1954 to 1967]
Colours—Blue and White Squares

Baker, Hugh
Barnes, D
Barns, Dennis
Barns, P
Brown, A
Byron, S
Campbell, Bruce
Campbell, P
Campbell, Phyllis
Carver, Mrs.
Collett, Bill
Craig Bar, Kit
DeVaal, Hendrick
Donaldson, I
Fingland, R
Grimstone, Julie
Grimstone, Penny
Harris, J
Hodgson, Mr.
Humphreys, Ken
Keene, Joan

Keith, Ian
Keith, Jill
Leared, Nick
McIlwain, John
McIlwain, Pat
Negri, T
Schlachter, B
Schlachter, H
Schlachter, R
Spotswood, Renee
Van der Hoven, G
Van Der Hoven, J
Van der Sluis, J
Van Tonder, R
Vissar, L
Warth, T
Wyrley Birch, K
Wyrley Birch, R

Ian and Jill Keith were farming just outside Marandellas in 1954 when they decided to start a polocrosse club in Marandellas. Ian Hodgson's father, who had seen the game played in Australia, came out to coach them for a couple of years and with the improved horses they were lent from the polo fraternity they were able to attend their first championships held at Glendale in the same year. Later they were given quality horses from the Worthingtons who ranched at Charter Estates.

Marandellas held their own tournaments over the Whitson weekends, which was later held at Ruzawi after the club closed down, and the club was able to field 12 lady players. Julie and Penny Grimston improved the standard of play as well as smartening their dress code. In 1959 the Marandellas B Team comprised five ladies and one man. These were Joan Keene, Pat McIlwain, Kit Craig- Bar, Isobel Donaldson, Jill Keith, and Bill Collet [who wore a wig and bra.

Nick Leared, as a young farm assistant working for Hugh Baker, was able to persuade his boss to play, thus starting three generations of Baker's into the game. Nick, at the time was courting Mary, who was teaching at Ruzawi School and later to become his wife and future player for Horseshoe.

Marandellas closed down around 1961, some players moved to Ruzawi whilst others like the Macillwains went across to polo, but later, in 1985, polocrosse started up again at the same club, only that the name was changed to Marondera.

MARONDERA COUNTRY CLUB
[1983 to 1988]
Colours—Dark Blue and Grey

Clark, J
Radley, G
Stockhill, F
Stockhill Grenville
Stockhill, M
Stockhill, R
Stockhill G
Stockhill P
Wright, C

Polocrosse was started a section of the Marondera Country Club situated just out of town on the Ruzawi road. The inaugural meeting was held on the 16th of January 1985 and the founding committee was Glyn Radley as chairman, Malise Stockhill as captain, Jenny Clark, secretary / treasurer and committee members, Clive Wright and Refred Stockhill.

MARONDERA NORTH
[1994 to Present)

Colours—Navy Blue with Sky Blue Sleeves

Baker A
Baker H
Baker K
Baker S
Baker Toppy
Baker, B.
Bouce, A.
Bowen, B.
Candy, D.
Dodd AM
Dodd F
Dodd G
Dodd K
Featherstone, A
Green, S.
Hickman, R.
Hopgood, M
Hughes, R.
Huxham P
Johnson A.
Johnson, C.
Johnson, S.
Kashula, C
Kay, B.
Kay, C.
Kay, D.
Kay, M.
Keith A
Keith P
King, D.
Lampard, K.
Lampard, S.
Lampard, T.
Lotta, B
Ludick H
Ludick, J.
Mannix A

Mannix C
Mannix Craig
Mannix D
Mannix J
Mannix M
Mannix, N.
Mansfield, R.
Morgan, Glen.
Morgan, L.
Norval, G.
Octeburgh, M
Panter, A
Panter H
Panter P
Pegley, K
Perreira, G.
Perreira, M.
Perreira, T.
Pocock H
Rowley, A.
Scott, Dale.
Scott, J.
Sharp, K.
Stanley, E.
Stanley, I.
Stockhill C
Stockhill Cindy.
Stockhill K
Stockhill Nicky
Stockhill R.
Stockhill, B
Stockhill, Fred
Stockhill, G
Stockhill, J
Stockhill, L
Stockhill, M
Stockhill, R
Thompson, D.
Thompson, G.

Walsh R
Watson, P.
Whaley, S.
Whaley, Squackie
Wiseman T
Woodhouse D
Worsley-Worswick L
Worsley-Worswick M.
Worsley Worswick, P.
Wright, B.
Wright, C.
Wright, L
Wright, N.

*Ant Keith, Margo Worsick, Craig Mannix, Howie
Baker, Clive Wright, Toppy Baker.*

MATEPATEPA
[1974 to 2002]
Colours—Green with yellow quarters

Becks J
Bellis, M
Birdwood, R
Bonthrone, Craig
Borland Shane
Braun, P.Brown P
Brown S

Chooks, B.
Crawford, R
Crawford, W
Cocker Brian.
Cocker Fern
Cocker Jo
Cocker Steven
Cocker Susan
Cocker Zingi
Cocker, Donald
Cocker, Gavin
Cocker, Jonathan
Cocker, Karin
Cocker, Karen
Cocker, Robert (bob)
Colley C
Colley S
Colley, M
Davies, S.
Digby, M
Dodd A
Dodd G
Elliot, G
Elliot, L
Elliot, S
Evans, J.
Fisher, R
Forrester K
Forrester N
Green T
Hall, M
Hamilton N
Hanmer, Luke
Hanmer Sheryl
Hanmer Quinton
Hanmer Kim
Harvey, R
Hill, R
Hind F

Hind, C
Hind, S
Hind Mandy
Hind, R
Homan, I
Homan, R
Hosack, Sam
Hosack, Benji
Hosack Adrian
Hosack Matthew
Huxham, I
Huxham, P
Huxham, T
Johnson, P
Keith, A
Landsberg, W
Logan Rory
Maldon, R
Mathews G
Mathews K
Mirams, G
McGladdery, G.
Mostert, P.
Rae Graham
Sergeant Greg
Sherwood, S
Simon, Clare
Simon, Conrad
Simon, Susan
Swan, W
Taffs, C
Taffs, J
Tate Slade
Tate, L
Tate, M
Tate, P
Tate, R
Taylor Ian
Taylor Mark

Taylor Natalie
Taylor Richard
Taylor Tanya
Taylor, Keith
Taylor, Les
Taylor, Ron
Thompson Noel
Thompson, C
Thurlow, B
Thurlow, G
Thurlow, Hornsby
Thurlow, L
Van Eeden S
Wakefield, C
Wakefield, D
Wilson Harris Ross
Walters Kevin
Walters, D
Wilson Harris

Guy Hornsby Thurlow was the prime mover behind Matepatepa starting up polocrosse in 1974 having played for Glendale prior to this. The first club was on Hornsby's farm behind Harry House where one compacted field was used. Ian Brown from Horseshoe and Iain Kay from Ruzawi went out to coach the players. The original pioneers of Matepatepa were Hornsby, Richard Tait, Don and Bob Cocker, Pat Johnson, Richard Hinde and Trevor Huxham.

In 1980, Bob Cocker allocated a piece of land on his farm to form a new club, and Margaret Crawford initiated fundraising in the district to start construction of the club facilities. One of the recognised methods of the day amongst tobacco farmers was to donate a bale of tobacco and the auction floors would collect the funds for them.

Ultimately, the club grew to four playing fields, an impressive building comprising: a pub, lounge, dining hall and kitchen, ablutions and a grandstand up on the roof overlooking the main field. Later a squash court was added.

Over the years Matepatepa fielded very strong sides both in the A and B divisions and producing a large proportion of the provincial sides as well as national. The Cocker brothers of Don and Bob with Richard Tait and Later Richard Harvey, were a powerful combination. Later Don's son, Gavin was to achieve the highest handicap of 10, the first in the history of Zimbabwe polocrosse.

Don, Bob and Gavin Cocker, Richard Tait, Richard Harvey and Ron Taylor made the National sides, whilst Lesley Taylor made the National Ladies. The Cocker family of Don, Bob, Gavin, Karen, Brian as well as 'Spud' Fisher, Ron and Les Taylor, Richard Tait, Richard Harvey, Simon Brown and Martin Colley made the provincial sides. Richard Tait was Mashonaland Chairman, whilst Don Cocker was Chairman of the National Executive Committee. Don Cocker was awarded his colours as a National Umpire.

The stalwarts of Matepatepa. Brothers Bob and Don Cocker.

*Matepatepa players who made the National sides in
2002. From Left to right bottom Row, Jo cocker, Ian
Taylor, Sally Anne Van Eeden, Top row Willie Swan,
Karen Cocker, Gavin Cocker, Brian Cocker, Ron and Les
Taylor*

*Winners of the Featherstone tournament from left to
right, Ron Taylor, Noel Thompson, Simon Brown, Don
Cocker, Gavin Cocker, Slade Tate,*

NYABIRA POLOCROSSE CLUB
[1975 to 1977]
Colours—Orange

Crookes, H

Davison, J
Fitzroy, J
Flett, D
Hammon, P
Hammon, N
Nokels, N
Robb, A
Roberts, A
Savory, P
Savory, T
Teede, J
van Reenen, A
van Reenen, H
Wallis, A
Whittaker, A

Nyabira's roots lie in Darwendale when ex Karoi farmer Hugo van Reenen relocated to that district. He registered a club under the name of Darwendale and for the first season played on his farm. The club then moved to the Nyabira country club where a piece of land was allocated to them.

The name was changed to Nyabira but whilst some top players passed through the club, it did not last for long.

OLD HARARIANS
[2003 to 2005]
Colours—Maroon, Grey and White

Borlase T
Crabbe G
Crabbe S
Curle J
Davinson, J
Dodd AM
Dodd F
Dodd G

Dodd K
Donavan M
Haasbroek A
Haasbroek F
Haasbroek J
Kneeharbour, C
Mallet B
Mallet L
Mallet M
Mallet M
Mallet N
Mallet T
O'Reiden, L
O'Reiden M
Parham B
Parham G
Parham S
Parham W

Old Hararians is yet another club to start up as a result of club displacements caused through the land grab exercise. Situated in the crotch of two roads that meet at an intersection in the Belgravia suburb of Harare, the vacant land where polocrosse was allowed to develop is a part of the main club.

Tony Borlace brought in his tractors and levelled a field whilst Wayne Parham supplied irrigation pipes. Gary Dodd and Mike Mallet were the other two founding members and between them security fenced the area and put up a shelter. Les O' Reiden designed the colours.

Old Hararians Polocrosse Club held the Family Tournament and in conjunction with the show jumpers, put on a gymkhana. The club provided the majority of the national juniors that were selected in the 2004 season.

Sadly the section was forced to close due to continual theft in which even the security fence was stolen.

RUWA

[1984 to 2004]
Colours—White with Red Collar/ Red and White
Stripes/ Green and Red

Agiotis A
Barnard S
Barnard Z
Barron, P.
Barron, S.
Bennett, B.
Blumears, D
Blumears L
Brooks, L
Castle, T
Chateris, M
Cossey B
Cossey K.
Cossey M
Crawford, L
Crawford, R
Crawford, W
Curle D
Curle J
Curle, K.
Davidson J
Davidson, A
Davidson, J
de Clerk, A
Dodd AM
Dodd G
England B
England L
Evans P
Ferreria, M
Field, C
Gail Matthews
Gaisford M

Gardner, H.
Gardner, J.
Gardner, R.
Grainger, D
Granger D
Hamilton, J
Hodges, D
Holloway, M
Hoostheizen, C
Hubbard T
Hubbard, B
Humphries, G
Jenkins C
Jenkins F
Jenkins J
Johnson, D
Johnston, G
Johnston, Glen
Johnston, W
Jolliffe, G
Kirkpatrick, B
Kirpatrick, B
Krienke, C
Kyle, B.
Linford, Aaron
Linford I
Linford R
Linford, A
Lombard P
Lombard, P
Ludick, H.
Ludicker, B
Mace, A
Mc Rae, I
Meyer, S
Nel A
Nel J
Nilson, M
Norval, P.

Norval, S.
Nyschens, I
Octebrough, M
Palmer, D
Palmer, R
Paweni, F
Phillips, E
Pocock, N.
Pocock, R.
Pocock, T.
Pocock, C
Reitz, D.
Rhodes D
Rogers, J
Rowe, S.
Schwind, Z
Sharp, L
Sharp, P
Slack, C
Small S
Small Sue
Snorte, S.
Stockhill, R
Surtees, P
Tait A
Tait J
Tantum, G.
Taylor D
Teale, D
Twine K
Twine M
Twine T
Twine, K.
Walker M
Walsh
Walsh R
Walsh S
Walsh, H
Waters, H

West, D

Zambra, S

Ruwa Country Club, built on land donated by the Cullinan family in the old English country style of expansive thatch, is a popular golf venue. Situated some thirty kilometres east of the capital Harare, Ruwa was for many years an exclusive club with strict dress codes.

Polocrosse came into being as a section of the club after Ken Linford approached the committee and asked if they could use the cricket field, which was no longer in use at the time. The small club house on the side was derelict and Gary Dodd re-thatched it whilst Richard Walton repaired the plumbing. The building was screened in two with the one half fitted out as a library and an adjacent building used as a veterinary surgery by Betty Sugden. The polocrosse half was turned into a pub and became their social centre as polocrosse players were not welcome into the main club house unless they adhered to their strict dress code.

When Harare Sports Club folded most of their players joined Ruwa. Mike and Julie Cossey became prominent members taking charge of the running of the section until it closed. The members raised money and Heather Walsh extended the ablution block to cater for the many tournaments held at Ruwa over the years.

International test matches were held here when New Zealand came out for the first time in 1989 and again when Australia toured in 1993.

During the high inflation period, Ruwa Country Club began to struggle financially and with the dramatically reduced membership, was heading for trouble. A local property developer joined forces with the club in a scheme to sub divide the attractive Msasa woodland around the golf course into plots for upmarket housing. This put the club back on its feet but with the dwindling number of polocrosse members a real threat existed that they could lose the two fields they were using.

The Zimbabwe Horse Society, representing the show

jumpers and dressage riders, approached the committee and asked if they could use these fields for their shows. This brought an uneasy alliance of the two different sports sharing the same facilities. I chaired a committee representing both sides in an effort to coordinate their different requirements but no common ground could satisfactorily be worked out and it wasn't long before the show jumpers left.

Ruwa polocrosse dwindled in numbers until the height of the land invasions when it finally closed. Marondera North polocrosse Club, unable to continue on the Worsley-Worswicks farm relocated to Ruwa and to this day continue to use the facilities.

Mike Cossey passing to Julie Cossey with Mandy Tanner in pursuit.

Stewart Baron,?, Rob Gardner, Julie Cossey, Mike Cossey,
Colin Jenkins.

Mike Cossey, Heather Walsh, Colin Jenkins, Rob
Gardner, Allan Agiotis, Stu Barron

Heather Walsh, Rob Gardner, Mike Cossey.

SALISBURY / HARARE
SPORTS CLUB [1979 to 1983]
Colours—White with Red Trim

Castle, T
Chateris, M
Colley, C
Colley, M
Colley, S
Cossey, M
Davidson J
Davidson A
Davison, A
Davison, J
de Klerk, A
De Robillard C
Field, C
Forrester A
Forrester F
Forrester R
Gardner, J
Grainger J
Grainger, D
Hamilton N
Hamilton, N

Hill J
Hill R
Hill, R
Hollaway, M
Humphries, G
Huxham I
Jennings H
Johnson, D
Johnston, C
Johnston, G
Johnston, Glenn
Johnston, W
Jolliffe, G
Krienke, C
Krinke, S
Lamb, N
Mace, A
Maldon R
Palmer, D
Palmer, R
Rodgers, G
Slack, C
Stopforth, P
Tex, I
Walsh K
West, D
Zambra, M
Zambra, S

Salisbury Sports Club initially, then renamed to Harare after the 1980 Zimbabwe Independence, was started by Gordon Johnson after Borrowdale Polocrosse closed. The main club is situated along North Avenue and has facilities to hold international cricket, hockey and rugby matches. Polocrosse was given premission to run a field at the back of the club and to run tournaments on the polo field that was situated across the side road and between the Prime Minister's official residence and North Avenue.

In 1980, the club hosted a sports expo in which polocrosse was one and this resulted in the club increasing its membership the following season.

Iain Kay, Charles Holland,?, Ken King, Mike Cossey and Sue Keene.

SALISBURY
[1957to 1964]
Colours—White Orange

Beak Mr.
Beak D
Bromley, G
Cameron, J
Coghill, J
Dankwerts. B
Davies, T
Floory, J
Gardener, Ret
Hamilton-Ritchie, D
Hamilton-Ritchie J
Hamilton-Ritchie, T
Hamilton-Ritchie, G
Johnson, Miss J
King, Don
Laurence, Don
Lawrence, J
Malcolm, D

McManus, R
Meeken, G
Meeken, H
Noakes, A
Proudfoot, B
Ramsey, C
Scotcher, J
Scotcher P
Soso, A
Thornton, S
Tilley C
Walker, A
Wilde, N
Wilson,
Wright, T

In 1957 the Polocrosse Association put on a demonstration match at the Salisbury Sports Club. The guests of honour were Sir Peveril William Powlett, Governor of Southern Rhodesia, and Lady Powlett who presented the prizes. This match had produced some interest amongst riders in the Salisbury area and it was Brian Dankwerts, who farmed out on the airport road that invited a number of people to join him in starting up a polocrosse club in Salisbury.

The first season was played on the open ground, which is now occupied by the Borrowdale Turf Club. A railway line ran along the side of the field, having come from the main terminus and heading out along the Gwebi valley to join the Banket line.

Among those early players were Dougie and Jill Hamilton Ritchie, Don Laurence, Atta Wallace and Rob McManus. After the first season, the club moved to another piece of wasteland on Armadele Road where they played for a further season before finding a more permanent home at the Borrowdale Country Club.

Peter Wright on his pony with father Ted at the Salisbury polocrosse Club where the Borrowdale Race Course is today. The view is looking back towards Borrowdale Village.

SHAMVA
[1980 to 1996]
Colours—Royal blue / red trimmings.

Agiotis, A
Alexander, S.
Brown, I.
Brundel, M.
Brundel, T.
Crawford, L
Crawford, R
Crawford, W
Crystal, M.
Fisher, K
Hoole, G
Hulme, G
Hulme, J
Kemp, D
Landsberg, W.
Laurent K
Laurent R

Laurent T
Logan L
Logan, A
Logan, K
Logan, R
McIntyre D
Mahon, R
Morkel, B.
Myburgh, B
Nash V
Nash, H
Pasco, R
Perreira, M
Ray G
Ray K
Ross S
Ross, M
Shand, D
Shand, Dell
Sweeting, M
Sweeting, R
Taylor, M
Taylor, S
Van der Myer, D.
Walters K
Willis, C
Willis, F
Willis, K.

Shamva was once known as Abercorn, named after the Chairman of the British South Africa Company, but dropped to prevent confusion with the town of the same name in the then Northern Rhodesia. Roy Welensky, uncle of Allen Willis, worked as a barman at the Abercorn Hotel before becoming an engine driver on the Shamva Railway line, and subsequently became the Prime Minister of the Federation. Shamva town is centred on a mine first pegged in 1893 on ancient workings along the summit of Lone Star Hill.

Polocrosse started in 1980 after young Shamva farmers, who had been in the mounted units, were looking for something to do with their trained horses. They approached the Shamva Club and were given a section of the golf course over the road and with farm labour and tractors the field was levelled and prepared. The first pavilion was built under the trees and then with the help of Brian James, the mine manager, a new pavilion was built, pushed down, and rebuilt again. The tin roof was donated by Paul Braun and timber by Aubrey Logan. Will Cook donated a hay rake.

The founding members of the club were G & J Hulme, D. Kemp, A.C.R. & L Logan, D. MacIntyre, M. Perrera, M & S Ross, M & S Taylor, C & F Willis, and H & V Nash. George Hulme, who came from Devuli Ranch, owned by his wife's parents, the Bridges, was possibly the only member who had any knowledge of the game, but nevertheless, Aubrey Logan, was sent off to Matepatepa on a crash course to learn the basics.

Shamva came into its own in 1981, with the arrival of the Laurent family and Robbie Pascoe and attended their first tournament on the old polo ground on North Avenue with all its members making up four teams. Tilly Laurent, well known for her coaching abilities, was invaluable to the club. In 1983 Shamva hosted their first tournament, and at about this time, Aubrey Logan purchased a job lot of 27 race horses and two stallions for two thousand dollars and used them to develop the club. Also at this time, the club expanded to three fields and was playing at B Division level, but a milestone was achieved a couple of years later, when their school boy team of Ross Laurent, Ian Brown and Rory Logan, won the open division at Horseshoe. Tilly Laurent deserves credit as a hard taskmaster in guiding the club to championship level.

The club ceased to operate in 1993, but in the relatively short period of time of thirteen years, became a formidable opponent at tournaments around the country. Graeme Ray, to my mind, became an exceptional umpire, and some top level and long standing players passed through the club, as with Robin and Walter Crawford and Kevin Walters. The two Logan girls, Stacey and Audrey, had their grounding in this club and achieved selection at different age levels in the national junior sides. Outside of this book Audrey went on to represent Zimbabwe at the World Test Series held in England.

SINOIA / CHINHOYI
[Registered 1961. Played 1978 to1984]
Colours—Chocolate Brown
Campbell, G
Freeman, C
Marillier, D
Marillier, W
McLaughlin, L
Morgan, M
Nuttal-Smith, D
Van Eden, B
Van Reenen, A
Williamson, T
Wilson, D
Wixley K
Wilson, J
Wixley, C
Wixley, G
Wixley, P
Zambra, M

Sinoia is an enigma! It applied and was granted registration with the Association in 1961. Despite paying their affiliation fees they never turned up to any tournaments. In fact at the A.G.M. no one knew who any of the members were.

It was only in 1978 when the club got going but only lasted for six years. Phil Wixley had moved up from Umvuma when he bought a farm in the Sinoia district. He set the club up with fields near the showground's and encouraged players from the district to join.

UMBOE / DOMA
[1986 to 2002]
Colours—Yellow

Alexander A
Alexander J
Alexander Z
Alexander, T.
Atwell B
Atwell K
Atwell M
Atwell, V
Brown C
Brown J
Brown S
Campbell, D
Cloetie, B
Cloetie C
Cloetie D
Cloetie G
Corbett, M.
Creamer, K.
Davidson, J.
Davidson, L.
Dodd A
Dodd F
Dodd G
Dodd K
Green T
Haasbrook, A
Haasbrook F
Haasbrook J
Hansen, T
Horsley, D.
Horsley, G.
Hulme D

Huxham P
Marais, C.
Marx, B.
Marx, S.
McKenzie, A.
McLaren, D.
Neiharbour, C
Nell B
Nell Daniel
Nell K
Roper, G.
Rouse ,W.
Rouse, S.
Scott, D.
Serra, D.
Seward, K.
Seward, Keran.
Seward, S.
Seward, T.
Straus A
Swan H
Swan J
Swan W
Tiffan, G
Tiffan R
Tiffan, Rolly
Whitefoot, F
Wixley P
Wixley, P.York A
York C
York Jr
York L

Umboe was an established polo club. Jeremy Brown, a top ranking polo player established polocrosse at the Doma Club to run parallel to polo . Initially called Doma Polocrosse Club, it changed its name to Umboe in 1988. The first year they had 7 players with 57 members passing through the life of the club.

VENTERSBURG / HARLEQUINS
[2002to 2008]
Colours—Black Shirt with Red Sleeves

Borlace, T.
Burbridge S. Burbridge T.
Clarke B.
Coetzee, A.
Crabbe, G.
Crabbe, S.
Dixon, A.
Donovan, B.
Donovan, M.
Durand, J.
Evans J.
Fisher J.
Fisher K.
Fungai.
Guimbeau, P.
Haasbrok, A.
Haasbrok J.
Haasbrok, F.
Harris C.
Harris D.
Harris H.
Harris M.
Kay, B.
Keith, G.
Keith, P.
Keith, T.
King, D.
Krynauw M.
Langley T.
Logan, A.
Logan R.
Logan S.

Lombard, M.
Lombard, B.
Mallet, B.
Mallet, M.
Mallet, T.
O Rioden, C.
O Rioden, L.
O Rioden, M.
Panter, A.
Panter, R.
Parham B.
Parham G.
Parham H.
Parham P.
Parham S.
Parham W.
Scott D.
Scott, K.
Sole, P.
Strauss A.
Swan D.
Swan J.
Swan C.
Swan K.
Swan W.
Swanepoel, J.
Ward, N.

Ventersburg is a Municipal farm used for the disposal of sewage water so ideal for irrigation. The main movers behind this club were Willie Swan and Henry Harris and they played under the name of Harlequins. Ventersburg as a venue closed down in 2008 and Harlequins relocated to Greendale Club where they went on to produce all eight squad members of the 2011 World Test Series held in England. Whilst this is outside of this books period, it should be noted that never before have a complete squad come out of any one club, and whilst this may have raised eyebrows at the time, the team went on to win the Silver beating six other nations, and came away with Kelly Redford as the top lady player in the world.

Looking through the names that passed through this relatively new club, one will realize where some of the influence came from to create this historical achievement. Henry Harris is a long standing and experienced national player with an eagle mind for tactical play. So too is Shannon Burbidge who Captained the Zimbabwe side against England with opposite captain, brother Jason. Both of these players gained a wealth of knowledge and experience from their fathers who likewise were top national players.

Willie Swan as well as Wayne Parham were the backbone of the club, providing transport, financial assistance, top horses and most importantly, discipline that every club needs. Willie became the National Coach and Wayne the National President for several years.

WATERFALLS
[1970 to1971]
Colours—Chocolate Brown

Crook, Graeme
Jonson, Pat
Wyde, George

This club existed on a farm on the outskirts of Salisbury as it was, and which is now the suburb of Glen Nora. George was the manager on this farm and laid out a dusty polocrosse field to practice on. Graeme at that time lived in Parktown and I went with him to one of their infrequent practices. Other casual players attended practice but I have been unable to get their names.

Graeme and Pat moved to Borrowdale whilst George took the job at Triangle Sugar Estates as their cattle manager and I believe, stopped playing polocrosse.

MATABELELAND PROVINCE

Chairman.
Owen Fitzroy [1972/79]
M. Sergeant [1980/2]
R. Hill [1983/4]
T. Wilmot [1985/6]
M. Sergeant 1987 to1990

Secretary.
A. Richards [1972/]

BULAWAYO

To tell the story of polocrosse in Bulawayo, one must follow the sequence from which the clubs were formed.

After Owen and Kathy Fitzroy, as well as Jon Webb, moved to Bulawayo they started polocrosse at the Bulawayo Hunt Club in 1968. There was a fairly large membership at this time including Malcolm Sergeant, Allan Molloy, Kenny Sinclair, Maizie Campbell, Tony Bonnett, Sylvia Campbell and many others.

For whatever reason it was agreed that the Bulawayo Polocrosse Club would split and the name BULAWAYO not used again. The two clubs formed were UMGUZA some twenty kilometres along the falls road on 'Pop' Hartley's plot, and LAKESIDE on the Kabot's family farm on the eastern boundary of the city. Initially more members joined Umguza and they became the stronger club while Lakeside had very few members, most of whom were very weak players.

Lakeside packed up and started a new club at Queensmead in central Bulawayo and with the war heating up; Umguza folded and joined forces with Queens. In the early '80's Queens closed and the members moved to Bulawayo Sports Club where it still is today.

With the return of Allan Malloy and Arlene Crook from South Africa a new club was formed at Riverside.

UMGUSA
[1970 to 1975]
Colours—Red Shirt, Black Band Across Chest with U.P.C. above it.

Ashford, Graham
Ashford, L
Ashford, Liz
Duvenage, M
Fitzroy, Kathy
Fitzroy, Owen
Hartley, John
Hartley, Pop
Jones, P
Kyle, F
Laurence, M
Malloy, A
Norvall, M
Norvall, R
Norvall, S
Perrott, J
Phillips, A
Phillips, H
Phillips, Alice
Robinson, Don
Robinson, G
Robinson, Kim
Sergeant, M
Sergeant, N
Shirley, A
Sinclair, Kenny
Spalding, Keith
Van Leeuwen, F
Van Reenan, F
Wilson, S

Situated some twenty kilometres out of Bulawayo along the Victoria Falls road, Umguza polocrosse Club was started on 'Pop' Hartley's smallholding before settling at the Umguza Cricket Club in 1970. Here was a community of small irrigation farms of about one hundred acres and which the water used was derived from the Umguza River. In its day, Umguza was a strong Club with top class players such as Richard Norvall, Pops and John Hartley, Allan Malloy, Malcolm Sergeant and Owen Fitzroy making a formidable side.

The club established two fields and was able to host the annual Matabeleland Provincial Championships in which the Gladiator Trophy was played for. With the war hotting up on their doorstep, it became impossible to keep the club going and the members moved to Queens.

LAKESIDE
[1970 to 1975]
Colours—Pale Blue Shirts with Brown 'V'

Ashford, G
Bonnett, T
Borland, J
Campbell, D
Campbell, M
Campbell, S
Fitzroy, O
Hartley, Pop
Smith, G
Wilmot, T

Lakeside was the brainchild of Mrs. Maizie Campbell who was a daughter of the famous Kabot family. The original membership consisted of many family members. Dougal Campbell, Sylvia Campbell , Tony Bonnett and another Kabot daughter. Tony Bonnett rode a black horse named Duke that he had purchased from Malcolm Sergeant's father and Geoff Smith.

The clubhouse comprised an old pontoon turned upside down on top of some 44 gallon drums where only tea and cakes were served with the proceeds being enough to pay for all the rail and trucking to tournaments. At this time Maizie Campbell encouraged Ted Wilmot and John Borland to play the sport to bring the players up to six members. This enabled the club to attend their first tournament at Umguza on Pop Hartley's lucerne field. Ted had borrowed a horse from Maizie Campbell and the horse was walked the twenty odd kilometres to the venue where they lost every game, but had impressed Ted, having never played a sport where the opposition helps and coaches while playing.

Owen Fitzroy, Graham and Liz Ashford and Pop Hartley came across from Umguza and with them came some good horses, one of which was Owen's Zeus of which the Zeus Memorial Trophy is still contested for the most outstanding horse in Matabeleland. Both Ted and Pop played for Matabeleland Province and both received their colours, but one must realize that Pop was seventy-four years old at the time and was a formidable horseman and player.

As Lakeside now had a fairly large membership and with stronger players their success grew, winning the B Division at Umvuma with Ben Slaghter in the side.

As more members joined the club the facilities became inadequate and with Pop as Chairman, the committee approached Queensmead Sports Club in central Bulawayo to be a section of the club. Geoff Smith and Tony Bonnett left the country and all the other members relocated to Queens. Lakeside then ceased to be a polocrosse club.

QUEENSMEAD
[1975 to 1980]
Colours—Maroon Shirt with Orange Collars and Sleeves, with Queens Sports Club Badge on the Pocket.

Ashford, E
Ashford, G

Ashford, L
Borland, J
Campbell, D
Campbell, G
Campbell, M
Campbell, S
Duvenage, M
Fitzroy, J
Fitzroy, K
Fitzroy, O
Hartley, J
Hartley. Pop
Howard Williams, R
Kyle, B
Kyle, D
Labuschagne, B
Labuschagne, L
Malloy, A
Mathews, R
Nell, P
Nortje, P
Norvall, M
Norvall, R
Norvall, S
Noves-Smith, D
Philips, A
Philips, H
Richards, A
Robinson, D
Robinson, G
Robinson, K
Sergeant, M
Sinclair, K
Snowdon, A
Spalding, K
Spalding, K
Spalding, M
van Blerk, M
Van Reenan, F

Wilmans, C
Wilmot, T

With the construction of new fields on the go, polocrosse was initially played at several small venues, one of them; Paddonhurst, was a bush clearing that later was used by Riversdale Club. When Queensmead was ready. Umguza folded and joined Queens and the membership grew once more with Malcolm Sergeant, Alan Molloy, Shirley & Malcolm Norvall to name a few. The better facilities attracted new members from the show jumping fraternity such as the Labuschagne sisters, Bev and Lynette, Lesley & Alison Todd, Cindy Smith and of course Roy Matthews who sat outside the fence for several months before joining. Pete Nel, the illustrious saddle, bit and racquet maker, known then as 'Petrocelli', and later 'Bomber Nel', joined Queens.

In 1976, Queens was the venue for the South Africa / Rhodesia test match and Ted Wilmot made the selection for the B side on his twenty three year old pony Billy Boy.

Most of the 45 players came from the eastern side of town and had to ride / lead (those without horseboxes) to Queens. Mandy and Gaye Wilmot, only very small then, had to ride and lead another horse there and back. This became a problem and a stimulus to look for a new venue closer to the majority of the membership. Queens finally closed in 1980.

BULAWAYO POLOCROSSE CLUB
[1980 to 1987]
Colours—Purple Shirt with White Collar and Sleeves.

Collins, D
Fitzroy, O
Garner, G

Garner, V
Howard Williams, R
Kyle, B
Kyle, G
Kyle, R
Labuschagne, A
Labuschagne, B
Louw, N
Mathews, R
Mathews, S
Moore, N
Moore, S
Nel, Bomber
Nel, J
Nel, P
Norval, S
Sergeant, M
Snowdon, A
Spalding, K
Thompson, K
Todd, L
Wilmans, C
Wilmans, J
Wilmans, N
Wilmot, T

As most of the players from Queens had to ride and travel through town it was decided to look for a venue on that side of town where most of the players were coming from.

The committee approached Mike McLean at Chip Chase Estates in Douglasdale to see if he would accommodate a polocrosse section. Two fields were graded, ploughed and planted by the members with Mike McLean irrigating both fields. A small pole and thatch clubhouse was built by the members amongst many laughs and drinks. Then 86 stables were constructed using Mukwa off-cuts from a member's timber contact.

As this venue was on a farm that included a riding

school and livery stables, even more members joined including Jane Woods, Kit Bawden and many others. Whilst the members were happy at this venue, the facilities were very basic and with the cold and wet and a small ablution block, a new venue was sought.

The committee then approached the Bulawayo Country Club where Keith Bowie was the chairman. He and his committee agreed to accept the section provided they increased their membership to 75. A huge recruiting exercise took place and they moved to the Country Club in 1988.

BULAWAYO COUNTRY CLUB
[1988 to present]
Colours—Light Blue Shirt with Dark Blue Collar and Sleeve Trim. African Hoopoe Badge on the Pocket. Later changed to Turquoise Shirt with Hoopoe Badge.

Bawden, L.
Bernard, M.
Blignaut, L.
Boyley, D.
Christianson, A.
Cocker, G.
Coetzee, C.
Cripps, M.
Cunnard, P.
Da Silver, M.
Devaris, A.
Ellman-Brown, A.
Ellman-Brown, G.
Ellman-Brown, K.
Ellman-Brown, R.
Evans, A
Evans, P.
Evans, R.
Garner, G.
Garner, V.

Ginns, M.
Greaves, J.
Heathcote, D.
Holzhauzen, D.
Holzhauzen n, J.
Holzhauzen, L.
Howard-Williams, R.
Howard, M.
Johnstone, J.
Joubert, J.
Joubert, Jill,
Keats, D.
King, B.
King, J.
King, R.
King, V.
Kyle, B.
Kyle, G.
Lassey, M.
Lombard, M.
Louw, N.
MacIntosh, B.
Mathews, K.
Mathews, R.
McBean, L.
McBean, L.
Moore, N.
Nesbit, I.
Nesbit, L.
Norvall, S.
Pretorious, J.
Reid, A.
Reid, S.
Rhodesdale, V.
Robertson, N.
Roper, P.
Rosenfels, J.
Sergeant, G.
Sergeant, M.

Sergeant, P.
Sergeant, S.
Shaw, U.
Small, Sue,
Snowdon, A.
Spalding, K.
Spalding, S.
Sparrow, R.
Staubesand, T.
Staubesand, T.
Staubesand, Tanya.
Thompson, J.
Thompson, K.
Till, T.
Todd, A.
Todd, L.
Vimpie Laurens.
Walker, J.
Wilmans, C.
Wilmans, J.
Wilmot, A.
Wilmot, G.
Wilmot, S.
Wilmot, T.
Wimans, N.
Wood, Judith.
Wood, M.
Woods, J.
Woods, S.
Wright, C.

It was agreed that polocrosse would become a section to the main club and that two fields could be marked out. Whilst they were not next to one another but far apart they would be maintained by the main club in line with the other facilities offered. These fields took a year to be grassed and grown to a standard where they could be played on. During this time the section played on the bush field used during the move from Lakeside to Queens.

As the membership was growing it was decided to put in two more fields across the road on a vacant piece of ground and this was done by Kabanga Enterprises giving the Club four fields. Later on a concrete 'Durawall' was erected around the "A" field and panels sold for advertising with the proceeds going towards the cost of transporting horses to far off tournaments. Some years later and after many humorous afternoons under the gum trees, it was decided to build a clubhouse and later, ablution facilities.

With the membership now at 75, it became the biggest polocrosse Club in Zimbabwe at the time and at one stage having the most national players. Colours were later changed to conform with the main club, keeping the Hoopoe emblem but on a turquoise shirt. The generosity of members made it all possible and Bulawayo are extremely proud of where they came from to where they are today.

RIVERSDALE
[1999 to 2006]
Colours—Purple with White Trim.

Crook, A.
Lombard, M.
MacIntosh, B.
Malloy, A.
Mathews, R
Sergeant, M

Riversdale polocrosse Club was formed in 1999 as a second Club in Bulawayo. They practiced on a piece of ground between Riverside and Douglasdale, hence the name Riversdale. The field was a piece of bush stumped and cleared by the members and their grooms and dragged with a chunk of steel behind Allan's Isuzu bakkie. The Bulawayo Turf Club lent their tractor and spike roller to level the field.

An old fig tree was made the clubhouse under which many hours of drinking beer and braaing meat was done. With only six members, selections was never a problem nor were positions, with Sarge and Mark being the 1's, Allan and Roy the 2's and Arlene and Bev playing the 3's. Who could argue about the selection of the team?

Riversdale travelled to every tournament throughout the country taking Allan and Arlene's three-ton horse box capable of carrying six horses. No reserve ponies and no umpire's ponies could be catered for and Riversdale acquitted themselves well wherever they went both on the field and in the pub.

Riversdale continued in this vein until 2000 when on the way from Umboe Tournament to Featherstone Easter Tournament the farm invasions started and they all decided to take up show jumping for the next year. When polocrosse started again in 2001, Bev and Mark moved to Harare and Roy to Cabora Bassa, this left Sarge, Allan and Arlene who moved the venue to the centre of the Bulawayo Turf Club Race Track but due to the lack of water this venue never really got off the ground. Finally they moved to Allan and Arlene's home.

Riversdale eventually came to an end in 2006 when Arlene went down to Plettenberg Bay to school polo ponies leaving Allan and Malcolm who joined up with Bulawayo polocrosse club.

ESSEXVALE
[1972to 1974]
Colours—

Curry, J
Gloss, C
Higgs, D
Howard Davies, T
Loxton, D

Renolds, J
Scaaf, D
Scaaf, I
Swailes, M

VICTORIA FALLS
[1995 to 2004]
Colours—Navy Blue

The Zambezi River flowing over the falls. Livingston in Zambia in the foreground and the Zimbabwean town of Victoria Falls in the back ground.

Baker. A
Blundell , S
Butler, G
Chassing, N
Crowther, G
Crowther, A
Cunard, P
Fergusen, G
Finaughty, A
O'Donnell, S
Olivier

Peter Jones, B
Phillipson, J
Reed, A
Reed, E
Rhodes, D
Rodwell, D
Rodwell, S
Saunders, C
Traicos, D
Weiman,

Situated in the north west corner of the country, Victoria Falls, a tourist resort, is remote from the main centres of polocrosse and other than safari trail horses, no other horse activities exist, which makes the town an unlikely venue for the sport. Despite this, in late 1995, two separate groups made a start simultaneously.

Alison Baker with her trail ponies and a bunch of French kayakers started their interpretation of polocrosse on a disused football field. Later Paula Cunard joined the group and introduced a few more rules. Numbers were made up and worn, more to protect their shirts than from any identity of position.

Adrian and Liz Reed were the initiators of the second group where they started playing the sport at the Victoria Falls Primary School. They played on a field at the shooting range and it was from here that Victoria Falls Polocrosse Club was formed. In early 1996, Ted Wilmot brought a number of players up from Bulawayo to coach and get the club off the ground, and at this point Alison Baker and her group joined up. Ted left behind a number of his horses for the club to use and eventually purchase. The Cossey and Pocock families also spent a weekend at the club playing and coaching.

In the same year, 1996, the club travelled to their first tournament at Bulawayo. Later they would travel to Featherstone and Ruzawi which was a long haul for the horses to get there. Dimitri and Jeremy had organized the use of the Elephant Hills driving range as a polocrosse field, and their first tournament was held at the end of the 1996 season. This was a sectional tournament, with players grouped according to ability and each section was sponsored by a local company to raise funds for the club. Victoria Falls tournaments would continue to be run according to this format and Liz Reed did an amazing job collecting prizes and organizing the event. Bulawayo their nearest club, were staunch supporters with a number of Zambians from Livingston attending.

In 1997 Victoria Falls Primary School asked the club to vacate their stables. Six horses were looked after by Alison until new premises were found at a game farm some 50 kilometres out of Victoria Falls on the Bulawayo Road. A long way out, but an excellent venue. Two fields were laid out on the airstrip, and the tournament was held there in September 1997. By 1998 Adrian had acquired land adjacent to the croc farm and a good deal of fund-raising was done to develop a field and club house. This became the permanent venue of the club until the last tournament in 2004.

The club flew in Henry Harris, a national coach, and with the efforts of Bulawayo's top players, particularly national player Ted Wilmot, the club standard of play improved dramatically. Adrian Reed, their strongest player achieved a 6 goal handicap playing on his top horses La Passion and Desert Rose and was a member of the veteran side.

Sam Rodwell had a natural ability in the sport. As a pilot he was most useful in that he would fly the team to various tournaments but after one season was relocated to Harare where he played for Greendale Polocrosse Club. He teamed up with Paul Huxham and Kim Mannix to play in a section for Karoi in A division. Another pilot, Craig Saunders went from strength to strength and won the trophy for the most improved player. Tragically he was killed in a plane crash in late 1997 and the trophy was renamed in his honour. He was a festive party animal and whilst sharing a tent with Adrian Reed he departed around the corner for a much needed pee only to notice

Adrian's boots posing invitingly as a urinal. Alison Baker was a 'mad hatter' on the field determined to cover every inch of ground as well as players.

Victoria Falls Polocrosse Club owes much to Adrian and Liz Reed as well as Alison Baker for without their enthusiasm and horses which they willingly lent, the club may not have started. Many of the players were pilots or involved in the tourist industry with irregular hours and certainly most did not own a horse initially.

Tragically, four of the horses, including Adrian Reed's top horse, Desert Rose, died in late 2004 and the club folded. The few remaining players moved across the border to play for Livingstone in Zambia.

A club tournament

Chris Pocock

Victoria Falls polocrosse Club House

MIDLANDS PROVINCE

President.
Dr. Strover [1972/]

Chairman.
A. Jenkinson [1972 to 1976]
R. Swift [1977]
W. Schultz [1978 to 1979]
J. Parker [1980 to 1982]
T. Savory [1983 to 1984]
S. Rick [1985 to 1986]
T. Savory [1987 to 1988]
J. Fairley [1989]

C. Wilmans 1990 to 1992
Secretary.
Neville Baker [1972 to 1976]
W. Paine [1977]
J. Parker [1978 to 1979]
C. Parker [1980 to 1982]
J. Mannix [1985 to 1988]
P. Fairly [1989]
N. Wilmans [1990 to 1992]
J. Mannix [1987 to 1988]

Midlands A 1988, T. Ferrera, R. Mostert, J. Jovner,
C. deRobllard, T. Dalton, J. Burbidge.

Midland A J. Fairly, R. Mostert, T. Parker, C. De Robillard, S. Burbidge, G. Burbidge

EIFFEL FLATS
[1977 to 1986]
Colours—Yellow

Edwards, P.
Jackson, D
Jackson, P
Lewis O
Mells, J
Payne, W.
Von Memerty, J.
Welch, G.

David and Trish Jackson started the club at Eiffel Flats together with Owain Lewis, John von Memerty and Wally Payne. John Mells joined shortly after.

David worked for Rio Tinto, (Rhodesia) Ltd., who

owned the Cam and Motor, a gold mine in Eiffel Flats. They gave permission for the club to use the abandoned rugby field, which the founding members extended and converted to a polocrosse field. The existing rough stalls were used to accommodate the horses before more respectable ones were built. The Rio Tinto Club house was used for entertainment, and the company provided a lorry to transport the horses to tournaments.

Trish ran a riding school and a number of teenagers would often join them at practice sessions but only Gill Welch and Paula Edwards traveled to tournaments. As numbers were down they would often team up with Rhodesdale.

Wally Payne, Gill Welch on Bush Baby, Trish Jackson on Mica

CAM AND MOTOR
[1987 to 1995+]
Colours—White with a Maroon Trim

This club was formed on the Cam and Motor Mine.in Eiffel Flats, on the same grounds as Eiffel Flats Polocrosse Club. At some stage play was moved out to Owain Lewis' farm but the date and reason for the move is not clear.

Barton, S.
Cremer, E.
Donney, D.
Downey, D.
Du Plessis, D.
Filton, D.
Grant, I.
Gundry E
Gundry L
Gundry, Liesel.
Halkier, K.
Hooper, Y.
Holtzhausen, D.
Holtzhausen, L.
Johnston, S.
Kettle, J.
Kruger, D.
Kruger, J.
Kyle, R.
Lewis, O.
Lewis, R.
Lewis, Robbie.
Lewis, Rowan,
Mannix, G.
Mannix, K.
Mannix, L.
Mannix, S.
McKennery, K.
Mee, D.
Miller, F.
Norris, G.
O'Connor, M.
O'Gorman, G.
O'Gorman, H.
O'Gorman, M.
Pistorious, D.
Pistorious, L.

Pistorious, M.
Rohm, C.
Rohm, D.
Rohm, F.
Rohm, H.
Rohm, H. Jnr
Rohm, L.
Rohm, S.
Rohm, T.
Rohm, Y.
Rohm, Zelda.
Taylor, F.
van der Merwe, N.
Van der Westhuizen, D.
Van der Westhuizen, R.
van Zyl, G
van Zyl, L
Van Zyl, S.
Wide, D.

Out of this club came a National Ladies player in the form of Lehanna van Zyl who rose from selection as reserve for the Midlands Provincial Schools side in 1988 to the National mixed side to tour New Zealand in 1992.

FEATHERSTONE
[1985 to 2000?]
Colours—Red and Black

Bailey, N.
Barnard, H.
Beeks, J.
Biggs, J.
Biggs, J. Jnr
Biggs, R.
Blighnaut, C.
Brocklehurst, D.
Campbell, C.

Campbell, G.
Campbell, K.
Campbell, K.J.
Coetzee, A.
Coetzee, M.
De Klerk, L
De Klerk, P
De Klerk, Paul
De Klerk, Peter.
Ferreira, H.
Ferreira, J.
Ferreira, L. Jnr
Ferreira, T
Gardiner, N.
Gardiner, N. Jnr
Gardiner, S.
Gardiner, W
Gorcher, W
Gundry, Lisa.
Halfpenny, R.
Halfpenny, L. A.
Ingrams, C.
Ingrams, S.
Jovner, D.
Jovner, J.
Jovner, L.
Jovner, T.
Lambert, T.
Lewis, S.
McLaughlin, M.
Maritz, L
Maritz, R.
Mee, F.
Mee, R.
Minter, C.
Minter, N.
Minter, S.
Mirams, C.
Muller, F.

Muller, J.
Muller, L.
Nel, E.
Nel, G.
O'Neil, H.
O'Neil, S.
Paynter, S.
Paynter, Sean.
Pearce, R.
Pio, J.
Schoultz, D.
Shaw, K.
Speedy, D.
Steyn, L.
Steyn, M.
Surtees, M.
Till, K..
Till, T.
Visagie, K.

Featherstone started when Beatrice packed up. Initiated by Lawrence Maritz who became the first chairman, Featherstone grew into a large club that at one point hosted the greatest number of teams at their annual Easter weekend tournament.

Their first season, they organized a successful mini demo tournament to encourage local players and by the second season, Paul and brother Pietman de Klerk with Wayne Gardiner were playing well enough to make selection for the Midlands Junior side. In that season the club won two B Division plate finals as well as the Midlands B Division Cup. Tom Ferreira was awarded the Doug King Floating Trophy.

Situated not far off the main Harare / Masvingo highway the club is situated on Norman Gardiner's farm. The soil is loose sands which made establishing fields difficult and for a time polocrosse was played in those conditions. With the development of irrigation Featherstone were able to have five fields of good quality.

FORT VICTORIA / ZIMBABWE
[1948 to 1962,]
Colours.—White with Blue Trimmings. Black
[Zimbabwe]

Austen, B.
Austen, S.
Bester S.
Bester, F.
Bester, M.
Bushell, W.
Caruthers, R.
Christopherson, A.
De Ploy, S.
Edridge, M
Edridge, Twink
Elvy, J.
Lapham, F.
Opperman, J.
Shaughnessy, R.
Strover, M.
Warth, Mrs. M
Warth, T.
Wheels, S.
Whitehead, C.
Whitehead, J
Whitehead, M.

Fort Victoria, later renamed Masvingo was the first
Fort to be established inside the country by the pioneers
on the long trek to Mount Hampden. East of the town is
the inland lake known as 'Kyle Dam', built to supply the
Lowveld Sugar Estates with irrigation water, and nearby
the ruins of Great Zimbabwe that was speculated to be the
hub of King Solomon's mines.

In 1948 Dr. Minto Strover, as Chairman of the Fort
Victoria Gymkhana Club suggested they might try
polocrosse, a game he had read described by the late

Tony Collins in the English Magazine "Riding". He then wrote to Portlock Vale in England for a book of rules, some sticks and balls, and polocrosse got under way in Rhodesia now Zimbabwe. Later, some keen riders from the Umvuma district came to watch the game and returned home to start their own polocrosse club that became Rhodesdale.

During the 1949 season they taught themselves to play this new game, which proved very popular as both men and women could play and only one pony was required. The first match ever played was between Rhodesdale and Fort Victoria in 1949. The teams were, Rhodesdale—Gordon Tolmay, Doug King, Barry Masson, Robbie Martyns, John Baird and John Stanley. Fort Victoria—Felix Bester, John Elvy, Frank Lapham, Jack Opperman, Martin Edridge and Dr. Minto Strover.

The first three ladies ever to play polocrosse in this country were Sheila Austen, Mrs. Strover and Molly Warth.

Sadly, and for some obscure reason, Fort Victoria collapsed soon after starting, and a breakaway section started a new club in the area and called it Zimbabwe. There is no trace of Fort Victoria attending tournaments and so one must presume it sat dormant. On the other hand, Zimbabwe competed in tournaments until 1960, and then in 1961 returned to amalgamate with Fort Victoria, but by 1962, the club finally collapsed and was not present at any of the venues again.

Phil Wixley, going down memory lane, recalls a particular final at the Rhodes and Founders tournament held around 1949. Barry Masson, playing at defence, threw a long high ball up field, well past the centre and caught by his No 1, Alan Lowe riding Joe Crowe in full flight. In two tics, he threw across the line, retrieved and scored. This same action reoccurred in 1984 in a final between Sebakwe and Ruzawi and in which Ken King, playing at defence, threw to his brother Jumbo. As Phil says, some people would say 'luck!' Yes—but combined with a lot of good judgment.

Ron Carruthers,   *Minto Strover*

Twink Edridge, Martin Edridge, Minto Strover, Felix Bester, Sheila Bester, Johnny Whitehead, John Elvy, Angela Christopherson, Frank Lapham, Jack Opperman

GUINEAFOWL

[1996 to 2008]

Colours—Red Collar and Cuffs, Royal Blue with White Polka Dots on the Body and Sleeve.

Beeks, D.
Beeks, R.
Beeks, S
Beeks, T.
Brockley, B.
Connolly, J.
Erasmus, J.
Erasmus, N.
Fairburn, B.
Mpofu, Leonard,
Nel, D.
O Connor, Megan
O Connor, Mona.
Petzer, C.
Petzer, D.
Rensburg, Brin.
Rensburg, K.
Rensburg, M.
Scheepers, A.
Scheepers, C.
Shaw, D

Shaw, N.
Shaw, S.
Taylor, A.
Van Der Linde, M.

Guinea Fowl started around 1996 on Bruce Fairburn's Divide farm where they practiced on a field that was mowed out of the bush. Gweru had packed up the previous year and so Tracey Beeks, Mitch Rensburg and Bruce Fairbairn, who lived in Shurugwi, were the forerunners in establishing this club.

At that early stage they only managed to field a team but with the help of the Rensburg transport they were able to attend tournaments. The club closed down soon after when the original three, Tracey, Mitch and Bruce, left for Harare.

In 2003, the club was resuscitated by Sally Beeks who became the chairman and Dave her husband was the coach. This time the site for the new club was on the Shaw's farm in Guinea Fowl. Sally designed the colours for the shirts which depicted the Guinea Fowl and Kershelmar Dairies sponsored the shirts.

Dave and Sally moved to Mozambique after 2005 and the club continued to run with Andre and Charne Scheepers taking over the reins. Charne did not like Sally's colours for the shirts and so removed the spots "so that they didn't look like clowns on the field."

There were no club facilities as such, only a field that Derek Shaw had prepared. Derek and his wife Sandy were not players but were the backbone of the club, being parents, grooms, cooks, supporters and transporters.

When Nikkie Shaw moved on to University, the club was relocated to Andre and Charne Scheepers dairy farm in Lalapanzi, midway between Gweru and Umvuma, where they had one good field and a little 'Lapa'. At times they went across to Antelope Park for practices. The club finally closed in 2008 when a number of players left the area.

Russell Stockhill, Andre Scheepers, Cindy Stockhill,
Charne Scheepers, Paul Huxham, Leonard Mpofu.

Leonard, Charne and Andre

The trophies the Scheepers' won.

*Derek and Sandy Shaw with their daughter Nikki and
Carmen Petzer at Chipinge*

GWELO / GWERU
[1964 to 1995]
Colours—[1] Black, [2] 1976 White / Blue Hoop

Almond, D
Almond, G
Almond, W
Almond, W
Bailie Barry, S
Beeks, D.
Beeks, R.
Beridge, P.
Beridge, Z.
Bezuidenhout, R
Bloom, L.
Botha, R.
Bother, Q.
Bushell, W
Button, R.
Corbet, J.
Cossey, M
Coventry, K
de Clerk, Z
de Klerk, A
Denton, J.
Downing, D.

Dredge, C.
Du Plooy, S.
Elvie, L
Fairburn, B.
Fenton,
Fenton, W
Field, C
Field, J
Fitzroy, O
Fritz, A
Fritz, Andrie
Fritz, E
Fromberg, N
Fromberg, R
Gardiner, R
Gardiner, Robert
Gardner, H
Gardner, J
Garner, G
Gaylord, D
Gould, C
Gould, J
Gould, M
Grainger, D
Hamman,
Hamman, D
Hamman, J
Hammon, B
Hapelt, C.
Hapelt, S.
Hartley, Pop
Hoy, R
James, C.
James, G.
James, J
Jenkins, A
Jenkinson, Gay
Jenkinson, L
Johnson, D

Johnson, J
Johnson, W.
Joubert, T.
Kruger, C
Lynch, J
McFadden, J
Marais, D
McGurr, G
McGurr, W
McLachlan, I
McLachlan, J
McLaughlan, K
Mee, D.
Meikle, R
Moore, M
Morraine, D.
Mpofu, Lennard
Nel, D
Nel, Dave
Nel, J
Nel, N
O Connor, M
Ongers, M
Pemba, A
Pemba, M
Pemba, N
Pemba, T
Penrose, R
Ranchod, V.
Rensburg, M.
Saddler, M
Schlachter, Ben
Shorp, B
Sinclair, P
Smith, J
Spiers, P
Spies, A
Spies, Bootie
Spies, L

Spies, M
Stocks, E
Streak, K
Tanner, D.
Tanner, G.
Till, K
Van Breda, M.
Van Rooyen, T.
Veendal, I.Warren, N
Weineck, J
Weineck, M
Wheels, S
White, B
Wilde, A
Wilmans, C
Wilmans, C
Wilmans, Colin
Wilmans, J
Wilmans, N
Wilmot, C

Gweru, the Provincial Capital of the Midlands, can be a freezing place in winter. Open and exposed to the westerly winds that start at Wedza there is little to check their pace as it blows across the open grasslands past Lalapanzi and on past Gweru to end at the barrier of teak forests in the Gwampa Reserve. Camping at Gweru tournaments can be quite stimulating and at times during the day cold enough to retain jackets over the shirts whilst in play.

Rhodesdale would accommodate their wives in the local hotel whilst Doug King would have all the men and their young son's camp at the field under tarpaulins. The National Championships held at Gwelo in 1967 was a particularly freezing year and motorists driving past the club would do a second circuit around the roundabout to have another look at these mad people sleeping out in the open covered with frost.

At that same tournament Phil Wixley recalls; 'The

night before the finals Alan and myself went to the stables (open to the elements!) to check on the horses. What a pitiful sight, hessian bags for numnahs, no blankets, and horses' coats long and shabby. We then moved to the Horseshoe lines where Mary Leared was in charge as usual! The horses were a sight, well-groomed and clipped and with blankets; altogether a nice sight. We were somewhat embarrassed that night as the finals were the next day and Rhodesdale were playing Horseshoe. We decided we had no chance so it was decided we would all tie carrots to our sticks and had the sticks in front of our horses noses as we went on to the field.

Phil Wixley, Charles Holland, Alan Lowe, Ian
Moffat, Ken King, Jumbo King.
Showing off their carrots that they rode onto the
Gwelo field insinuating their mounts were donkeys.

We did win the championships and the B and C Divisions. The Rhodesdale team was chosen as the Midlands team for the Inter-provincials and won that as well. In the Inter-provincials, playing Horseshoe (The Mashonaland team) Robin Wyrley-Birch was brilliant as the number 3. With Alan having outplayed him in the area Robin rode straight for the goal and as Alan threw the ball, stood on his saddle and deflected the ball.

Gweru Polocrosse Club started around 1961 out towards Lalapanzi on Debshire Estates owned by Mr. and Mrs. Till. Soon after it moved to the Gwelo Sports Club were Ken Till, Al Jenkins, Meyer Spies, Ian McLachlan, Owen Fitzroy, Bob Gardner, John McFadden and Don Gaylard were the first pioneering members. The first national championship tournament the club attended was in 1966 held at Glendale, and in 1970 the Gwelo Municipality assisted the polocrosse section by building a permanent pavilion with grandstands and scorer huts.

Liz Stocks who recently worked at the Antelope Park outside Gwelo where a walk with the Lions was a speciality, assisted a lot of the youngsters start their career in polocrosse. Lenard Mpofu was the son of her groom that Liz sponsored and coached as he developed into a very handy player. Mitch Rensberg is another who has a deep sense of gratitude towards Liz for getting him off to a good career in polocrosse.

Gweru Sports Club polocrosse finally closed when the fields were taken over for soccer. The last tournament in Gweru was the Nationals in 1995.

Of interest, Bob and Sheila Gardner moved to Ruwa to live with their family. Bob always wanted to outstrip Pop Hartley who played polocrosse at the age of 74 and this he achieved. At the age of 84, Bob still mounts up and rides around the farm.

HARTLEY
[1958 to 1965]
Colours—Light Blue

Castlet, P
DeKock, Betty
Fairley, J
Ferguson, Helen
Ferguson, Ian
Francis, J

Francis, K
Gordon, Molly
Higginson, G
Howe Ely, Mike
Smith, D
Smith, Jeremy
Smith, M
Smith, Prinea
Smith, R
Stevens, R
Van Zellar, P
Vowles, John
Webb, Jon

A number of competent riders lived and worked in the Gadzema farming community, some twenty kilometres outside Hartley, now Chegutu. They would gather at Mike Howe Ely's farm, Morning Star where, in 1958 they started to play polocrosse. Rhodesdale had heard about them and offered to assist in getting them going as a club. By August of that year they were allocated a piece of wasteland at the Hartley Sports Club and the members marked out a field and erected pole stalls for the horses. Rhodesdale then sent a team, including their top players of Alan Lowe and Gordon Tolmay, to intermingle and coach the players.

By the second season, the club travelled to tournaments at Marandellas, Umtali and to Rhodesdale. They had advanced to such a degree that by the end of the season Jon Webb had achieved a 6-goal handicap, when at the time, the highest was an 8. By 1960, Hartley held its first tournament in which Rhodesdale fielded an A Division team with a young fourteen-year-old Ken King playing for the side. The rules prohibited children of fourteen and under from playing unless parent's permission was given.

Sometime after, Hartley held the National Championships in which the Colonial Governor, Lord Dalhousie and his wife arrived to watch the finals. The cavalcade duly drove up in front of the field with the requisite pomp and glory and disgorged its contents of eminent humanity under a plumage of feathers. The players, lined up and dismounted, stood to attention with their helmets held across their chests. On the other hand, the umpires, Nick Leared and Bill Cossey, remained mounted on their horses, with their backs to the distinguished guests and smoking and chatting away as though the Queens representative was of no consequence. Having known them both well, I can tell you they were very eccentric characters and relished in rebelling any form of ceremony. The game went on to play, and as Mary says, Nick and Bill were the "worst" umpires imaginable, but none the less the Dalhousie's, not understanding the rules of the game, thoroughly enjoyed watching it.

Ian Ferguson was the Hartley Polocrosse Chairman and in 1963 was elected Chairman of the Rhodesia polocrosse Association with Joan Webb as secretary.

After the Unilateral Declaration of Independence in 1965, with the resultant world sanctions, many members left the area. Some switched to polo and played for the Chakari Polo Club, but the end result, Hartley ceased to exist as a polocrosse club.

The Webbs moved to Bulawayo in 1968 and together with Owen Fitzroy, introduced polocrosse to Bulawayo at the Hunt Club. By 1979 the Webbs left for England to a place called Beccles in Suffolk where Jon helped to found the Silver Ley polocrosse Club at Lliketshall Hall near Beccals. A second move in 1999 brought them to St Breward, North Cornwall, where again Jon helped establish Camel Valley polocrosse team playing on a ground not far out of Wadbridge. Jon was an active player up till 2007 when he retired at the age of seventy-four.

HIPPO VALLEY
[1966 and still going.]
Colours—Black

Agnew, K.
Auld, B
Auld, J
Baker, E.
Barrett, S.
Barry, G.
Barry, J.
Beverley, J.
Blake, A
Blake, E.
Bonnet, C.
Budgen, S
Burbidge, B
Burbidge, G.
Burbidge, H
Burbidge, I.
Burbidge, J
Burbidge, M.
Burbidge, Mike.
Burbidge, R
Burbidge, S.
Burbidge, T.
Burnett, G.
Church, S
Coghill, L
Coghill, M
Crook, A
Crook, G
Cunningham, L.
Curwen, P.
Dabbs, A
Dalton, I.
Dalton, J
Dalton, T.
Dates, C
Davies, A
Davies, D
Davies, J.

Davies, M.
Davies, S.
De Klerk, Paul.
De Robillard, C
De Robillard, M.
De Robillard, V.
De Vries, G.
Edridge, A.
Fairlie, P.
Fairlie, J.
Fairlie, Jack
Fairlie, R
Fayde Herbe, B.
Fayde Herbe, L.
Forrester, A ~ M
Gage, Judy.
Garrs, D
Gilpin, B.
Gower, S.
Graham, J
Griffiths, A.
Griffiths, B.
Griffiths, E.
Griffiths, N.
Grobelaar, L.
Groenewald, A
Groenewald L.
Guimbeau, P.
Halse, R
Hamman, D
Hammon, C
Hardmore, G
Hayler, L.
Hayler, D.
Hendreston, G.
Henning, G.
Hind, S
Hitchcock, R.
Holland, C

Holland, O
Holland, P
Holzer, D.
Holzer, G.
Horton, I
Hulme, D.
Humphries, D.
Jenkinson, A
Jenkinson, L.
Johnson, Paul.
Keller, J.
Kemper, M.
Kemper, P.
Lamont, D
Lancaster, R
Malloy, A
Mare, M.
Mare, Y.
Maritz, F
Maritz, P
Maritz, R
Mason, B
Michael, C
Michael, H
Michael, L.
Michael, S.
Michael, T.
Mostert, D.
Mostert, J.
Mostert, O.
Mostert, R.
Muil, J
Muil, R
Muir, J
Mullen, D
Murray, L
Pallister, G.
Pallister, K.
Parker, J.

Parker, T.
Pascal, D
Phelan, K
Philips, N
Preston, A.
Preston, E.
Rees, M.
Reynolds, A.
Reynolds, J.
Ridout, D.
Rose, H.
Rose, M.
Rose, V.
Rudolph, T.
Schultz, Vim
Schultz, W
Scott, R
Taylor, I.
Taylor, L.
Taylor, P.
Trembath, P
Wallace, S.
Walsh, A
Warth P.
Warth S
Warth, G
Warth, T.
Wenham, P
Whitehead, C
Wide, G
Williams, G
Williams, R
Willows, W
Wolfee, W
Yeatman, G
Yeatman, B
Yeatman, K.
Yeatman, L
Yeatman, Lloyd.

Yeatman, R
Yeatman, Ron.
Yeatman, S.
Zambra, M

Hippo Valley Sugar Estates, one of two main sugar producers in the country, lies adjacent to the small town of Chiredzi. In the early years roads were gravel with a sticky layer of molasses sprayed on the surface to keep the dust down that gave such a lovely aroma and so unique to the Lowveld. There was such an abundance of molasses coming out of both cane estates, Triangle and Hippo, that to dispose of it was a problem. The solution was to spray the roads with molasses to keep the dust down, whilst the remainder was stored in earth dams specially built for the purpose. Later, they were to use molasses and cane tops in a formulated stock feed manufactured by T.A.F. and known as 'Voermol' and very sort after by horse and stock owners. Ultimately, years later, the molasses dams were pumped out and used for the ethanol plant in production of fuel and alcohol.

In the early 1960's, all field staff on Hippo Valley were issued horses as their only means of transport. Amongst them were a number of horse enthusiasts in this group who formed the Hippo Valley Saddle Club. This started in 1966 at the Chiredzi show grounds on the outskirts of that town with the original members of the club being: Simon Budgen, Barry Burbidge, Tony Blake, Harry Yeatman, Des Mullins, Chris Hallimore, Harry Yeatman and Farther Joe Keller, a Roman Catholic priest. At the conclusion of the large sugar cane expansion program there was a piece of land to the east of the sugar factory which was not suited to irrigated sugar cane production, and in 1975 the members applied to the company management to move the club there. This was approved on a 99 year lease agreement and overhead irrigation equipment was purchased with some given to the club. Soon there was a large piece of land planted to couch grass, and a small rustic club house was erected around a large Baobab tree. This was then the home to many gymkhanas, and was on the show jumping circuit.

In 1966, Simon Budgen visited Rhodesdale club where he watched a polocrosse tournament over the weekend and came home fired up with enthusiasm to start polocrosse at Hippo. He met with solid resistance as most club members were set in their ways but Simon was resilient and soon had a handful of people trying this new sport. Simon could not recall the dimensions of the field layout, so the game started on a field of 160 yards long and 60 yards wide. There were no 30 yard areas, and no 10 yard circles in front of the goal posts which were set at 8 yards apart. At least he had the correct number of people in a chukka, three, all of whom could use the whole field, and anyone could score, much like polo . The game under Simon's rules and field dimensions was played at great pace.

1967 saw Hippo attend its first national championships held at Gwelo over the Rhodes and Founders weekend. This turned out to be a most memorable weekend as on arrival at the field, they were all surprised that there were two 30 yard areas and circles clearly marked in front of what were very narrow goal posts. All was not lost, as Doug King, who became their mentor, took them under his wing and assured them that the field was correctly marked out. He further pointed out that only the attacking number1 and the defending number 3 could play in each respective 30 yard area, that the number 2 was restricted to the centre field, the number 1 could only score a goal after bouncing the ball over the 30 yard line, or take a pass from the centre field, and that he had to be out of the circle placed in front of the goals. He also mentioned that the players needed numbers on their shirts to depict their respective positions, so a quick trip to town was required to purchase the relevant material. It took most of that night to put players into position, as they all wanted to play number 1.

It was possibly the coldest weekend Gwelo has recorded, with all the players wearing heavy coats over their shirts and making it impossible to identify teams. Hippo, having lost all their games, probably incurred the greatest number of penalties as they could not resist hitting sticks down. The finals of the A Division was won by Horseshoe against Rhodesdale who had superior stick work, but the better quality horses from Horseshoe made an impression on the Hippo players to purchase Thoroughbred ponies.

Minto Strover relocated to work for Triangle Sugar Estates in 1968 and came across to Hippo to coach and get the club going. The National C Division Championships were held at Gwelo that year in which Hippo, represented by Barry Burbidge, Harry Yeatman and Tony Blake won the tournament. The rest of this year they achieved good results in B Division.

Two top players from Rhodesdale, Ian Moffat and Charles Holland, joined Hippo in 1969 and the team became the National Champions having climbed the ladder from the weakest position to beat Horseshoe in the finals. This title they held for the next three years. Minto returned to Fort Victoria in 1970 where he retired.

Hippo was a polocrosse legend in the '70's, winning most of the A Division trophies. Dressed in their colours of black shirt, white johds and white pith helmet with a black band, they demonstrated the efficiency and strength of a cohesive team disciplined in positional and tactical play. Barry Burbidge, a skillful 1 at speed, with Harry Yeatman at 2 and Tony Blake, who could out maneuver his opponent before he considered the move himself, made a tactician's dream come true. The other section of 'bulldozer' Charles Holland, who liked to train his horses to push him into position, played a different style to Barry, but no less efficient. Behind him came big and tall Ron Yeatman who would dominate the lineout, followed by dynamic brother Les Yeatman. The combined effect was a team of formidable strength and enormous spectator value to watch.

In 1970 Hippo were the first to introduce sponsorship to tournaments by inviting Mobil Rhodesia to sponsor the

Mobil Annual Tournament that lasted for a number of years. In the same year Hippo travelled to South Africa with two teams and played at Ladysmith, Estcourt and Richmond.

With the Club at the top of the 'leaderboard', it was not surprising that it should attract new members, a large number of whom were employed by the Estate. Some of these would become top national players and compete for positions in the top team, such as Graeme Crook, Jim Parker and possibly the best 2 of the time, Mark De Robillard.

Hippo would travel to tournaments in style. Horses would arrive in big articulated trucks flying their club banners down the sides and grooms attired in smart coloured overalls. Transport was often sponsored by the estate and probably made possible by members who were in senior positions in the company and in which Barry ultimately became the General Manager.

The water table sits very high at Chiredzi and one year, Billy Hughes' lorry and trailer bogged down as it was approaching the ramp at the original club in the show grounds. Unable to remove it, a huge four-wheel drive Cameco tractor was brought to the rescue from a nearby cane field. As it towed both truck and trailer, the trailer sunk progressively deeper until the axles were under ground and which ultimately bent the rear axle of the trailer. The horses were offloaded by literally stepping them out. Hippo was renowned for its manicured fields that resembled bowling greens. But the high water table would be a persistent problem for them as the grass roots could not penetrate deep and anchor the top layer of soil, resulting in the turf giving way under foot.

*Rich Mostert in possession for Hippo with Rich Palm
from Chipinga in defence in the 1979 A finals. Umpire
Iain Kay in the back ground.*

MASVINGO
[1981 to 1993]
Colours—Pale Blue

Baker, Toppie
Binder, B
Brown, C
Brown, R
Burger, D
Crocker, R
Crocker, V
De Robillard, E
Edward, J
Evans S.
Gundry, E
Gundry, L
Gundry' T
Jovner, H
Jovner, J
Jovner, L
Knowles, K

Landsberg W
Meadon, Kendrick, F
Phillips, G
Webb, B
Weineck, G
Weineck, Meg

MARTIN SPUR
[1993 to 1995]
Colours—Red, White and Blue

Coetzee, A.
Coetzee, M.
Cotrel, D
Holtzhausen, D.
Holtzhausen, L.
Kruger, D.
Kruger, J.
Kruger, J. Jnr
Lowe, D.
Lowe, R.
Mannix, G.
Mannix, K.
Mannix, L.
Mannix, S.
Taylor, F.
Van der Westhuisen, D.
Wallace, S.

MIDDLE SABI
[1974 to 1984]
Colours—White

Bailey, L
Bailey, L
Baker, N
Banks, P
Blighnaut,

De Robbillard, C
Durand, J
Forrester K
Forrester, A ~ M
Forrester, Frans
Forrester, Kyle
Forrester, M
Forrester, Rolf
Forrester, Sonia
Hallows, P
Hallows, Pixie
Smith, P
Smith, P
Thompson A
Williams, G

Below the Chipinge escarpment is the Save River Valley, the land of giant baobab trees and the 'Middle Save Irrigation Scheme'. This was a post-war settlement scheme to settle farmers on square blocks of four hundred acres of alluvial soil, irrigated by canal from the Save River.

Here Mike Forrester farmed Sabi Star and was instrumental in getting the Middle Sabi Club off the ground. Mike was one of those players who kept a string of top quality thoroughbred horses and was generous to a 'tee', helping out new members. He provided his lorry and trailer to transport the horses on tour to South Africa in 1975 despite the fact that he had no family or club member participating in that tour

RHODESDALE / SEBAKWE
[1949 to 1995+]
Colours—Green

Abrams, C
Ashmore, J.
Austin, A.

Austin, D.
Austin, N.
Baird, E.
Baird, J.
Barnes, J.
Bester, R
Blundell, H.
Botha, M.
Botha, R.
Bowles, B
Bowles, B.
Bundell, H
Bunnet, T
Bunnett, C
Burgher, D
Burke, D
Bushnell, S
Bushnell, W.
Campbell, Cathy.
Campbell, Charles.
Carney, L.
Caulback, P
Christensen, C
Clarke, R
Coetzee, D
Coetzee, G.
Dalton, B.
Drury, R
Duffy, J
Fairy, C.
Fritz, A.
Fritz, E.
Fritz, K.
Fritz, T.
Goby, R.
Grant, T.
Halkier, A.
Halkier, D
Halkier, K.

Halkier, T.
Hamman, N
Hammon, D
Hardwick, R.
Hassel, J.
Holland, C
Jenkinson, A
Johnson, S
Jury, W
Kent, J
King K [Jnr],
King S
King, C.
King, Claire.
King, D.
King, Dougie.
King, J
King, James
King, K
King, Karen
King, R
King, V.
Kok, M.
Kok, T.
Kyle, R.
Landman, K.
Laret, K
Levell, H
Lewis Mrs. R
Lewis Mrs. R
Lewis R
Lewis R [Jnr],
Lewis S
Lewis, O
Lewis, O.S
Lowe S
Lowe, A
Lowe, Anne
Lowe, C

Lowe, D.
Lowe, E
Lowe, R
Lowe. C.
Mannix, C
Mannix, G
Mannix, I
Mannix, J
Mannix, K
Mannix, N
Mannix, Z
Mason B
Masson, A.
Masson, D
Masson, Debbie
Masson, E.
Masson, M
Masson, R.
McCarrick, T.
McGuir, W.
McKennard, K.
McKennery, S.
Mee, D.
Mellet. Liz
Meyer, P
Moffat, B
Moffat, I
Morkel, C
Morkel, J
Nairn, Mrs. J
Norton, T
O'Connor, M.
Opperman, A.
Painting, K.
Palmer, S.
Pocock, C
Rick, J.
Rick, S.
Savory T

Savory, A.
Savory, B.
Savory, G.
Savory, M.
Savory, P
Shentall, W
Skipforth, R
Small, R
Stanley, J
Stevens, E
Stevens, E,W
Stevens, J
Swift, J
Swift, L.
Swift, N.
Swift, R.
Tolmay, D
Tolmay, G
Tolmay, J
Toms, B
Van der Berg, B.
Van der Berg, K.
Van der Berg, R.
Van der Walt S.
Vaughan, H
Vaughan, J.
Vickery, N.
Waters, H
Watson, A
Watson, M
Waymark, J
Wevell, H
Wilmans, C.
Wilmans, N.Wixley, P.

Brigadier Andrew Dunlop learned about polocrosse in 1949 from someone he met in Fort Victoria. The first polocrosse meeting took place at the King's home with Brig Dunlop, Guy Savory, Gordon Tolmay, Cliff Morkal,

Don Waymark, Barry Masson, and Doug King. It was decided to form a polocrosse club, and until they were able to get land for the club, each farmer would take turns in having the game played on his own farm. Thus the first game was played on Chinyika Ranch, then rotated on Morkels', Tolmays' etc.

Later, Don Waymark was kind enough to give a piece of land on his property to use as a permanent field and also the use of one of his barns for meetings to take place in, and in typical Rhodesdale fashion, the usual hilarious Saturday evening bottle parties.

Polocrosse was a real poor man's polo in those days with farm horses being used, and the game rather resembled an egg and spoon race played on horses. The first tournament was played against Fort Victoria and the team consisted of: - Gordon Tolmay [3] Brig. Dunlop [2] Barry Masson [1] Doug King [3] Don Waymark [2] James Baird [1]. In those days only under arm throwing at goals was used and it was James Baird who was the first to use the over arm method.

Around 1950 the members applied to the government to rent a disused farmhouse and piece of land to establish a permanent club and this was granted and so Rhodesdale Country Club was born. It was only in 1981 that the club was able to irrigate the fields, prior to that they were simply carved out of the veldt and mown short with Barry Masson's sheep. The ball would not bounce true with the presence of thick tufts of bush grass, but it gave rise to an excellent training ground for players to learn to retrieve a difficult ball off the ground.

The second generation of players put Rhodesdale well and truly on the map in the environment of greater national competition. Alan Lowe as a 9 handicap was probably the best number 1 in the country at the time with Ken King amongst the top number 3's. Not far below them were some very talented players that with the combined effect produced a national champion side. The likes of Bob Swift, Jumbo King, John Tolmay, Tim Savory and Dave Masson all of whom were talented and skilled players that made provincial and national sides.

Rhodesdale had a hard upbringing in its early formative years. An unrelenting field aside, the founders were true 'salt of the earth' type of cattle ranchers who put their all into everything they did, social activities included. Doug King, who rode a chestnut swayback with a head carriage like a giraffe, and Barry Masson, who could throw the ball from the back line and into his scoring area, were two characters out of a western movie. Probably these were the two that set the tempo for the future.

Here was the Rhodesdale I knew. Riding in cricket longs with cowboy boots, and mounted on gawky cattle ponies with floppy ears and names like 'Toilet', they could remove a tick from under your tail before you realized you had it. The customary team photograph witnessing yet another tournament victory with players beaming toothless grins. These were the wild boys of polocrosse. It has been said that Barry Masson would have his feet tied together under the horse's belly to prevent him falling off when he had had that one too many, and his son Dave, having had his leg broken at an Umvuma tournament, made an enlarged stirrup iron to accommodate the plaster of Paris so that he could take his place in the team for the nationals.

Phil Wixley remembers the man behind Rhodesdale and these are his words.

"Doug King, man of men, was the man who kept us together, if your horse went lame, Doug would lend you whatever he had. At tournaments he would have a complete camping site and we were expected to eat with him. One night, during a polocrosse season, Ian Moffat, Charles Holland and I stayed with Doug and Nina for the night as we were quite a distance from the club. It was the last weekend before the championships and team announcement. We all left, eventually, with Doug. At the farm, had a bath and then bed. Next morning Doug comes into the bedroom with a tray of Lion and Castle asking who would like tea or coffee!

"All too soon Doug passed away and we all met up at the church and then to the wake, Robert and Ken did everybody proud and after a few drinks we could look back on Doug and what a man he was."

Some Clubs have their very own special supporter. Flash Vickery was one such man. Although he did not play the sport, he would follow his club around all the tournaments, looking after all their wants, drinks behind the goals, getting Dave Masson to tournaments on time and cooking for the whole Sebakwe contingent.

In the early '80's, cattle ranching was not as lucrative as game ranching and Sebakwe district switched over to game with many of the men becoming hunters, some of whom were instrumental in establishing the original guidelines and rules for professional hunters, to guide their foreign clients in a fast expanding tourist business. John Tolmay and Alan Lowe were amongst them. Hunting is a dangerous profession, not only from the exposure to wild animals but from protecting inexperienced foreign clients in that environment. Ken King survived being crushed by a rhino as it had him pinned to the ground after he had diverted a charge from a client but Alan Lowe was not that lucky when his life was taken in an effort to save a client from an elephant charge. Alan was hugely popular in the community and left a void at his passing.

Alan and Brian Bowles had been capturing game for relocation in the lowveld and had stayed overnight with Simon Budgen. By now out of clothes, Alan had borrowed a shirt from Simon which Eleanor, Alan's wife, had washed prior to returning and had discovered a Hippo Valley Stores purchase order for 1 gross of condoms. Her suspicions roused, she confronted Alan thinking he had been capturing a different sort of wild life. In fact Simon had purchased these condoms as free handouts to the workers but from then on he was known as 'one gross' to his Rhodesdale friends.

*Back row, Steve Johnson, Chris Pocock, ?, Dave
Masson, Bob Swift, Tim Savory, Harry Waters,
Front row, Don Burgher, Ken King, Leon Snyman,
John King, Roy Small.*

Alan Lowe on Bruno   *Doug King on Joe Crow*

Steve Johnson, Simon Rick, Chris Pocock playing for Rhodesdale against Hippo

RISCO

[1968 to 1974]
Colours—White Shirt with Vertical Black and Green Stripe on Right Shoulder to Waist

Auld, J
Brandt, G
Buck, F
Buck, W
de Klerk, S
Dew, C
du Wet Lombard, J
Flanagan, E
Groenewalt, B
Jenkinson, A
Jenkinson, G
Jenkinson, L
Joubert, D
Kyle, B
Lawrence, N
Lombard, J
McFaddon, J
Moffit, B
Mostert, J

Mostert, D
Mostert, P
Mostert, R
Rhosedale, D
Rick, S
Rom, S
Roos, W
Rosedale, A
Rous, D
Shentall, J
Shentall, W
Stevens, S
Stevens, G
Streeter [Jnr],
Streeter, J
Streeter, R
Van der Walt, N
Van der Walt, W
Watkins,

Risco, situated just outside Kwe Kwe on the main Bulawayo road, is the centre where Iron Ore is mined for the production of steel that meets the requirements for the country as well as for export. On the road in to the mine complex, on the right, is the club with excellent stables and facilities that were used primarily for gymkhanas in which Risco were high on the leader board nationally.

By 1972 the club moved to a new site where four fields could be established and the Club was able to field 5 teams.

SHABANI
[1970 to 1977]
Colours—Blue with White Quarters.

Abrams, H
Albasini, D
Brown, C

Buchanan, A
Buchanan, G
Drummond, J
Du Plessie, P
Hollicke, J
Holland P
Keats, D
Martin, A
Minnie, R
Plotz, J
Rawston, B
Rawston, P
Robinson, K
Robinson, M
Sealy, R
Sealy, B
Shepherd, B
Shepherd, S
Siebert, S
Smith, M
Snowdon, A
Stachan, M
Summersgill, C
Sutton, K
van Wyk, P
von Pechman, T
von Pechman, Mrs.
Warwick, A
Webb, J
Webb, N
Webb, Noel

Shabani is a mining town east of Gweru and the dress the club members wore depicted this. With the use of mining helmets and mining boots they looked quite a 'nigged' lot. It appears that Brian Shepherd, the Railway Stationmaster was the man who got the Club off the ground, but soon after became dormant until it was revived by Paddy Holland in 1976. Their first tournament was held 1973.

UMNIATI
[1979 to 1984]
Colours—Gold / blue trimmings

Campbell, C
Clark, A
Davies, A
Garner, H
Lewis, O
Lewis, R
Lewis, Robbie
Lewis, S
Lowe C
Lowe, K
Lyon, J
Lyon, K
Lyon, K
Maertens, M
Mannix, C
Mannix, G
Mannix, I
Mannix, J
Mannix, K
Mannix, S
Mannix, Z
Myburgh, P
Nicolae, W
Ogilvey, H
Ogilvey, I
Ogilvey, W
Payne, W
Rick, S
Ross, C
Self, M
Stephens, D
Stevens, D

Toms, B
Toms, N
Welsh, J

Ian and Jenny Mannix, together with Bruce Toms started the club on Bruce's ranch in Battlefields in 1979. Later, the club moved to Umniati on Henry Garner's, Kopjies Farm, and a small clubhouse was built. The members pooled together enough money to buy a Thames Trader lorry that they used to transport their horses to tournaments. In 1984, the Club was going to move to the C.S.C ranch in Umniati and a field was prepared, but with the players dispersing, the club folded.

UMVUMA
[1959 to 1980]
Colours—Yellow with Black Quarters.

Allison, M
Ashmore, B
Baillie Barry, S
Bayley, D
Bester, J
Bester, R
Cloete, H
Cossey, M
Davies, D
De Klerk, A
De Klerk, T
Gilpin, G
Hamman, B
Hamman, D
Hamman, I
Hamman, J
Hamman, S
Hamman, P

Hammon, W
Jefferies, W
MacArthur, B
MacArthur, I
Marillier, E
Mentz, M
Mentz, T
Meyer, J
Nielson, O
Pinkney, E
Rooken Smith, R
Savage, B
Small, R
Snoek, H
Spindler, M
Stopforth, C
Till, K
Till, R
Van Den Berg, R
Van den Berg, S
Waters, H
Wells, M
Wixley, P
Wixley, C
Wixley, G
Wixley, W

Records show that the second club to start playing polocrosse after Fort Victoria was known as Umvuma but this referred to the startup of what was to become Rhodesdale and in which the venue was alternated between Bemthree, Mahamara and Chinyika. In fact Umvuma only started in 1959 with two registered members.

Horse activity started in the '50's on the old airstrip with gymkhanas and later race meetings at a venue across the Umvuma River on Central Estates where they had a mule cart race won by Charlie Christenson. Charlie in fact had not started his career in polocrosse until he went to work for Gordon Tolmay of Rhodesdale. It appears that the first Umvuma club was based at Fairfield, Mtao Forest on a field behind the forester in charge's house but with very little activity until 1971 when it was revived at a new venue west of the Umvuma Golf Club.

At this time, a number of Chaplin School players would stable their horses at the showground's and sometimes on the Till's farm where there would be occasional weekend practices during the term and over the school holidays. The club was then relocated to a piece of ground belonging to Central Estates just across from the golf course. Johan Bester provided earth moving equipment to level two fields and a pavilion was built.

Phil Wixley and John Hammon were the driving force of those days and Umvuma would host the Easter tournaments that made for a great weekend of polocrosse. Horses would arrive by train and those that came by truck would be offloaded at the railway siding and walked across the way to the club. The evening's entertainment would be held in town at the Umvuma Club where many a raucous party would be held. Some people even camped in the car park outside this small stage post venue.

Tim Savory gives a highlight of one of those wild parties in the Pub;

"Some story involving Dave Masson i.e. the time at Umvuma Midlands Championships when his horse Ginger fell and he broke his leg, He was not going to miss the party in the pub that night so sat in a chair having used copious quantities of alcohol to dull the pain. The highlight of the night was when Mike Cossey came back from the toilets with only his Hippo shirt on and his little wee willy peering out every time he took a step. This was too much for his partner at the time Cynthia Field and she stormed out, passed him and gave his cheeky arse the most thunderous slap on his bare bum. He proudly wore the badge for the rest of the night. That party was one of the most infamous as the bar games degenerated into who could slide the furthest down the bench seat and along the bar floor much like the Canadian game of Curling. In the time honoured practice drink was used to lubricate the path. In no time it was too much like hard work to pour the beer out so full bottles were just thrown down in the path of the contestant. The next day there was a sorry sight of bad hangovers, sliced feet and chests. But the greatest pain was the belly muscles from having laughed so hard for so long."

The small town of Umvuma is one of the early settlements centred on the aging Umvuma gold mine that had a smelting tower constructed of brick perched on top of a small hill. In the early years, gold would be shipped in by ox wagon from the Copperbelt in Zambia for it to be smelted there. This tower could be seen from some distance on the approach to Umvuma and many a parent would distract their restless kids by rewarding the kid who spotted it first on the distant horizon. Today the tower is no longer used and is gradually crumbling.

The surrounding district was made up of cattle ranches that by nature were spread over a large part of the countryside and therefore the club was not able to draw on a lot of members. This was a factor that curtailed the lifespan of the club, but despite this, the club produced some very talented players in the likes of Sonny Hamman, Rudy Van den Burg, Oscar Nielson, Ken Till and Phil Wixley. In 1978 Phil achieved a 9 handicap riding an amazing chestnut called Shannon and went on tour to South Africa representing his country.

Rob Rooken Smith, who ranched in the area, had a herd of horses that had bred wild and free roaming on his ranch. Devuli Ranch in the lowveld was another of these places that a number of entrepreneurs would round up these 'Brumbies of the bush' by the R.M.S. lorry load, break them in and sell them off. I was able to purchase a shipment from Rob, but due to fuel rationing at the time, had to resort to the railways, where they were herded straight into a cattle truck and railed off to Lochinvar siding just outside Salisbury. From there I was able to move them by roping them in pairs and herding them to their final destination. Not being able to coordinate their dash to freedom they were reasonably easy to control and the use of a good polocrosse pony made it possible to direct them with the odd 'ride-off'

ARMED FORCES
Colours—Military and Police Uniforms

In 1971, the polocrosse Association of Rhodesia embarked on an exercise to promote polocrosse as a sport in the armed forces. The Army, Air Force and Police were approached but with little success as horses were not an integral part of the military at that time. Police had horses but for some reason the sport did not take off. Llewellyn Barracks in Bulawayo where national servicemen received their training had a few horses for recreation purposes and with polocrosse players doing their training at the time, were able to form a club. Although the club was registered with the Association it was not able to progress to attend tournaments and soon fizzled out.

By 1974 Captain Frazer McKenzie from the Motor Transport Unit of the Rhodesian Army had the idea that a horse mounted unit could be effective in the guerrilla war being waged at the time. He approached the Army Staff Headquarters with his ideas and was granted permission on a trial basis to see how effective it would be. A piece of land was allocated at Inkomo Barracks and Captain Stevens became the first C.O. of the then named Mounted Infantry Unit before being renamed the Grey's Scouts, with Captain Frazer McKenzie as his second in command. Recruiting among the territorial forces was carried out from polocrosse clubs as it was felt that polocrosse players had the right horsemanship skills needed for the purpose.

Whilst the Grey's Scouts did manage to attend a few tournaments, it was not practical to sustain as, for one, the mounts were not suitable and secondly, the time required was prohibitive. Captain Stevens then formed a recruiting section of a few well known show jumpers to ride their own mounts and compete at shows under military colours.

I was one of the original founding members and can relate an amusing story on the use of polocrosse to break in and train wild horses that were acquired through the 'Friends of Rhodesia Association' from South Africa. These beasts arrived with long winter coats and tethered with bull halters to gum poles buried in the ground. Naturally we all ran around selecting the mounts we wished to ride, but Squadron Sergeant Major Ken Till would have none of it and allocated each his mount to much grumbling.

The first order of the day was to groom these hairball animals into something resembling military shine. Then came the saddle-up which erupted in saddles flying in all directions as irritable mounts bucked and attempted to murder their keepers. Eventually the impossible was done and time to mount was ordered. From irritation to fright the mounts took off for the horizon bucking in a desperate attempt to rid their riders, and in most cases they achieved their goal. Medics were busy occupied in patching up the injured whilst those beyond patching were rushed to hospital. Graeme Crook sustained a broken collar bone when his mount wiped him off against a tree.

I, on the other hand, was not issued with anything so exciting, much to my irritation. I had Oakley, who, despite his aristocratic name, resembled a mule and 'Mules' became his nick name. He was that idle that he refused to buck. In fact he would not leave his stall, let alone buck off into the distance. It required Phil Wixley to whack him from behind with stirrup leathers to coax movement out of him, which he did in reverse.

S.S.M. Till now decided that a game of polocrosse would be the ideal distraction to get these animals into the right frame of mind for training. So off we headed to a bare earth piece of ground. We lined up on Till—crowded is a better word—six a side, and in came the ball. No one went for the catch. It was more prudent to hang on as the mounts took off as if it was a grenade that had been lobbed in. They disappeared in a cloud of dust, bucking as they went In all directions and over the horizon. All that is, accept 'Mules' who had entered the lineout backwards. As soon as the dust settled, there was the ball in front of me, some six paces away. Could I get Mules there? Certainly not, he was content to stay where he was, alone in this dust patch of Rhodesia.

Somehow, and I don't know how, the rest of the mob returned from all corners of the field as fast as they had left. Over the ball they criss-crossed with amazing precision, only to disappear in the opposite direction from whence they came. Once again there I was on that lonely piece of dirt, amazed that no head-on had occurred. That ball was still in front of me and a stubborn 'Mules' still refused to budge.

Mules and I became the firm friends that constant contact tends to produce. He would be at my heels wherever I went and would sleep on my sleeping bag with me trapped inside. He learnt to dance to Elvis Presley's 'Blue Suede Shoes' and was one of the horses that survived the duration of the war.

The Grey's Scouts was not disbanded after independence in 1980 and in peacetime conditions, it was used for anti-poaching patrols. Around 1994, the executive, under President Jock Kay, tried to revive polocrosse amongst the armed forces and Sally Rowe was sent out to Inkomo Barracks to coach the Greys. They attended a couple of tournaments but soon faded away through lack of interest.

The lead horse is Oakley, 'Mules'.

NGESI POLOCROSSE AND GYMKHANA CLUB

Three members of the Club turned up at the first annual general meeting held at the Sebakwe Hotel, Que Que in 1953. Nothing further was heard of them.

SELOUS

[1961 to ?]
Started with 12 members

MTOKO

I came across a snippet that suggested that polocrosse was played on one of the farms in the Mtoko farming area in the mid '60's. It is doubtful if it survived very long and probably was influenced from some Virginia players. The commercial farming community ceased to exist soon after independence as the Government purchased the farms for resettlement.

LEWISHAM

[1973]
Lewisham was the name of a riding school just above the vlei line in Chisipiti, a suburb of Harare. Ray and

Anne Adams owned and ran the school and introduced polocrosse as an exercise.

Sadly, Ray was killed crossing the main Enterprise Road with his pupils when a car crashed into his horse. Anne continued to run the school.

TRELAWNEY
[1987]

No information available.

CHAPTER 15

EXECUTIVE MEMBERS

PATRON
Mr. Clifford DuPont 1974 to 1978
Mr. N.D. Campbell 1979 to 1989
Received R.C.C.B. Silver Medal for services to polocrosse
Mr. Jock Kay, 1990

HONARY LIFE PRESIDENT
Dr. M. Strover

HONARY LIFE VICE PRESIDENT
Mr. Gordon Tolmay
Dr. Hamilton Ritchie 1964
Mr. Leo Teede
Mr. Simon Budgeon 1978
Mrs. Phyllis Campbell 1979
Received R.C.C.B. Silver Medal for services to polocrosse

PRESIDENT
Dr. M. Strover 1951 to 1955
Sir Rupert Bromley 1956 to 1963
I. Ferguson 1964 to 1965
N.D. Campbell 1966 to 1979
J. Kay 1980 to 1991
R. Tait 1991
B. Burbidge
J. Whaley

A. Keith
A. Jack
R. Taylor
R. Mostert
W. Parham

VICE PRESIDENT
Dr. M. Strover 1956 to 1962
G. Tolmay 1963
F. J. Barry 1964 to 1965
W. Cossey 1966 to 1982
I. Keith 1983 to 1984
J. Harris 1985 to 1987
D. Cocker 1988 to 1989
R. Tate 1990 to 1991
B. Burbidge
A. Jack
T. Wilmot
R. Gardini.
C. Wilmans

HON SECRETARY
Mrs. Strover 1951 to 1955
Mrs. C. McKersie 1956 to 1962
Mrs. N.D. Campbell 1966 to 1979
Mrs. S. Harris 1980 to 1981
Mrs. C. Parker 1982 to 1988
Shirley Harris 1989
Mrs. P. Fairlie 1990 to
Pam Whaley 1997

COUNCIL CHAIRMAN
John Elvy. 1951 to 1955
J. Kay 1978 to 1987
J. Harris 1988 to 1989
J. Fairley 1990 to
H. O'Neil

COUNCIL VICE CHAIRMAN

J. Harris 1983
D. Cocker 1984 to 1988
J. Fairlie 1989
M. Davies 1990 to

TREASURER
J. Harris 1980 to 1981
J. Parker 1982 to 1987
C. Bouwer 1988 to 1990
Sally Harris 1997

PUBLIC RELATIONS OFFICER
P. Scotcher 1970 to 1972
J. Fisher 1973 to 1975
J. Parkin 1976 to 1977
J. Crawford 1978 to 1982
S. Rick 1983
I. Taylor 1984 to 1986
R. Tait 1987 to 1989
C. Johnson 1990 to
Rowena Fairley 1997

CHIEF UMPIRE
Ian Keith 1968 to 1976
Charles Holland 1977
John Harris 1978 to 1981
Iain Kay 1982 to 1983
John Harris 1984 to 1990
Rich Games 1991 to
Allan Malloy
Richard Mostert 2002 to 2003
Rod Fennel
Allan Malloy
Richard Mostert 2006 to present

DEPUTY CHIEF UMPIRE
I. Brown 1978 to 1979
A. Keith 1980 to 1983
Iain Kay 1984 to 1986

Anthony Keith 1987 to 1989

Rep to Colours Control Board;
O. Fitzroy 1971 to 1981
Al Jenkinson 1971
L. Morcell 1972
M. Sergeant 1982 to

? [N.Z]R. Coorey [N.Z]. ? [Aus], T. Blake [Aus] A. Keith[Zim] J. Harris[Zim] Lawrence Tye[NZ]Max Walters [Aus] ? J. Kay [Zim]

CHAPTER 16

FROM THE MINUTE BOOK

1951

Fort Victoria, Rhodesdale and Glendale held their second meeting in 1951 under the Chairmanship of Dr. Strover and it was decided to name the association the Polocrosse Association of Rhodesia. The annual subscription was fixed at one pound per club together with a member's subscription of 2/6d per head, and colours were allocated to the three clubs.

Advertisements announcing the formation of the association were placed in all the local newspapers and anyone interested was advised to contact the Secretary [Mrs. Strover] at Fort Victoria.

1952

The first Annual General Meeting was held at Umvuma on 22nd June 1952. It was at this meeting that it was decided that each club send two representatives to council with the Chairman, Secretary and Treasurer being ex officio members. The council quorum was fixed at four.

1953

The first Council Meeting with John Elvy in the chair was held in April 1953. Glendale appears in the minutes as having replied to the chairman's circular. The organization of the championships came under discussion and it was decided that they should be held at a different club each year over the Rhodes and Founders weekend. Clubs were asked to provide at least one umpire to officiate at the championships and to nominate one member for the handicapping committee.

The second Annual General Meeting held at the Sebakwe Hotel, Que Que, on Sunday 12th July 1953, was quite a big affair with no less than 27 members present. Glendale Polocrosse Club put in a lot of hard work during the session, as when the venue for 1954 championships was discussed, Glendale put forward their claim against Fort Victoria who also wanted it. After a vote was taken Glendale's offer was accepted.

A ruling was introduced whereby a team was allowed 9 ponies

1955

At the Annual General Meeting of 1955, it was decided to draft our own Rulebook, as there was dissatisfaction with some of the Australian rules.

The women complained that they were not coached in the use of the stick and that husbands and boyfriends took away the ponies that they had schooled up and given farm hacks. Also ladies trophies played for at tournaments were taken away and given to the men.

It was decided at this meeting by 14 votes to 11 that the championships be played from scratch, but that handicaps should be allotted for matches and tournament play.

1962

The ruling of number of ponies reverted to one pony per player.

1963

A proposal was made to fit a cross bar on the goal posts 17 ft. high. The three points to this suggestion was; to give the No 3 a better chance at defence, to help goal umpires in their decision, and to speed up the game.

1966

The first revision of the Rulebook was done

by Dr. Hamilton Ritchie.

Balls made by Dunlop Rubber Co Australia cost one pound and were of inferior quality.

1967

The Inter Zone tournament became the Inter Provincial tournament.

1969

The first National Selection Committee was elected.

Introduced an under 13 tournament.

1970

The polocrosse Association was now affiliated to the Rhodesia Colours Control Board.

1971

Virginia started the under 13 Tournament in conjunction with the C Division Tournament. Mrs. Rutherford donated a cup.

A proposal was made that The Polocrosse Association should have its own tie.

1972

Ponies were to be registered with the Association accompanied with a registration fee of 10 Dollars.

The C Division age group was raised from 11 to 13 years of age.

1973

Executive committee was formed to take the load off the president by being the policy maker, law enforcer and to deal with management issues.

Common rule book was drawn up with South Africa. Ruling made on the restriction of the depth of the net.

Polocrosse balls were made locally at a better

quality and at the affordable price of 85 cents. Johnson's Saddlers were appointed the agents.

1974

At the March Council Meeting in 1974, the age limits of players were amended to be at the discretion of the captains of the clubs concerned. A robust and well-mounted player of 14 years could play in A or B Divisions at the discretion of his captain and with his parents' written permission.

1975

Two coaches from Australia visited.

1976

First International Polocrosse Council meeting held in Australia with David Campbell and Charles Holland as delegates from Rhodesia.

It was decided that a club captain must pay $10, 00 as a deposit against his team defaulting in their goal and line judging duties.

Delegates were sent to Australia by invitation of their association to discuss the Rulebook. The parallel form of lineup was adopted, and the over-arm throw retained.

1977

Gwelo Club was approached to provide a permanent home for polocrosse. Gwelo delegates said that their club was very keen on the idea provided that national tournaments were held at Gwelo, as it would require a great deal of financial expansion. Mr. Jock Kay spoke of changing the 'home' every year; the trophies etc. and the test matches could go to any club that could offer the necessary facilities.

Security for the championships. Hippo Valley was busy organizing armed convoys for clubs competing. It was agreed that nowhere could complete safety be guaranteed, and despite the fact that some

Borrowdale parents would not allow their children to go, the meeting decided not to change the venue.

Council approved the Chief Umpire's proposal to allow past A and B Division players to take part in C Division Tournaments.

1978

Former President of Rhodesia and polocrosse patron the Hon Clifford W DuPont died.

1980

At the Council meeting Mr. N.D. Campbell suggested that a dress up ball should be held at the National Championships instead of the usual 'disco and jeans'. He also proposed that a Miss Polocrosse competition be held just as other sports do.

1983

Hippo requested that A Division games should be held as sectional tournaments as there were few A Division players to field full teams. This proposal was rejected but left to Hippo to change their own tournament if they wished.

It was decided at executive that helmets in current use were dangerous and that from next year players would not be allowed to play without safety straps on the existing helmets. John Harris, with the assistance of the Bureau of Standards, was looking into a new helmet being designed.

Hippo proposed that accident insurance be included into tournament fees.

1984

Two Australian coaches arrived.

1986

International Polocrosse Council meeting was held in Australia with John Harris attending as Zimbabwe delegate. Conditions on the depth of net removed.

1987

International polocrosse Council meeting held in Australia to discuss the International Rule Book was attended by Jock Kay, John Harris and Anthony Keith.

A proposal from Midlands Polocrosse Association to change the allocation of votes at the March Council meeting was adopted to one vote allocated to each club that was fully registered and paid up. One further vote allocated to each club for every six fully paid up playing members of the association.

Tournament fees raised from $4.00 to $5.00.

1988

The involvement of the Police and Grey Scouts in the game of polocrosse still to be pursued by Richard Tate.

Mashonaland Polocrosse Association proposed that the present restriction on the depth of the net in Zimbabwe be reviewed with the idea of adopting the international rule, but maintaining the over-arm throw.

Mike Cossey proposed the idea of introducing a mixed team division at the National Championships and handed over a trophy for this event.

Players required to vaccinate their horses against Equine Flu and keep the receipt on hand as evidence.

1989

Rothmans Sports Council funded the fares of two Australian Coaches to a total of $3,000.00.

B Division at the National Championships was dropped to a 6 goal team.

Penalties for misbehaviour of players and spectators at tournaments to be enforced with a year's banning.

1990

Bulawayo proposed that the maximum length of chukkas be reduced from 8 minutes to 6 minutes. Decision was left with host clubs holding tournaments.

Iain Kay proposed that a committee of past and present administrators be set up to define and interpret in detail the responsibilities of all national office bearers, to provide a guideline for future officials.

1991

Three Zimbabweans attended the Australian National Sports Centre where they qualified as Level 2 coaches.

Six Americans visited Zimbabwe to gain experience and were seconded to various clubs for a three week period.

1994

Seven provinces formed from the previous four to follow the political provinces.

CHAPTER 17

NATIONAL CHAMPIONSHIPS VENUE

1954 Glendale
    1957 Umtali
    1959 Fort Victoria. A Division, Founders Cup.
Ladies Champs, Strover Cup.
    1961 Umtali with Civic sundowners
    1962 Hartley introduced on trial mixed section and
asked the Barry's to consider Umtassa Cup transferring
to this.
    1963 Marandellas.
    1964 Rhodesdale
    1965 Umtali
    1966 Glendale
    1967 Gwelo
    1969 Hippo. Matama Natal club attended. Hippo won
champs.
    1970 Ruzawi..
    1971 Hippo Valley
    1972 Karoi.
    1973 Ruzawi River Association made ruling that the
top 16 teams on handicap presented to executive play at
champs and divided into A and B.
    1974 Hippo Valley
    1975 Umvuma
    1976 Ruzawi River,
    1977 Hippo Valley
    1978 Glendale

1979
1980 Ruzawi River
1981
1982 Hippo Valley

CHAPTER 18

TROPHIES

THE FOUNDERS CUP
Presented by Mr. V. Demetrious of Fort Victoria as a floating trophy for the winners of the A Division National Championships
1955, Rhodesdale
1956 Rhodesdale
1957 Old Umtali
1958 Rhodesdale
1959 Rhodesdale
1960 Rhodesdale
1961 Rhodesdale
1962 Marandellas
1963 Marandellas
1964 Marandellas
1965 Marandellas
1966 Marandellas
1967 Marandellas
1968 Horseshoe
1969 Hippo Valley
1970 Hippo Valley
1971 Hippo Valley

MAKORI CUP
Presented by Major Sir Rupert Bromley Bart for the winners of the B Division National Championships.
1959 Marandellas

1960 Umtali
1961 Glendale
1962 Salisbury
1963 Horseshoe
1964 Old Umtali
1965 Rhodesdale
1967 Gwelo
1968 Rhodesdale
1969 Gwelo
1970 Rhodesdale
1971 Borrowdale

SLADE TAIT MEMORIAL TROPHY
Presented by Richard Tait

ZEUS FLOATING TROPHY
Presented by Owen Fitzroy

DOUG KING FLOATING TROPHY
Presented by Doug King for the most enthusiastic supporter

BARRY FLOATING TROPHY
Presented by Fred and Sheila Barry for the winners of the Inter Provincial Tournament. Originally presented as the Umtassa Trophy for the winners of the 1959 Marandellas Women's Tournament, it was transferred by request of the Association.

THE STROVER TROPHY
Presented by Strover for the winners of the A Division, Hippo Valley Mobil sponsored tournament.
1964 Mashonaland
1967 Midlands
1968 Mashonaland
1969 Mashonaland
1970 Mashonaland

THE STROVER SHIELD
Most improved player National Championships

BUDGEON TROPHY, later renamed BRAZERO FLOATING TROPHY.
Presented by Simon Budgeon in 1971 for the best pony of the year.

BESTER CUP
Presented by Felix Bester for the winners of the C Division
National Championships.
1966 Virginia
1967 Gwelo
1968 Hippo Valley
1969 Hippo Valley
1970 Chipinga
1971 Hippo Valley

MANICA SHIELD
Presented by Umtali polocrosse and Saddle Club for a Handicap Tournament
1968 Borrowdale
1969 Rhodesdale
1970 Borrowdale
1971 Umguza

SIMPSON CUP
Presented for the winners of the Mashonaland Championships
1972 Horseshoe

GLADIATOR TROPHY.
Umgusa Tournament

CAMPBELL TROPHY
Ruzawi Whitson

KIRCOS TROPHY
Umtali Eiberg, most improved player.

THE STACHEN TROPHY
Shabani tournament

THE RICHARD SEALY TROPHY
Shabani tournament

BONES TROPHY
Gwelo tournament

THE HUXHAM TROPHY
Copper Horse [Matepatepa.1976]
Donated by Trevor and Thora Huxham for the most
improved junior player

T.A. FLOATING TROPHY
Presented by Tobacco Auction for the winners of the
Family Tournament

HAMILTON RITCHIE CUP
Presented by Dr. Hamilton Ritchie for Mashonaland
15 and under

BRIAN HARRIS TROPHY
Championship A Division winners

CAMPBELL TROPHY
Championship B Division winners

DOUG YEATMAN TROPHY
Best turned out team National Championships

PAUL SCOTCHER TROPHY
Mashonaland Provincial Handicap Section.

FORRESTER TROPHY
Family Tournament

McLAREN TROPHY
Umtali Eiberg, most improved player.

CALL BOY TROPHY
Mutare Eiberg, hardest trying player.
TROUT STREAM TROPHY
Horseshoe B Division

FERREIRA FLOATING TROPHY
Featherstone. Most improved player

CANE KNIFE TROPHY
Hippo. N. Richards Tournament, C Division

IAN BROWN MEMORIAL TROPHY
Horseshoe A Division

SIDNEY TROPHY.
Sebakwe. A Division

FRIDAY TROPHY
Sebakwe. B Division

TICKEY TROPHY
Sebakwe. Most improved pony.

MENTZ CUP
Sebakwe. Most improved player.

FISHERMAN CUP
Sebakwe. Most accomplished rider and pony.

DOREEN HUGHES TROPHY
Horseshoe. C Division

ARTHUR BURBIDGE MEMORIAL TROPHY
Hippo N. Richards B Division

N. RICHARDS TROPHY
Hippo. N. Richards D Division.

BROMLEY SHEILD
Glendale. A Division

FITZROY STIRRUP
Glendale B Division

COSSEY SHIELD
Glendale C Division

JOKER CUP
Ayreshire B Division family tournament

BURNETT ~ SMITH TROPHY
Ayreshire C Division family tournament

SHANNON CUP
Ayreshire. Family tournament. Most improved player

ABOUT THE AUTHOR

Chris was born on the 18th of November 1950 and attended Melsetter Junior School and Umtali Boys High School. He learnt the art of horse riding as a 15 year old from Sheila Barry who had just started up her riding school on their Old Umtali Farm, Umtassa.

Started with show jmping, but soon got the polocrosse bug. He went on to play for Umtali, Borrowdale, Karoi, Glendale, Rhodesdale, Horseshoe and Ruwa. He played for Midlands and Mashonaland Provinces and then at national level in 1975, 1980, 1982, 1985 and selected to play in 1987 but withdrew for work commitments.

He managed tours to New Zealand and South Africa in 1993 and was the fourth Provincial Chairman for Mashonaland and a member of the National Executive.

Chris was an active member in polocrosse administration becoming a national selector, was on handicapping, umpire and rule book committees as well as being Chairman and Captain of a number of clubs. He received his colours as a National Umpire and umpired test matches in New Zealand and the South African Quadrangular Tests.

Married to Heather who still plays polocrosse

He has 5 children, Roger, Tara, Nicholas, Ryan and Scott who have all played polocrosse. Ryan is currently playing for North Club.

You Self Publish

Editing, Formatting, Cover Design, Self-Publishing Assistance and Website Services

Trish Jackson

Author of several romantic suspense fiction novels and...

For more information and to find out how I can help you please visit my websites

http://www.youselfpublish.com

www.trishjax.com

Made in the USA
Middletown, DE
01 April 2017